THE

HEART

AND

THE

FOUNTAIN

THE
HEART

An Anthology of
Jewish Mystical Experiences

AND

Edited by
Joseph Dan

THE
FOUNTAIN

OXFORD
UNIVERSITY PRESS

2002

OXFORD
UNIVERSITY PRESS

Oxford   New York
Auckland   Bangkok   Buenos Aires   Cape Town   Chennai
Dar es Salaam   Delhi   Hong Kong   Istanbul   Karachi   Kolkata
Kuala Lumpur   Madrid   Melbourne   Mexico City   Mumbai   Nairobi
São Paulo   Shanghai   Singapore   Taipei   Tokyo   Toronto

and an associated company in Berlin

Published by Oxford University Press, Inc.
198 Madison Avenue, New York, New York 10016

Oxford is a registered trademark of Oxford University Press

Library of Congress Cataloging-in-Publication Data
The heart and the fountain : an anthology of Jewish
   mystical experiences / [edited by] Joseph Dan.
      p. cm.   Includes bibliographical references.
   ISBN 0–19–513978–X
      1. Mysticism—Judaism.
      I. Dan, Joseph, 1935–
   BM723 .H36 2002
   296.7'12—dc21   2001055485

9 8 7 6 5 4 3 2 1
Printed in the United States of America
on acid-free paper

CONTENTS

PREFACE

An anthology usually is a selection of texts from a well-defined whole. This is not the case with this volume. Jewish religious culture does not contain a distinct subdivision of "mystical texts" from which such a selection can be made. The term *mysticism* does not have a Hebrew equivalent, and the concept, which developed in Christianity since the third century, has never been defined within Judaism. Using this term consists of the imposition of a foreign category by modern scholars on the vast body of Jewish spiritual literature, declaring—each scholar following his own individual definition—some texts as analogical to what in Christianity is regarded as "mystical." The works presented here are exactly that: Using my own definition of mysticism, which is explained in the introduction, I have selected texts that I believe express, analogically, the religious attitudes and experiences that in a Christian context are regarded as mystical.

The common identification of the kabbalah—which is an authentic, internal Jewish religious phenomenon—as "Jewish mysticism" is completely wrong. The kabbalah is a Jewish esoterical tradition of contemplation of divine secrets, believed to have been given by God to Moses on Mount Sinai, which includes spiritual expressions of a variety of disciplines and characteristics. Some of these can be analogically categorized as mystical, but most are not, while at the same time there are many Jewish spiritualists who wrote mystical works who were not kabbalists. This anthology should not be regarded as a selection of kabbalistic texts. About half of the authors of the texts presented here were kabbalists. Even so, in several cases the works from which the texts were selected would not be regarded by their writers as "kabbalistic." In fact, if I were to prepare a representative anthology of the kabbalah, there is only one text from this volume that I would include in it (chapter 12, "Zohar: The Beginning"). The first eight chapters are taken from works written before the beginning of the kabbalah in the end of the twelfth century. The last two chapters are taken from the works of writers who regarded themselves as nonreligious. Several others are selected from autobiographical works and others from ethical literature that usually is not included in kabbalistic literature.

The experiences, visions, dreams, and apocalypses presented here demonstrate, I believe, that in any large group of religious writings it is possible to discern spiritual phenomena that are analogical in their characteristics to what is described in a Christian context as mystical literature. The difference is that while the Christian writers, in most cases, identified themselves or at least related themselves to the phenomenon of mysticism that is part of their tradition, the Jewish writers did not, because the concept was completely absent from their religious worldview. Because of this, the selection of the texts is unavoidably subjective; the editor is loyal not to the intrinsic dynamics of Jewish religious expression, but to external criteria, incorporated in the contemporary concept of mysticism.

I would like to thank the Rockefeller Foundation in Bellagio, Italy, and its director, Giana Celli, for the invitation to be their guest in the summer of 2000, a most enjoyable period that I dedicated to writing a part of this book. Several of my colleagues assisted me with good advice, especially Dr. Mor Altshuler-Suleiman, and I thank all of them very much. Ms. Na'ama Mizrakhi assisted me in collecting the material. My partner, Professor Miri Kubovy, demonstrated her usual patience and tolerance in the many months in which I was completely absorbed in this work.

Joseph Dan
The Hebrew University, Jerusalem
November 2001

THE

HEART

AND

THE

FOUNTAIN

INTRODUCTION

I. Religion, Mysticism, and Language

Mysticism, as it is usually understood, is a religious phenomenon, yet the relationship between the two is very
difficult to define. In current usage, the term is often
used as designating the depth of one's faith: Someone
who prays is religious; someone who really means it is a
mystic. This makes the relationship between mysticism
and religion a quantitative one: Mysticism is religion,
but a little more so. The terms by which mysticism is
often described—a way to approach God, to sense his
presence, an intense emotional response to him, be
united with him—are actually religious ones, promised
by most religious establishments, but within the framework of mysticism they are "really" taken seriously.
Mysticism has often been described as the pinnacle of
religion.[1] Catholic scholars, especially, tend to view the
mystical experience as expressed by the great Carmelite
mystics of the sixteenth and seventeenth centuries as the
maximal expression of faith, striving for a complete spiritual union with God and the human soul's immersion
within the Godhead.[2]

If it were so, it would be difficult to explain the insistence of mystics themselves on the separate, different
nature of their approach to God. A historical analysis of
the subject of mysticism,[3] however, tends to reveal
meaningful tensions between established religion and
mysticism, sometimes leading to a conflict between
them. Despite the reverence shown by many Catholics
to mysticism, it is a fact that there was never a pope who
was a mystic, and hardly any cardinal. As will be dis-

cussed below, the basic premises of a mystical attitude to religion are often contradictory to those of established religion, though the nature of mysticism is such that it successfully avoided, with few exceptions, an open clash with the church.

The three so-called monotheistic religions, which are better described as the religions of revelation or scriptures, are recognized by their deep faith in the communicative power of language. In all of them, God spoke, and people recorded his words in texts, and these texts reveal understandable meanings that have to be obeyed. Isaiah, Jesus, and Mohammed are described as having spoken, and their words were followed or disregarded, but not misunderstood. The founders and prophets of these religions spoke in public; they did not whisper secrets in the ears of the selected few who had particular spiritual or intellectual qualities. The scriptures of the three religions are portrayed as understandable and communicative for all; even the portions that later generations and modern scholars found difficult to understand are not presented as such. The words of divine revelation included in the sacred texts have sometimes been disobeyed, but not misunderstood, according to the traditions of these religions.

The adherents of these religions are required to listen carefully to the divine message incorporated in scriptures, to follow the leadership and directions of their religious leaders, and to perform what is required of them, and then they can be confident that they will achieve the maximum possible spiritual rewards promised to the faithful. No provision is made to a possibility of language being a barrier between man and God; rather, the language of the sacred texts is believed to be accessible to all people of good will, without any difference concerning background, gender, education, and even age. Young and old, women and men, can share the communication offered by the word of God.[4] It is evident, therefore, that the three scriptural religions are based on the concept that language should communicate to anyone with open ears and heart the full meaning of the divine message that will save his soul and provide him with all the benefits that such communication promises.

The starting point of the mystical attitude to religious truth is the deep doubt—or, very often, complete denial—that communicative language can reveal divine truth to a believer. Mysticism, above anything else, is the result of the certainty that language, as spoken by people, cannot serve as a vehicle for the revelation and communication of the nature of God and the truth of his message to humanity. Only nonlinguistic means can glean some aspects of the hidden divine truth.[5] The term *mysticism* itself is a negative term: It does not denote anything specific, but rather the absence of something. *Mysticism* is a seemingly positive term that denotes a negative, as the word *darkness,* which seems to be a positive term, denotes only absence—the absence of light. It is not knowledge or perception, but their absence. Yet not every kind of ignorance is mysticism; the real question concerning the meaning of mysticism is: the absence of what? A mystic is someone who does not know, but does not know what? The most prominent absence that the mystics describe when they discuss their own uniqueness is that of the meaning of communicative language. A nonmystic is someone who believes that when truth is explained to him in words, he should understand that truth. The mystic is someone who knows that real truth, meaningful truth, can never be fully expressed in words.

It is not only language that the mystic distrusts, but the whole range of means by which people acquire knowledge, especially the senses. logic and thought. The best one-sentence expression of this attitude may be found in the "secret" that the fox reveals to the Little Prince in Antoine de Saint-Exupéry's tale: "This is my secret, and it is really very simple: That which is really important is hidden from the eyes." If we understand "eyes" to mean the totality of human perceptions, sensual and intellectual, we may have a glimpse of the mystic's attitude toward the world. If something is revealed, obvious and understood, it cannot be "really important." Only the trivial, or the false, can be communicated and understood. Truth is beyond comprehension, it is eternally hidden from the senses and the mind, it is "mystical."

People who like what they see, who enjoy learning and understanding, who willingly join conversations and communicate their feelings and thoughts, who are dialogical and well attuned to the world around them, will not become mystics. Mysticism is characterized by a deep pessimistic attitude toward the universe and human existence in it. This is not a pessimism resulting from a particular state of affairs that can be changed, but an existential attitude, which results from their disbelief in the possibility of linguistic communication. The belief in the ability of human beings to communicate with each other is based on our faith in the common nature of our sensual and intellectual experience. If we believe that our eyes perceive colors in the same way, and that our minds grasp syllogisms in an identical way, then we can use these shared perceptions to give words meanings that will bridge one mind with another. If, on the other hand, we do not believe that the senses and logic penetrate into the real truth that is hidden from us, we are unable to communicate, at least concerning meaningful and important things. Each soul is isolated in its own realm, in quest for a truth that even if it achieves a glimpse of, it cannot share it with anybody else, lacking a means of communication.

It is very probable—though there is no way of knowing or proving it—that as a result of this attitude most mystics are silenced by the paradox of their own denial of communication. We shall never know that, because anything that is not communicated is "lost" as far as history and culture are concerned. No one will ever know how many silent mystics dwell around us, in the same way that we shall never know how many of our neighbors and acquaintances write poetry and burn the pages or hide them in drawers. The mystics whom we know are those who found a way to break out from their shells of silence and create some kind of communication with the surrounding world. These are the mystics who are committed to any of the three scriptural religions. These religions not only enable them to do this, but actually impose it on them, because to be a believer in one of these religions one must accept that language is not a human means of communication but an aspect of divine wisdom, which God chose first and foremost as his tool for the creation of the universe, and then addressed humanity by it. If God used language, it must be possible to communicate truth by language, because God's word must be true. The scriptural believer who is also a mystic cannot, therefore, deny language totally. He has to accept that language can convey truth—at least when it is shaped and used by God.

This may seem to be a bridge that brings together mystics and nonmystics within the structure of a scriptural religion. It does not. On the contrary, it identifies and emphasises the differences between mystics and nonmystics. They may share the same scriptures, use the same prayer book, listen together to the same sermons, and identify their faith by the same terminology. Yet they differ from each other in the most drastic manner because the nonmystic believes that he understands the text of the scriptures on the levels of communicative language, while the mystic knows that these denote, at best, the trivial and superficial if not that which is completely false, whereas the real meaning, the mystical message of scriptures is beyond communication. It is hidden within the text, but it can be glimpsed only by mystical means. A sensual-intellectual approach to the text of scriptures is either irrelevant or wrong. Only the mystic, by his metasensual and metaintellectual perceptions or experiences, can achieve a glimpse of the hidden truth. It can be said that *the mystics and the religious are two kinds of believers who are separated by a common language.* A religious person believes in the word of God incorporated in scriptures, and is certain that he understands it, or at least that its core, its most important meaning, has been absorbed by him. The mystic knows that various levels of communicative interpretation—including allegory, analogy, etc.—cannot reveal the hidden divine truth, which can be achieved only in nonlinguistic ways.

What is that mystical truth? What is that mystical, metalinguistic way of achieving it? What is the mystical experience that opens it for the mystic? At this juncture the historian must stop explaining, if he follows the mystics, because they claim consistently that the mystical is that which cannot be conveyed in words. When a scholar tries to formulate the inner nature of mysticism in positive terms (we have, up to this point, used only negative terms—discussing what mysticism is not rather than what mysticism is), he puts himself in the position of knowing better than the mystics themselves what they have experienced, and succeeding where they say failure is inevitable—expressing the inexpressible in communicative language. This approach, I believe, is a wrong one, unacceptable on methodological grounds. If the mystics insist that this is beyond words, it is the duty of the historian to accept it, and stop his research at this point. Mysticism is that which cannot be expressed in words, period.

This injunction is valid only concerning a general definition or description of mysticism. It is different on the contingental level, dealing with individual or groups of mystics in particular historical contexts. When this approach is adopted, a lot can be learned from the study of the sources of the mystic's terminology and images, from his references to the cultural and historical reality surrounding him, from his choice of emphases and denials, and many other aspects of textual study and criticism. But even then, it is impossible to ask: What did the mystic really mean? What vision was presented to him? Do all mystics share the same experience, or does every mystic have his own hidden spiritual world, distinguished from all others? When one answers such questions, one expresses his own dispositions, ideology, and faith, rather than describing the world of the mystics he is reading. *The mystical text, for the nonmystical reader (e.g., the historian) is a set of signifiers without signifieds.* The signifiers cannot be reached by any other means in order to check or verify them, and comparative study of mystical texts is even more misleading because there is no way to verify that the various sources represent the same or similar experience. If two sources use similar terminology, this does not denote that they have "seen" the same thing; the similarity of words and images is the result of shared cultural background rather than proof of the identity of experience.

One may ask: If so, how do we know that the mystical realm ever existed? How do we know that the mystics mean anything? Maybe there is just nothing there, nothing to explore, nothing to discuss. This may indeed be the case: We have no way of confirming that the mystic did indeed envision this or experienced that. Yet this does not mean that historical study of mysticism is pointless. We cannot put ourselves in the place of the mystic and share his visions and experiences. Yet we can do something that may be much more meaningful: we can place ourselves in the position of the mystic's readers, those nonmystics who read, listened, and were influenced by the mystics, and acted to shape their own worldview and culture as a result. We cannot know what the inner truth of mysticism is. We can and should investigate and learn how mysticism operated within the history of religion and culture. There may not be "mysticism" as such, yet no one can deny that hundreds of people who believed themselves to be mystics, and hundreds of thousands of people who were their adherents, believed in the existence of the mystical realm, and shaped their own lives and cultures being influenced by the words of these mystics. We shall never know whether the medieval readers—or modern ones, or even scholars—really understand what the mystics meant, and whether their words really portray their hidden, mystical realms. But we can know what their nonmystical readers and followers understood, so that we can follow the impact of their words in history, culture, and religion. Mysticism as a spiritual experience may be forever hidden from us, but mysticism as an operative, dynamic force in shaping religion and culture can be studied and understood.[6]

II. Jewish Mysticism

The term *mysticism*, when applied to a Jewish religious phenomenon, is different from when it is used to denote a Christian one, because the Hebrew language does not have a term parallel in meaning to *mysticism*; nor is there in Jewish culture any concept that can be identified as equivalent to *mysticism*. The same is true concerning Arabic and Islam. When something is described as *Islamic mysticism* the designation is not authentic but imposed by the analogy to similar Christian phenomena. *Mysticism*, the term and the concept, is authentic only in the framework of Christianity; using it outside the cultural context of that religion is analogical, imposed by contemporary scholarship. No Jew or Muslim, at least until the last few decades, ever knew that he was—or was not—a mystic, whereas the word and the particular kind of religiosity associated with it were present within Christianity from antiquity. It developed within Christianity since the second century, and took shape in the third one, both in Greek and Latin, Eastern and Western branches of that religion. Because of this, how "mystical" a certain Jewish phenomenon is cannot be decided by intrinsic, immanent characteristics. Contemporary scholars evaluate such phenomena according to their similarity to its authentic Christian counterpart, and then decide whether it is appropriate to use that term. Therefore, nothing in Judaism is "really" mystical, because no Jewish religious writer ever described himself in this way. The concept of "Jewish mysticism" is the invention of contemporary scholars dealing with comparative study of religion.

It has become commonplace since the middle of the nineteenth century to identify the kabbalah with Jewish mysticism, and in a similar way to identify Sufism with Islamic mysticism. This is wrong and misleading, causing numerous misunderstandings. Kabbalah, in Judaism, is an authentic term—thousands of Jewish religious teachers and writers identified themselves as kabbalists (as did many Sufis in

Islam). What they meant by this term was a concept completely different from the Christian concept of mysticism. *Kabbalah* in Hebrew means "tradition"—any tradition, including legal, exegetical, historical, etc.[7] In this context, *kabbalah* means a particular kind of esoteric, secret tradition concerning the divine world, which the kabbalists believed was given to Moses on Mount Sinai and was transmitted secretly from generation to generation. *Kabbalah* is an abbreviation of "secret tradition concerning the divine world." Kabbalists may sometimes reveal in their works the characteristics usually identified as "mystical" in a Christian context, but they do not do it because they are kabbalists: It may be even said that kabbalists may become mystics in spite of, or in denial of, their being "kabbalists." A pertinent example may clarify this.

One of the greatest kabbalists—arguably, the greatest—in Jewish history was Rabbi Moshe de Leon, who lived in Castile in the second half of the thirteenth century (d. 1305). He was the author of the book *Zohar* ("Brilliance"), the most important, rich, and influential kabbalistic text, which became in the late Middle Ages a sacred text and established in the same category of sanctity as the Bible and the Talmud. De Leon was destitute most of his life, and used to sell copies of portions of the *Zohar*. He claimed that the book was an ancient one, written twelve centuries before by Jewish sages, and that a manuscript of that lost work was brought to Europe and is now in his possession; in other words, he wrote the *Zohar* as a pseudepigraphy, and claimed to be its copyist rather than its author. When he died, his widow and his daughter were left without any means of support. A rich Jew heard about their situation, and offered them a large sum of money for the original manuscript of the *Zohar*, from which De Leon claimed to be copying. The widow responded to this offer by saying that she could not do that because there never was such a manuscript; "He was writing from his head," she said about her late husband, not copying an ancient manuscript.

This story, recorded by an early fourteenth-century kabbalist,[8] may be understood as identifying the difference between kabbalah and mysticism. Moshe de Leon himself claimed to be a kabbalist, a traditionalist: He was not doing anything original, just copying and transmitting an ancient tradition, as written twelve centuries before him, and including truths that were as old as the divine revelation to Moses on Mount

Sinai. His widow, on the other hand, claimed (unknowingly) that he was a mystic. He was not transmitting, but inventing and experiencing the fascinating visions included in the *Zohar*. Moshe de Leon was either this or that; he could not be both. There is little doubt that the widow was correct, and that de Leon was one of the most creative mystics who ever wrote in any religious context. He claimed to be a kabbalist but he was really a mystic—a term that he did not know, expressing a concept of which he was never aware.

It is not surprising that within the closed, esoteric circles of the medieval kabbalists mystics have found a haven, and therefore many of the Jewish mystics flourished within the framework of the kabbalah, pretending to present ancient traditions while they were actually having spiritual experiences that were often similar in nature to those of the Christian mystics. Yet the phenomena that may be characterized as mystical were not confined to the kabbalistic circles. Jewish mysticism began a thousand years before the appearance of the kabbalah, in late antiquity, in talmudic times. The kabbalah appeared only in the High Middle Ages, in the last two decades of the twelfth century, and flourished especially in the thirteenth and early fourteenth centuries, before it surged and became the dominant worldview in Judaism in the seventeenth and eighteenth centuries. In that late period, when almost every Jewish writer, thinker, and leader was versed in the kabbalah, there certainly was no identity between mysticism and kabbalah. Judaism became, in modern times, almost completely kabbalistic, but certainly not completely mystical. There is a link between kabbalah and mysticism: For several centuries from the High Middle Ages to modern times, most Jewish mystics found their natural habitat within the framework of kabbalistic traditionalists. Yet Jewish mysticism flourished also outside the confines of these circles and independently of them. There is no intrinsic connection between kabbalah and mysticism, even though many Jewish mystics were indeed kabbalists.

III. The Jewish Concept of Language: The Midrash

One of the most stubborn barriers that separates Judaism in general and Jewish mysticism in particular from the Christian-European culture is the vast, radical difference in the basic conception of language, resulting from the completely different experiences of language in the cultures based on these two religions. The following paragraphs are an attempt to explain this, yet my experience has taught me that the chances of succeeding in it are very remote. The Jewish concept of language is so far from the intuitive attitudes of European culture (now shared also by that of modern Hebrew, which adopted completely the European concept of language), that no amount of explanations can bridge it.

Judaism differs from Christianity in that it believes that it has recorded, in its scriptures, the actual word of God in its original language. Christianity, on the other hand, is based on the word of God in translation. The Hebrew bible included tens of thousands of words, believed to be the actual syllables uttered by God or inspired by him. The New Testament includes thousands of words said by Jesus Christ or inspired by him, not in their original form but in their translation to Greek. Only six words uttered by Jesus are recorded as they were actually pronounced—"Talita kumi," and, "Eli eli lama shavaktani." As we all know, translation is interpretation, and a selective one at that; the words of Jesus as preserved in the Christian scriptures contain, at best, one of the possible interpretations of the meaning of the original. The rest is lost.

The language of Christ as preserved in the New Testament is the one put in his mouth by his human translators-interpreters. The Hebrew bible, according to Jewish and Christian faiths, includes the word of God as actually uttered by him even before humanity was created. When God said, "Yehi or," he did not only convey the message "Let there be light," he actually uttered these syllables, and as a result there was light. God's utterance was not a semantic one: There were no people, nobody could be listening, it could not be an order because there was no one to carry out the order. The very utterance was the deed, the cause of the emergence of light. Its semantic interpretation came later. It is the human conclusion that if the sound *yehi or* makes light, then it must carry the meaning "Let there be light." It is as if we interpreted the click of the light switch as an order for the lamp to light up. But in the case of the lamp we know that the switch releases an electric current that heats a wire and causes it to glow. How did the sound *yehi or* switch on the universe? This is divine wisdom, forever hidden from us. The syllables *yehi or* include not only a sound, but also a picture of six letters of the Hebrew alphabet. They include vocalization marks (*nekudot*) and musical signs (*teamim*). The letters are decorated by little crowns (*tagin*). The letters also include a numerical value, because writing words and numbers was done in Hebrew (as in Arabic, Greek, and Latin) by the letters of the alphabet. It could also be an acronym, possibly of the names of the letters—*yod he yod aleph vav resh*—which are also derived from divine wisdom, because they pre-existed in God before the creation. Each of these components could be the decisive one in the creation of light. We can never know their hierarchy of importance and meaningfulness because we cannot introduce such a hierarchy into divine, infinite wisdom. All we can know is that the totality of the linguistic phenomenon—the sound, the picture, the music, the "decorations" (the term indicates that this is a secondary element, which of course cannot be within divine infinity), and all the other elements combine into the essence of language as a creative—rather than communicative—instrument.

When *yehi or* is translated into any language carrying the semantic message "Let there be light," all these elements are lost. There are no vocalization marks, crowns, or musical signs. The sound is now different, and the shape of the letters is different. The numerical value is changed. The only component that remains is the assumption—an arbitrary one—of a semantic message. The concept of language as essentially a communicative device for semantic messages in Western culture is the result of the historical accident that Christianity was based on the word of God in translation into existing languages that had a vast pre-Christian literature that was essentially semantic. Hebrew and Arabic viewed themselves as languages identical with their religions. Christianity could not do that, because it integrated itself into existing languages—Greek and Latin—that sustained great civilizations that were not dependent on Christianity.

Once language is recognized as an aspect of infinite divine wisdom, it cannot have finite meanings. In the same way that no one can ever know the "real" meaning of *yehi or* from the divine point of view—one can only view the earthly result of the utterance—so one cannot glean the real, finite semantic message of any word of God. It is impossible therefore to present the "true" meaning of any biblical verse. One can only search further and further, digging deeper into the infinite layers of divine wisdom, never reaching the end. Exegesis is an infinite process, and no new discovery negates the previous ones. Different, or even contradictory interpretations have equal validity, because the laws of exclusion have no relevance within divine wisdom.[9]

These principles became of vital importance after the most crucial change in religious perception that brought forth religious faith as we know it in the three scriptural religions, namely *the end of prophecy*. From the first words that God spoke to Adam to the last words of Hagai, Zecharia, and Malachi, God was ever-present in human affairs. According to the biblical narrative, he was always available to direct and guide, to chastise and reprimand. There were always people who were inspired by him and spoke for him—prophets and judges, elders and priests. When God is present in such a way, scriptures are superfluous: You do not have to browse in the Bible to find an answer because a prophet or a priest will tell you what to do. Mysteriously, however, this divine presence came to an abrupt end in the early days of the Second Temple, in the sixth century B.C.E. From then on, no new revelation can be relied on; the old collection of divine utterances becomes the only tool of guidance for present and future religious authority. Exegesis now replaces revelation as the expression of divine will. God can no more be envisioned, there is no direct dialogue with him. It is necessary to interpret his words to Isaiah in particular circumstances many centuries ago in order to surmise what he wishes us to do now.

The transition from direct, constant divine presence to scriptural exegesis was a long and complicated one. Some religious phenomena seem to have been attempts at preserving the old order even though they accepted the norm that prophecy has come to an end. Thus, the great pseudepigraphic literature of the Second Temple period presented new divine revelations, but ascribed them to old, biblical figures—Adam and Abraham, Isaiah and Moses. People still claimed from time to time to having experienced visions and revelations, "the holy spirit" and messianic aspirations, but they did not acquire a position of communal leadership and were not regarded as legitimate representatives of divine messages.

The greatest expression of the rebellion against "the end of prophecy"—though even that was not a complete and radical one, was early Christianity. It represented the belief that God has appeared again and spoken again to the people in the most authoritative way. Yet even the writers of the Christian Gospels, who represented the believers who actually experienced divine presence and message—could not refrain from adding to that direct relationship an element of exegesis. Each step in Christ's life is accompanied, in the text of the Gospels, by a verse from the prophets of the Hebrew bible that predicted it. It is as if the direct divine revelation is not authoritative enough if it had not been predicted by the ancient prophecies. Several decades later Christianity joined Judaism in the denial of constant divine revelation and its substitution by textual exegesis—though this was an exegesis of a different kind, because it was based on a nonoriginal, human translation of the divine message.

In Judaism, the most potent bridge between constant divine revelation and complete reliance on exegesis was the concept of the oral Torah, the tradition given to Moses on Mount Sinai that was transmitted from generation to generation, from elders to judges, from judges to prophets, from prophets to sages, thus making certain that a divine message, which was at the same time ancient and contemporary, was always available. The Mishna—the most prominent expression of the Jewish legal, religious, and social system is given authority by oral tradition. These two elements—oral tradition and exegesis, were united in the phenomenon of the *midrash*, which became the dominant component of Jewish religious culture, besides the *halakhah*, the law, from the early centuries of the Common Era to the present.

The typical midrash consists of an opening sentence that claims that rabbi so and so said, in the name of rabbi so and so, thus establishing a link with the ancient tradition that leads to Moses. Then a verse from the Hebrew bible is quoted, and the speaker offers his exegesis, often relying on other verses as well. Midrashic sections are frequently connected to each other by the term "another statement" or "another possibility"—*davar aher*), offering a different interpretation for the same verse. In many cases we may find long series of such sections that offer half a dozen or more different interpretations of the same verse. Obviously, none of these present the one-and-only, ultimate meaning of the verse: that is impossible, because the verse expresses infinite divine wisdom that can never be exhausted. This gives scriptural exegesis its eternal power: Divine truth can always be gleaned from the verses, even when each has scores of interpretations already. The term *midrash*, and the concept of midrashic exegesis, cannot be translated to another language, because in a European cultural context exegesis and interpretation are inherently connected with the concept of the quest for the one ultimate truth, the correct meaning.[10] The notion of multiple, different, and even conflicting meanings does not conform to the attitude toward language prevailing in a world dominated by the Christian conception of semantic language. The awareness of this difference in the concept of language and scriptures is essential for the understanding of Jewish traditional culture. One has every right to ask, "What did Christ really mean when he said that?" but one cannot ask, "What did Moses really mean when he said that?" because the first question may have an ultimate answer, whereas the second has an infinite number of equally correct ones.

Furthermore, whereas Christian exegesis may use the words of the scriptures and their possible meanings, the Hebrew midrash treats the verse as a full semiotic phenomenon. Midrashic interpretation may take into account not only the different meanings of the words in different contexts, but also the letters of the alphabet that constitute it, the shape of the letters, their names, their "crowns," their numerical value, the shapes and names of the vocalization marks, the shapes and names of the musical signs, and numerous other elements.[11] It is no wonder that when Christian scholars were exposed to Hebrew midrashic methodologies in the Christian kabbalah of the late fifteenth and the sixteenth centuries,[12] they regarded them as highly mysterious and representing ancient esoteric wisdom. They used the term *kabbalah* to describe all postbiblical Jewish culture, including the Talmud, the midrash, and medieval rationalistic exegesis, and this meaning persists in European languages to this day. Whereas inside Hebrew culture it is rather easy to distinguish between traditional midrashic methodologies and the unique, medieval ideas of the kabbalah, in a Christian context the distinction is lost; thus, numerology has become a most representative constituent of the "kabbalah," even though it is an unavoidable method in a language that has no immanent system of numerals. In fact, the earliest such computation—called in Jewish tradition by the Greek term *gematria*—known to us is found not in the midrash or kabbalah, not even in a Hebrew text, but in the Greek text of the book of Revelations in the New Testament, where the "number of the beast," 666, is the result of the computation of the Hebrew letters of the name of the Emperor Nero.[13]

How does Jewish mysticism fit into this picture? Actually, it does not. The mystic is the rebel, the nonconformist, he cannot accept the midrashic-exegetical monopoly on divine truth. The mystic craves for a closer relationship, for a direct spiritual contact, with divine truth, a craving that midrashic scriptural exegesis cannot satisfy. Some Jewish mystics—especially the early ones, the "descenders to the chariot," openly rejected the dominant midrashic methodologies and claimed to ascend spiritually to the divine world and envision God and his surroundings in an unmediated fashion. Others, especially the kabbalists of the Middle Ages, used the midrashic form as a convenient cover. The midrash allows, after all, an infinite number of correct, legitimate interpretations. A mystic who pretends to be a midrashic exegete can easily present his own truth as if it were one more midrashic interpretation, without danger of exposure and sancture. It is he alone, or together with a few pneumatics in his closed circle, who know that what he presented was not "one more" interpretation—(davar aher) but the result of a unique experience, a spiritual meeting with the divine realm. The mystical truth gleaned by him in this experience cannot be presented fully in words, but it can be hinted at, for the cogniscanti, using the midrashic methodologies. He cannot be accused of breaking the rule of "the end of prophecy" when he writes "one more" midrashic commentary, nor can he be accused of hubris, pretending to know what others do not, placing himself in a superior rung of the spiritual religious ladder. Yet he knows that the other, nonmystical exegetes, when they present the fruit of their work, are far away from the true knowledge of divine secrets, which were opened to him in his spiritual experience. That experience cannot be shared, because it is metalinguistic, but it can be hinted at, in obscure and enigmatic ways, using the midrash as a cover. Indeed, a perfect case of two worldviews separated by a common language.

IV. Historical Outlines: Late Antiquity

It is very difficult to indicate a particular point in which Jewish mysticism began. Several sections in ancient Jewish religious texts can be characterized as mystical—some psalms, for instance, or some visionary chapters in the Apocrypha and Pseudepigrapha of the Hellenistic period. Such characterization, however, may often be just an exercise in the implementation of a preconceived definition of the subject. One decides first what are the characteristics of mysticism, and then proceeds to search for them in the texts before him. If we wish to understand the historical development of a religious culture, we should look for phenomena that represent definite historical outlines: a group of people, a group of texts, distinct terminology, dynamic practices, and all other expressions of a historically active religious group. Such a phenomenon did present itself in ancient Judaism; it is known as the mysticism of "the descenders to the chariot," *yordey ha-merkavah*, who flourished between the third and seventh or eighth centuries.

The mystical texts that reached us from this ancient school of mystics are incorporated in a library of esoteric treatises, about two dozen works, known traditionally as the literature of *Hekhalot* and *Merkavah*—"celestial palaces and the chariot." This appellation reflects the frequent occurrence of the words *hekhalot* and *merkavah* in the titles of several treatises in this literature.[14] These treatises cover a wide range of subjects, which can be grouped in four categories:

1) Cosmogony and cosmology, treatises and parts of treatises dealing with the process of the creation, the structure and nature of the universe, the celestial bodies, astronomy and astrology, and the ways in which God conducts the universe. A prominent example of such a work in this library is the *Seder Rabba de-Bereshit*, "The Great Design of Genesis,"[15] but almost every work includes sections and chapters dedicated to this subject. Some works of a more midrashic nature can be included in this category, like the *Midrash Konen* and *Midrash Tadsheh*. A special position in this context should be given to the *Sefer Yezira*, the ancient "Book of Creation."[16]

2) Magic. Almost all the treatises in this library include an element of magical information, incantations, and lists of potent angelic names by which earthly purposes may be achieved. A major treatise dedicated exclusively to a list of magical formulas—hundreds of them—is *Harba de-Moshe*, "The Sword of Moses." Another is *Sefer ha-Razim*, "The Book of Secrets," which is divided between magical information and descriptions of the celestial realms and the angelic powers governing them.

3) Merkavah exegesis. The first chapter of Ezekiel was regarded as the most detailed revelation of celestial and divine secrets in the Hebrew bible, and it seems that the tradition of expounding it and using it as a starting point for the description of angelic and divine realms is an early one. It has even been suggested that the "second chariot" (Ezek. ch. 10) is the first such exegesis.[17] Hekhalot and Merkavah treatises deal with this subject extensively. An example of a work dedicated to it is *Reiyot Yehezkel*, "The Visions of Ezekiel,"[18] in which Ezekiel is described as standing on the bank of the river *Kevar* and envisioning a series of chariots in the various heavens, as they are reflected in the water in front of him. Discussions of the nature and number of the holy beasts and the other powers surrounding the chariot, the throne of glory and the wonders above and below it and similar subjects abound in most treatises of this literature.

These three subjects exhaust almost all the material in the Hekhalot and Merkavah literature that reached us. They are all traditional, well-established subjects of spiritual speculation in Jewish culture; all of them can be found, for instance, in the Apocrypha and Pseudepigrapha, as well as in the Dead Sea Scrolls and early Christian literature. Particular details may reflect new concepts, but the subjects themselves are constant ones in Jewish religious writings. None of them can be characterized as "mystical"; exegetical speculation about the chariot, for instance, is midrashic activity that does not necessarily reflect mystical experience.

4) The mystical component in this literature, which also represents the first distinct mystical historical phenomenon in Judaism, is the fourth subject, found in several treatises in this literature. It is the practice of the "descent to the chariot," a subject that is found for the first time here, and it is different from the traditional subjects in that it includes a dynamic element, an activity, that is not found in any previous source: the ascension of the sage from heaven to heaven, from "palace" to "palace," overcoming difficulties and dangers, until he reaches the supreme palace, the throne of glory, "faces God in his beauty," and joins the celestial powers in their hymns of praise to the creator.

The sections dealing with this practice are found in four of the treatises of this literature: *Hekhalot Rabbati* ("The Greater Book of Divine

Palaces"), which is the most extensive work in this group, at the center of which is the ascension of Rabbi Ishmael;[19] *Hekhalot Zutarti* ("The Lesser Book of Divine Palaces"), which is probably the oldest work in this group, at the center of which is Rabbi Akibah's ascension;[20] *Ma'aseh Merkavah* ("The Work of the Chariot"), which is an anthology of hymns and practices of the "descenders";[21] and *Third Enoch* or the *Hebrew Book of Enoch*, describing the revelations given to Rabbi Ishmael by Enoch in his ascension to the divine world.[22] These four treatises are characterized by several elements, all of them new, that are not found in the talmudic and midrashic literature nor in the other treatises of the Hekhalot and Merkavah literature:

1) They describe a group of sages, headed by Rabbi Akibah, Rabbi Ishmael (the two principal sages of the mishnah), and the head of the school, Rabbi Nehunia Ben ha-Kanah (a rather obscure sage who owes his prominence here to his being the teacher of Rabbi Ishmael). This group is described as convening in Jerusalem and holding common rituals. An extensive description in one of these treatises attributes to these mystics unmatched magical powers that enable them to overcome all their opponents and vanquish all enemies.

2) Distinct, unparalleled terminology, like the term *hekhalot* in the plural as signifying the seven layers of the celestial realms within the seventh heaven. The word *hekhal* may refer either to the temple or to a kingly palace (see below).

3) A systematic angelology that may have developed into a concept of pleroma of eight angelic-divine powers.[23] These higher powers are distinguished by the addition of the title "Lord God of Israel" to their angelic names, a title not found anywhere in previous literature as applying to anyone but God himself.

4) The distinct, paradoxical terminology describing the mystical practice itself, the "descent" and "ascent" to and from the chariot.[24]

5) Another element that is found in a fifth treatise: the concept of the *Shiur Komah*, "the measurement of the height," describing the magnitude of God and his limbs in stark anthropomorphic terms and mysterious names. This concept may be the most important one that ancient Jewish mysticism introduced into Jewish thought, and it became a central one in all subsequent Hebrew mystical and esoterical literature. The concept of the *Shiur Komah* is not found explicitly in

the other four treatises describing the mysticism of "descent to the chariot," but it may be assumed to be a part of the concept of God of these early mystics.[25]

6) A new interpretation of the biblical book of Song of Songs as a self-portrait of God. The *Shiur Komah* concept is based on Song of Songs 5:10–17, the physical description of the (male) lover, and other elements in this literature seem to be based on an identification of the Song as a self-expression of God. The meaning of the term *hekhal* is dependent on this new concept: It can be conceived as a reference to the celestial temples,[26] or, if the stronger influence is that of the Song of Songs, it should be understood as the divine counterpart to Solomon's palace.[27]

7) A unique concept of history, which deviates in a meaningful way from the traditional historical narrative of talmudic-midrashic literature. Thus, for instance, Rabbi Ishmael, who was born about the time that the second temple was destroyed in 70 C.E., is described as a "high priest the son of a high priest" who officiates in the temple in Jerusalem. The circle of mystics is described as convening in the temple itself, and the names of the participants include some that could not be together in the same age. It is difficult to understand this concept, and the authors of these treatises seem to have had a unique attitude toward history to which we have no key.[28]

8) A treatise close in some of its characteristics to the literature of the "descenders to the chariot" is the *Sar Torah*, "The Prince of the Torah," which describes the mystical experience of the builders of the Second Temple who had just returned from Babylonian exile, headed by Zerubavel ben Shealtiel. The treatise is centered around the revelation of a mnemonic magical formula that enables people to retain in their memory all that they have studied.[29]

The most important distinctive element of this mystical literature is its departure, or it may even be described as rejection, of the norms of the midrash. The authors of these treatises seem to have rebelled against the concept that divine truth can be reached only by tradition and exegesis, and demanded a direct experience of God, an actual spiritual meeting with him, and an experiential awareness of the divine realms. This literature is completely visionary and experiential, and the sages often present their visions in the first person. It includes numerous hymns that the mystics heard in the divine world or have sung themselves in the context of their spiritual journeys. There are harsh and cruel descriptions of the terrible fate awaiting those who failed in the mystical enterprise. The combination of all these elements serves as basis for the claim that this literature represents a distinct mystical phenomenon, a novel and to some extent a revolutionary one, within Jewish religious culture.

It is very difficult to present the chronological development of Hekhalot mysticism. We do not have in all these texts even one personal or geographic name, or a reference to an event, which may serve as a chronological starting point. Yet it seems that the phenomenon had it roots in the late second century C.E. or the beginning of the third, probably in Palestine, and it continued to exist as a closed, marginal circle or circles till the seventh or eighth centuries; it is probable that the later phase of its existence occurred in Babylonia. The earliest treatise in this small library may have been *Hekhalot Zutarti*, in which only Rabbi Akibah plays a part, following the talmudic parable of the Four Who Entered the Pardes. The peak of creativity of this school may be represented by *Hekhalot Rabbati* and the *Shiur Komah*, in which both Rabbi Akibah and Rabbi Ishmael participated, and the circle is portrayed as being led by Rabbi Nehunia ben ha-Kanah. *Ma'aseh Merkavah* is close in character to these two, while *Third Enoch* and *Sar Torah* seem to represent a later, Babylonian stratum.

It should be mentioned that this period is parallel chronologically to that in which Christian mysticism began to flourish, first among the Greek church fathers and somewhat later among the Latin ones. Such chronological proximity naturally raises the question of a possible influence in one direction or another, but there seems to be no basis to that. If the list of eight main characteristics of Hekhalot mysticism is reviewed, it is obvious that only one of them may be relevant to a comparison between Judaism and Christianity—the new interpretation of the Song of Songs, but even concerning this the details are radically different.[30] On the other hand, the dominant factors in the emergence of Christian mysticism, namely the beginnings of desert monasticism, the concepts of virginity and celibacy are very far from the worldview and the experience of the Jewish mystics. It is meaningful to note that Jewish mysticism first appears when Judaism was about a millennium and a half old, whereas mysticism in Christianity began when this religion was hardly a century and a half old.

A similar problem is presented by the chronological-geographical proximity of Hekhalot mysticism to Christian Gnosticism, which peaked in the Middle East in the second and third centuries. Gershom Scholem pointed out some aspects of typological resemblance between them, yet no historical point of contact between the two religious phenomena has been established. Neither do we have any evidence that there was a Jewish Gnosticism that preceded and served as a source for Christian Gnosticism. It is a matter of taste and semantics whether one is inclined to use this term as an adjective describing ancient Jewish mysticism; historically, we do not find any contact between it and the other major religious movements that flourished at the same time.

The Hekhalot texts do not seem to have had a meaningful impact on Jewish religious culture during the many centuries of late antiquity and the early Middle Ages. They are hardly mentioned in late midrashic collections, and their characteristic terminology cannot be discerned in subsequent texts. There are a few compilations that included Hekhalot material, like the *Alphabet of Rabbi Akibah*, but the actual mystical practice of "descent to the merkavah" did not express itself in later texts. The concept of the divine figure as the gigantic *Shiur Komah* made more of an impression, and we have evidence of that both in internal sources and in external ones.

Another important Jewish esoterical work that was written at the same time that the Hekhalot mystical treatises first appeared was the *Sefer Yezira*, "The Book of Creation," which had very little impact during late antiquity and the beginning of the Middle Ages, but later became one of the most influential texts of medieval Jewish mysticism and, subsequently, of the Christian kabbalah. *Sefer Yezira* cannot be described as a mystical work in the usual sense of the term, because it is clearly oriented toward an investigation of cosmogony and cosmology. It achieved its unique place in the history of mysticism and esotericism by its development of the concepts of the power of the letters of the alphabet and of the harmony between God, the cosmos, and man.[31]

Sefer Yezira does not use the terminology and concepts that characterize Hekhalot mysticism, and should not be regarded as belonging to that school. It developed a unique terminology, to which we do not have any parallel, including the term *sefirot,* which was destined to play a central role in the medieval kabbalah a millennium later. It is similar to the Hekhalot texts in that it represents a rejection of the dominant culture of midrash, of oral tradition and biblical exegesis. Unlike the Hekhalot it did not present experience as a substitute to midrash, but speaks authoritatively without relying on any source (it has been later attributed to Abraham the Patriarch, but this is not found in the ancient text itself). It uses only a handful of biblical verses, and does not mention the traditional rabbinic commentaries on the creation. Not only that, but it seems to ignore the creation narrative in the book of Genesis itself, using only a few terms (especially those in Gen. 1:2).

It is impossible to describe here the enigmatic and complex ideas of this small treatise. Suffice it to say that the main concept is the development of the idea of creation by language into a scientific system. The author claims that if God created the universe by language, then the laws of the universe are those of language. Natural science is identified with grammar. Every linguistic element is identified in this work as representing divine power that is expressed in the world on three levels: cosmic (planets, elements, constellations); time (days, weeks, months); and man (limbs, orifices, senses). They are all operated by letters and groups of letters governed by the laws of grammar, and including, in a way not clarified in the text, the first ten numbers, 1–10, called here *sefirot* and given roles in the creation of the universe.

This enigmatic treatise, probably frowned upon by rabbinic culture, was discovered by Jewish scientists and rationalistic philosophers in the tenth century, who found in it a source for Jewish authentic scientific tradition that could be used when they tried to integrate Judaism with the prevailing rationalistic-scientific civilization of medieval Islam. They wrote many commentaries on the treatise from this point of view, but in the end of the twelfth century and during the thirteenth they were replaced by medieval Jewish mystics and esoterics who developed new, sometimes mystical, interpretations of the ancient text.

It is impossible to point out a central, dominant Jewish mystical phenomenon during the Gaonic period (sixth to eleventh centuries). We have evidence that esoteric speculation continued on the margins of Jewish culture, dealing mainly with holy names, angelology, magical formulas, and possibly merkavah and genesis speculations, which were not incorporated in definite worldviews and treatises. There are Hebrew manuscripts from the High Middle Ages that contain scattered material, brief treatises, and notes, which may have originated in this period. It is evident, however, that medieval Jewish mysticism was a new phenomenon, a new beginning on different premises, even though it relied heavily on the traditions of ancient Jewish mysticism.

The Sufi mystical circles had a marked influence on Jewish thinkers in the eleventh, twelfth, and thirteenth centuries, even though they did not coagulate to create a distinct Jewish Islamic-inspired mysticism (as did Jewish rationalistic philosophy from the tenth century onward, which created a full-fledged Jewish religious-philosophical culture that dominated Jewish intellectual life in southern Europe for several centuries). Yet works like those of Bahya Ibn Paquda in the eleventh century and Rabbi Abraham Maimon, the son of Maimonides in the thirteenth, may be regarded as chapters in the history of Jewish mysticism. The medieval chapters in this history took shape in the second half of the twelfth century, in Christian Europe.

V. Historical Outlines: The Middle Ages

Jewish esoterical speculations had a second resurgence in the High Middle Ages, after being relatively dormant for several centuries, and this happened in two parallel centers in about the same time. One was centered in the Rhineland, the participants known mainly as *Hasidey Ashkenaz* or the Jewish Pietists in Medieval Germany, and the other, in Provence and northern Spain, is known as the Kabbalah.

A. The Esoterics of Medieval Germany

The term *Hasidey Ashkenaz* is a traditional one that was adopted by modern scholars as well to denote Jewish esoteric, mystical, and pietistic groups mainly in medieval Germany in the twelfth and thirteenth centuries. It is not a very good term, because it tends to hide the independence and divergence of these schools, which often did not know even of the existence of each other, so that combining them into one phenomenon is highly misleading. Some of these are represented by isolated, anonymous treatises, like *Sefer ha-Hayim* and *Sefer ha-Navon*.

Others are distinct schools that produced numerous treatises (though most of them are anonymous), like the school that attributed its traditions to the fictional figure of Joseph ben Uzziel (known also as the "unique cherub" circle, the name of the main divine figure in their theology), and based its teachings on the ancient *Sefer Yezira*. The most prominent school was that which flourished mainly in the Rhineland, and most of the scholars associated with it belonged to the Kalonymus family, the dominant family in German-Jewish culture in that period.[32]

Like the parallel circles of the kabbalists, the Kalonymus family esoterics did not follow the ancient Jewish mystics in presenting experiential, visionary mystical texts. Their avenue of expression was exegesis—including the interpretation of the Hekhalot and Merkavah texts that reached them. A perplexing problem is presented by their attitude to the practice of the "descent to the chariot." The texts of this mystical activity reached us mainly from thirteenth-century manuscripts, or copies of such manuscripts, which were studied, edited, and paraphrased by Jewish-German esoterics of that period. Yet in none of the numerous original volumes of their writings that reached us do we have any reference to the mystical practice of the "descent." From a textual-historical point of view, this is quite incomprehensible. All other aspects of this literature are presented and discussed, but the mystical practice seems to be nonexistent. This can be explained by one of two possibilities: Either by a mysterious textual history the "descent" texts did not reach them, and were added to the manuscripts somewhat later, or they were familiar with these texts but decided to ignore and hide this practical aspect completely. The first possibility is very difficult to accept on textual grounds, and the second seems to be nearly impossible. How could several writers hide so completely a central subject in such a consistent and perfect manner? Was it because they disregarded it, or was it because of its importance, relating to their innermost religious experiences? The subject of the meanings of the tetragrammaton was regarded by them as sacred and dangerous, yet Rabbi Eleazar of Worms wrote a comprehensive monograph on it; could the descent be regarded as even more holy and esoteric? This is one of several historical-philological enigmas that haunt our understanding of the emergence of Jewish mysticism in medieval Europe.

The leaders of the Kalonymus school were the most prominent

sons of this family in three generations: Rabbi Samuel ben Kalonymus, known in the unusual title "the saint, the pious, the prophet," who flourished in the middle of the twelfth century; his son, Rabbi Judah, who moved from the Rhineland to Regensburg, and their relative and disciple, Rabbi Eleazar ben Judah ben Kalonymus of Worms. The main contributions of this school to the development of Jewish mysticism can be presented in the following subjects:

1) **The Development of the Concept of a Multiple-Powers Divine Realm.** At the center of the Kalonymus circle's theology stands the figure of the divine glory (*kavod*), which is different from the supreme Godhead, often called "the creator" (*ha-bore*). This divine glory is conceived as a divine emanation, which is indicated in the Bible by the tetragrammaton, and whose main function is the revelation to the prophets and being the subject of all anthropomorphic references in ancient texts. Rabbi Judah the Pious presented this theory in the context of a paraphrase of Rabbi Abraham Ibn Ezra's Commentary on the revelation to Moses in Exodus 33,[33] as an exegetical response to the textual-theological problems raised by those verses. It is clear that in this case it was not a spiritual experience or a vision that gave birth to the concept but the pressure of theological needs, the necessity to preserve divine infinity that does not allow any change or form, and the need for preserving the divine nature of the revelation to the prophets. Both Ibn Ezra and Rabbi Judah found in that concept a response to the problem of the stark anthropomorphism of the *Shiur Komah*; what Rabbi Ishmael described in that ancient treatise was the image of the glory, not that of the infinite creator. The functions of the *kavod* were extended to include response to human prayers and revelation to the righteous in the next world. Another circle, the "unique cherub" school, developed the concept further (even though there is no evidence that they were familiar with the Kalonymus concept), and distinguished between two emanated powers: the glory, which responds to prayers, but has no anthropomorphic features, and the "unique cherub," which sits on the throne of glory(!) and is revealed to the prophets and serves as the subject of the *Shiur Komah* speculation. Again, theological drives seem to have been dominant in the evolvement of these concepts rather than experiential-visionary ones. It is

clear, however, that in this historical juncture, in the late twelfth century, the concept of the unity of God underwent a dramatic change, and it allows from now on the existence of emanated powers besides the supreme Godhead, which have their distinct functions and serve as subjects of worship in religious rituals.

2) **Prayer.** Interpretation of the prayer book was one of the main esoteric concerns of the writers of the Kalonymus school. Rabbi Judah and Rabbi Eleazar wrote extensive commentaries on the prayers that are the earliest such works known to us (Rabbi Judah's was lost, Rabbi Eleazar's was preserved in several manuscripts). Rabbi Eleazar's disciple, Rabbi Abraham berabbi Azriel of Bohemia, wrote a voluminous commentary on the synagogue hymns (*piyyutim*), Arugat ha-Bosem.[34] They conceived of prayer as the spiritual everyday approach to God and contact with him, and made the subject central to their spiritual activity.

Rabbi Judah the Pious developed a unique, original concept of a mystical prayer in his lost *Commentary*, from which we have only quotations. He believed that the text of the prayers represented, in every letter, word and name in it, a universal numerical harmony that extended to every realm of existence—history, anthropology, the celestial realms, and every passage in the holy scriptures. This harmony becomes apparent when the numerical value and other semiotic characteristics of the text are analyzed. Therefore, it is forbidden to change even one letter from the traditional wording, because the most minute change destroys the whole harmonious structure. It seems that Rabbi Judah did not find adherents to his concepts even among his closest disciples, and his original mysticism, viewing all existence as a harmonious divine text, remained a dead end in the history of Jewish mysticism.

In an opposite direction, some writers of the Kalonymus circle, most prominently Rabbi Eleazar of Worms, developed religious expression in the form of individual prayer, a direct address delivered by a person to God, either in the context of repentance or even without a particular cause. The sanctity of the prayer, so strongly emphasized by these writers, helped place this ritual in the heart of Jewish mysticism, and the attitude of the kabbalists was very similar to theirs despite the different surrounding structure. It should be remembered that on the surface, prayer and mysticism seem to be markedly distant and even

antagonistic toward each other. Mysticism requires an individual relationship with God, segregated from society and seeking unique, experiential circumstances, whereas traditional prayer was a public ritual,
constantly repeating exactly the same words and phrases, representing
a communal relationship with God. The Kalonymus circle's varied
attempts at spiritualizing and personalizing the ritual of prayer had an
impact on subsequent Jewish mystical phenomena.

3) **Pietism.** The writers of the Kalonymus circle expressed the terrible
trauma of the vast persecutions of the Jews in the period of the
Crusades in Europe, which started in the mass murder of Jews in 1096
and was repeated in several waves in subsequent generations. They
developed, in response, a system of ethics and pietistic way of life,
extremely harsh and demanding, which was intended to prepare the
faithful for the ordeal of having to sacrifice their lives for the "sanctification of the Holy Name" and be martyred (*kiddush ha-shem*). This system was presented in several of Rabbi Eleazar's works, and especially in
Rabbi Judah the Pious's "The Book of the Pious" (*Sefer Hasidim*),
which probably includes, in its first chapters, a presentation of that system written by Rabbi Samuel ben Kalonymus, Rabbi Judah's father.[35] It
seems that Rabbi Judah even tried to organize a movement or a sect
that will follow this way of life and be separated from other Jewish communities, but this endeavor did not become a reality, and was not sup-
ported even by Rabbi Judah's most faithful disciples.

B. *The Emergence of the Kabbalah*
In many respects, the appearance of the kabbalah in Provence and
northern Spain in the end of the twelfth century and the beginning of
the thirteenth resembles the flourishing of the schools of esoterics in
central Europe at almost the same time. Both are recognized, first and
foremost, by the new concept of God that is centered around a system
of emanated divine powers with specialized functions to participate
together in the new conception of divine unity. Both gave new emphasis to the element of prayer in Jewish ritual and endowed it with
renewed spiritual power. Both presented themselves in the garb of
exegetical works, some of them pseudepigraphic and anonymous, while
others were written by well-known scholars. Both relied on narratives —

mostly fictional—of ancient sources and roots that connect them to biblical and talmudic times. Both used these new esoteric concepts to solve current theological problems, mostly arising from the adoption of the basic contentions of rationalism and neo-Platonism. Most of all, both of them expressed themselves in terminology and images derived to a very large extent from the Hekhalot and Merkavah texts and especially from the *Sefer Yezira* (though again, the specific terminology of the "descent to the chariot" is absent from both of them).[36]

The kabbalah is different from the Ashkenazi esoteric circles by the power of the new myths that it introduced into its literature. The most potent ones—found already in the book *Bahir*, the first text of the kabbalah (written about 1185)—are those of the ten divine emanated powers that are portrayed anthropomorphically as the *Shiur Komah*, the image of the divine world as a huge tree (upside-down, its roots above and its branches toward the earth), and the tenth divine power, the *shekhinah* (identified with the *kavod*, which is revealed to the prophets), which is conceived as a feminine power, in juxtaposition to the other nine powers that constitute the male figure. The scope and power of these and other relevant images far acceeded the theological needs that were raised by the domination of the relatively arid rationalistic thinkers. While most of the ideas of the Kalonymus and related circles can be understood in the immediate medieval cultural circumstances, the emergence of the kabbalistic myths is very difficult to confine in such boundaries.

Historians in the nineteenth century, and some later ones, tried to explain the appearance of kabbalistic mythology in the heart of medieval Judaism as an expression of a reaction against the rationalists, a resurgence of the powers of darkness against the light of reason engulfing Jewish culture. There is indeed such an element in the early kabbalah, though it is accompanied by other elements that try to reconcile and combine philosophical concepts and terminology with the kabbalistic myths. The dominating component of this new religious phenomenon is its insistence on tradition rather than reasoning (or mystical experience), and its endeavor to reinterpret all previous Jewish texts in the light of the new world of images, which claims to be the oldest and most authentic Jewish conception of the divine realms. The midrashic form was adopted by several early kabbalists, most notably

the author of the book *Bahir*, who not only used the midrashic methodologies and language, but by presenting Rabbi Nehunia ben ha-Kanah
as the speaker in the first paragraph, claimed to be the direct continuation of Hekhalot traditions.

Where did these new myths come from? Several scholars, including Gershom Scholem (but also others before and after him), tended to
assume that there may be some justice in the claims of the kabbalists,
and that some components of the new myths may be derived from
ancient traditions that were transmitted orally or in lost treatises. Some
even identified these lost sources as Gnostic, being the result of the
influence of early or late Christian Gnosticism, or a continuation of
ancient Jewish Gnosticism that may even have been the original source
of Christian Gnosticism. Elaborate speculative systems have been
developed in the attempt to find such internal or external sources for
kabbalistic terminology and imagery.

From a methodological point of view, it seems that such speculations have reached a dead end. After nearly 150 years, no meaningful
source of the new kabbalistic concepts has been identified. While it is
impossible to prove a negative, namely that there were no ancient
sources, it is time now to accept the current state of affairs and say that
as far as we know today the ideas of the kabbalah were developed by the
early kabbalists themselves, especially by the author of the book *Bahir*
and the first known kabbalist in the Provence, Rabbi Isaac ben
Abraham "the blind." If tomorrow some new material will be discovered, this conclusion should be reconsidered, but until that happens, it
seems that we have to describe the new kabbalistic myths as the result
of intense new speculations by the medieval writers who authored the
new kabbalistic treatises. Reliance on "oral traditions" as a source is
actually a declaration of ignorance. When someone says, "They may
have received it by oral tradition," one actually says, "I do not have any
idea where this came from, nor shall we ever know," because oral tradition is a postulation that can never be proved right or wrong. As far as
we know today, the kabbalah is a combination of ancient, known,
Jewish sources, especially Hekhalot texts and the *Sefer Yezira*, contemporary philosophical terminology and ideas, and original contributions
of writers of the High Middle Ages in Provence and Spain, some of
which may have been the result of mystical experiences.[37]

The early kabbalistic circles in the end of the twelfth century and during most of the thirteenth were very small: The author of the *Bahir* probably was an isolated individual mystic, whereas in Provence we know about two generations of a handful of kabbalists. The first meaningful center of kabbalistic study was established in the Catalonian small town of Gerona, near Barcelona, where several scholars were active in this field in the first half of the thirteenth century; the most prominent figure among them was Rabbi Moshe ben Nahman (Nahmanides), who was a leader of Spanish Jewry and wrote an extensive, influential commentary on the Pentateuch, using sometimes esoteric kabbalistic terminology and ideas.

In the second half of the thirteenth century there is a surge in kabbalistic creativity in Spain, represented first by a circle of kabbalists in Castile, headed by the brothers Rabbi Jacob and Rabbi Isaac, the sons of Rabbi Jacob ha-Kohen, and later by the circle of Rabbi Shlomo ben Adrat (known by the acronym Rashba). Parallel to them, a lone mystic, Rabbi Abraham Abulafia, tried to spread his experiential-alphabetical system that rejected the mythical concepts adopted by most other kabbalists.[38]

The kabbalah in Spain reached its peak near the end of the thirteenth century in the circle from which the book *Zohar*, the most important and influential work of the kabbalah, emerged (this monumental work is presented and discussed in several selections in this anthology). It was written by Rabbi Moshe de Leon, possibly in some collaboration with a close colleague, Rabbi Joseph Gikatilla (who was previously a disciple of Abulafia), and several other people may have contributed to the work of this circle.[39] This was the only age in the three centuries of the kabbalah's existence in Spain in which several scores of kabbalists may have been at work at the same time; it declined swiftly in the fourteenth century, and the kabbalah remained closed in very small and scattered circles until nearly the end of the fifteenth century.

These kabbalistic circles were marginal in Jewish culture in Spain, having very small impact. Some kabbalists became famous because of their leadership positions, like Nahmanides and the Rashba; others composed popular works of ethics, like Rabbi Jonah Gerondi and Rabbi Bahya ben Asher. The kabbalists may have had some impact on the several waves of antirationalistic polemics and controversies that influenced Jewish discourse in Spain and Provence in this period. In all their activities they exhibited an adherence to tradition, insisting that the ancient sources, when properly interpreted, include the correct answers to contemporary problems. From the second half of the thirteenth century and the early fourteenth, some kabbalists are found in other countries, first in Italy (Rabbi Menachem Recannati), Near East and North Africa, and the Byzantine empire. In the last decades of the thirteenth century the kabbalah began to penetrate the esotericists' centers in central Europe, and scholars tended to fuse together the new kabbalistic terminology with that of the esoteric doctrines of the Kalonymus circle. Their impact, however, was minimal. If it were not for what happened later, the kabbalah would have been remembered as a minor, almost marginal, component of Jewish culture in southern Europe.

C. The Expulsion and Safed

The dramatic change occurred when the long and mostly prosperous sojourn of the Jews in Spain was approaching its end, beginning with the mass persecutions of 1391 and culminating with the expulsions of the Jews from Spain in 1492 and their forcible conversion to Christianity in Portugal in 1497. A large part of the Jews of that period were converted to Christianity, the others went into exile, completely impoverished and dispirited; many perished in their hazardous journeys seeking refuge. The geography of Judaism in Europe was completely transformed: the Jewish population in Italy increased meaningfully as did that of North Africa and the Near East, and numerous new communities were being established and expanding in the relatively tolerant and vigorously spreading Ottoman Empire, in the Balkans, in Turkey and in the Holy Land, Syria and Egypt.[40]

This upheaval had also spiritual and cultural consequences. Jewish philosophical rationalism, the dominant worldview for half a millennium, was discredited: it was blamed for weakening the Jews' adherence to the practical, ritualistic aspects of Judaism, and by emphasizing the spiritual-intellectual aspects made it easier for many—especially the more affluent and educated parts of society—to convert to Christianity. This brought to an end a long and illustrious chapter in Jewish philosophy and theology, which was gradually replaced, during the sixteenth century, by the increasing interest in the kabbalah, and especially in the *Zohar* (which was printed twice, in Mantua and Cremona) in the 1560s, after an emotional controversy whether it is permitted to make the secrets of the kabbalah public. Schools of kabbalists appeared in various centers in Italy, in Greece, and elsewhere. This was integrated with a new surge of messianic speculations and expectations that began in the second half of the fifteenth century, and most of the writers of apocalyptic and messianic works, which abounded in this period, used the terminology and used the myths of the kabbalah. Within a short period—two or three generations—the kabbalah has been transformed from a marginal component of religious culture into a central worldview, supporting and giving expression to the cravings of individuals and communities, and the nation as a whole. Kabbalah became the language of Jewish culture, used in sermons and commentaries, ethical treatises, and messianic speculations.

This process was accompanied by the establishment of a great center of kabbalistic learning in Safed, a small town in the Upper Galilee. Safed attracted to it kabbalists from all over the Jewish world because of its proximity to a site that was believed to be the tomb of Rabbi Shimon bar Yohai, the second-century talmudic sage to whom the *Zohar* was attributed. Its atmosphere of isolation from the real world contributed to the flourishing in it of radical ideas and extreme, demanding ethical practices. Here Rabbi Moshe Cordovero, one of the greatest kabbalists of all generations, wrote his classical summary of the Zoharic kabbalah, *Pardes Rimonim* ("An Orchard of Pomegranates") and his extensive, voluminous commentary on the *Zohar*, *Or Yakar* ("Precious Light"). Another mystic, who believed that a divine presence is revealed to him frequently and directs him in all his deeds, wrote the most important legal work of modern Judaism that directs Jewish law and ritual to this day—the *Shulhan Arukh* ("Laid Table") by Rabbi Joseph Karo, a great lawyer and mystic. Messianic expectations abounded here, and there was even a concerted attempt by Safed kabbalists and scholars to enhance the arrival of the messiah by reenacting the lost line of rabbinic *semichah*, divine ordinations, which was lost in the early Middle Ages.

In this atmosphere the kabbalah underwent a revolutionary transformation, brought about by the new kabbalistic myth that was developed by Rabbi Isaac Luria Ashkenazi (d. 1572; known by the acronym
ha-Ari, "the Lion") and his closest disciples, especially Rabbi Hayim
Vital. Luria arrived in Safed from Egypt in 1570, when he was thirty-six
years old. About a dozen of Safed's kabbalists assembled around him
and heard his sermons and commentaries, which he never wrote down.
Two years later he died in a plague. This brief episode, however,
changed the character of the kabbalah and transformed it into the dominant religious worldview of traditional Judaism in the next three centuries. Subsequent major developments, like the messianic fervor of the
Sabbatian movement, or the emergence of the Hasidic sects, were all
based on Lurianic concepts.[41] To this day, there is no other Jewish
orthodox system of thought that rivals Lurianic kabbalah.

In Gershom Scholem's words, what Luria did was to turn the kabbalah around, from a nonhistorical quest for the secrets of the primordial process of creation, to the historical quest for ultimate redemption.
The Lurianic myth of divine, cosmic, and human history contains the
blueprint for the achievement of messianic deliverance, in which each
individual participates and each has to contribute his spiritual and
physical powers to its successful accomplishment. The uniqueness of
this worldview can be discerned even from this basic starting point.
Earlier kabbalists, like almost all other theologians, assume that before
the creation, before the beginning of cosmic or divine history, there was
a state of perfection, which should be reinstituted in the redemption.
Luria, however, postulated that there was never a state of perfection,
even when the Godhead alone existed; there was an innermost, hidden, potential crisis within the eternal Godhead, which the emanation
of the divine powers and the creation of the universe and humanity
were intended to resolve. Perfection, therefore, will be achieved for the
first time in the future, as a result of the endeavors of all the participants
in the process. A seeker of perfection should not withdraw from history
and try to unite himself with eternal unity of God as it existed before
everything, but should rather turn forward, into history, and take part in
the spiritual struggle which it represents, which is the only vehicle for
the achievement of perfection.

Luria introduced into the kabbalah a series of terms that represent his concepts of drama and myth that characterize divine and earthly processes. The first occurrence, before everything, was the *zimzum*, the divine withdrawal from a certain segment of space in order to allow the emergence of other beings, thus making evacuation and exile of the infinite divine power the characteristic of all existence. Into that empty space then flowed divine light intending to create the divine entities, the *sefirot*, as they were described in the early kabbalah. This process, however, failed, because some elements, always hidden in a potential manner within the Godhead, rebelled and refused to assume the constructive function designed for them. This primordial catastrophe is described in Lurianic kabbalah as "the breaking of the vessels," the *shevirah*, which caused the emergence of a dualistic divine existence, in which the lower part is dominated by the rebellious elements that now have assumed the character of the powers of evil, a demonic realm that strives to destroy the holy realms in the higher parts of the formerly empty space. This myth, which is described in great detail in the writings of Hayyim Vital and other of Luria's disciples (especially Rabbi Joseph Ibn Tabul), contains dramatic new concepts hitherto unknown in Judaism, like the limitation of divine omnipotence and the postulation that the roots of evil existed potentially within the eternal Godhead.

The most powerful concept introduced by Lurianic kabbalah is that of the *tikkun*, the "mending" (of the broken vessels). Everything that happened from the *shevirah* to this day, and everything that is going to happen in the future until complete redemption is achieved, is part of the process of the *tikkun*. After the "breaking of the vessels," the emanation of the divine realms, the creation of the universe, the creation of humanity, the choice of Abraham, the giving of the torah to Israel, the building of the temple in Jerusalem—all represented divine attempts to bring about the *tikkun* using different tools, and all have been in vain up to now; in several cases such attempts ended with a crushing new catastrophe, another "breaking," like Adam's sin in paradise or Israel's worship of golden calf near Mount Sinai. The process, however, goes on, and the Lurianic circle was confident that the time of final success was at hand: Many believed that the sacred year *shiloh* (1575), would see its culmination. Rabbi Hayyim Vital was absolutely confident that he himself was destined to be the messiah, to be crowned the king of the universe once redemption is completed and revealed.

The Lurianic myth is revolutionary and innovative, using terms and images that seemed to be foreign and impossible in a Jewish context. Yet its practical message was highly conservative. Immersion in the project of the *tikkun* meant complete dedication to the performance of Jewish commandments, precepts, and ethical norms, in the most traditional and conservative manner. During the shevirah sparks of divine light were captivated by the powers of evil. These should be set free and returned to their original place in the divine realms. The way to liberate such sparks is the performance of the commandments. Each righteous deed frees a captive spark, while every sin condemns another spark to captivity. The dedication to the process of the *tikkun* did not demand understanding and knowledge of the myth of which it is a component; just by doing it—praying on time in the prescribed circumstances, helping the poor, eating kosher, and observing the sabbath are enough, even without any inclination concerning the wider context and meaning of these deeds. In this sense, Lurianic doctrine is both conservative and democratic: It does not demand a change in behavioral religious norms, and it allots the power of redemption to every individual. While redemption is the paramount concern of this kabbalah, it is not messianic in the narrow sense of the term: Redemption is not dependent on the messiah and his employs, but on the religious performance of every individual. The messiah is the result of the completion of the *tikkun* rather than its cause. Because of this, the disciples of Luria did not try to publicize their revolutionary teachings; to the contrary, they tried— especially Vital—to keep them in strict secrecy. Good people were contributing to the tikkun even if they knew nothing about this term and its context. Orthodoxy was the important factor rather than spiritual awareness of the cosmic Lurianic myth. In this sense Lurianism is not Gnosticism, even though some other aspects of this doctrine may seem to be surprisingly close to some traditional Gnostic concepts and terms. Redemption did not depend on knowledge and understanding, but on a conservative, traditional way of life.

Luria's teachings did spread widely in the first half of the seventeenth century, being disseminated not only by kabbalistic monographs but mainly by hagiographic narratives concerning Luria and his disciples and many ethical popular works that presented or hinted at the new revolutionary concepts. It did, however, lay a very difficult burden on the shoulders of every single believer. The redemption of the whole universe, even that of the divine realms, depended on every single deed of every single person in every moment of his life. Each prayer, each ethical deed, might be the clinching one, releasing the last spark and bringing forth the messianic salvation. Each sin, each impure thought, may, on the other hand, plunge the universe into another catastrophe, strengthening the powers of evil and delaying the redemption. Individual responsibility knew no bounds. This system was probably suitable for the select group of dedicated pneumatics assembled in Safed, but it was very difficult to adopt as a way of life for normal, average communities all over the world. This may have been the reason why the democratic, egalitarian Lurianic theology gave rise to the first Jewish systems of religious, even mystical, leadership.

VI. Historical Outlines: The Modern Period

A. The Sabbatian Movement

The year 1666 marks a crossroad in the history of the kabbalah and of Judaism as whole. In this year the kabbalah broke the last barrier between its early origins as a marginal, esoteric spiritual phenomenon and became the dominant factor not only in religious worldview but in Jewish history as well. Three major events occurred during that one year: Nathan of Gaza proclaimed himself to be a prophet and identified Shabbatai Zevi as the messiah; the belief in Nathan the prophet and Shabbatai the messiah engulfed most Jewish communities, from London to Poland and from Amsterdam to Yemen; Shabbatai Zevi, threatened by the Ottoman Sultan, converted to Islam, forcing Judaism to confront the paradox of a converted messiah. In the next century and a half, up to the beginning of the nineteenth century, numerous sects of believers in Shabbatianism flourished in most of the major centers of Judaism, many of them esoteric and hidden, but together they constituted a major unsettling force, which caused—together with other historical changes—a radical upheaval in Judaism and gave it the diverse character it has today.[42]

The history of the Shabbatian movement has been studied in great detail, and its implications, spiritual and historical, were masterfully presented by Gershom Scholem. Three great mystics of this movement are portrayed in the selection presented in this volume—Nathan of Gaza, Jacob Frank, the archheretic who converted to Christianity in 1760, and Moshe Hayyim Luzzatto, who used some Shabbatian ideas in the formulation of his own messianic mission. One point, however, should be stressed because of its importance to the position of mystics in modern Judaism.

The messianic teachings of Nathan of Gaza were completely based on the Lurianic myth. The main theme was the duty of each individual to participate in the process of the uplifting of the scattered sparks, the result of the breaking of vessels, the primordial catastrophe, this enhancing the redemption. He presented one meaningful deviation, which was the source of major historical consequences. According to Nathan, the process of *tikkun* as described by Luria has been completely accomplished by 1666, and the universe was on the verge of redemption. There remained, however, one point, one inner core in the realm of evil, which was so tough that the usual procedure of correction could not overcome it. In order to transform this core of evil a divine emissary was sent, the messiah, who is destined to overcome it, but even he cannot accomplish it on his own: He must have the assistance of the whole people to support him. This they can do by putting their faith in him, enabling him to serve as the focus, concentrating the spiritual power of the nation in order to overcome evil. Faith in the messiah was therefore the added theological demand that Nathan introduced into the Lurianic system. By doing that he inserted into Judaism an idea that was almost completely absent for many centuries: the concept of mediated spiritual activity, a relationship between the believer and God that is not direct but is mediated by another person-entity, in this case the divine incarnation of one of the sefirot in the image of the messiah Shabbatai Zevi. A new concept of religious leadership thus emerged within Judaism, that of the mystical mediator between humanity and God, the mystical-messianic leader.

The numerous sects and groups of the Shabbatians during the generations following Shabbatai Zevi (d. 1676) were led by people who claimed to be the reincarnation of the messiah or his heirs in various forms. The new concept of leadership was thus exercised and diversified, to become a comprehensive phenomenon characteristic of the period. It was destined, however, to have its maximal impact in the new resurgence of Jewish spirituality and mysticism associated with the Hasidic movement, the most powerful expression of Jewish mysticism and Kabbalah in modern times.

B. Modern Hasidism

Rabbi Israel ba'al Shem Tov (1700–60), known by his acronym, the Besht, who is regarded as the founder of the Hasidic movement,[43] may be regarded as a paradigmatic Jewish mystic. He did not introduce a new system of thought, nor did he deal with traditional kabbalistic theosophy. His ethical teachings do not constitute a system of hierarchical values. He was an autodidact (though several legendary figures were described as his teachers—the prophet Ahia ha-Shilony, for instance, and Rabbi Adam Ba'al Shem), who did not write any treatise. His teachings are known to us from quotations preserved by his disciples, especially Rabbi Jacob Joseph of Polonoi, the first writer of the Hasidic movement, whose works were published more than twenty years after the Besht's death. The one document that reached us which may be regarded as authentic—a letter he wrote to his brother-in-law Rabbi Gershon of Kutov—is clearly a mystical document in form and content. It describes an "ascension of the soul," an experience in which he was visiting the celestial realms, and conveys a mystical message concerning language and religion. These facts had an impact on the vast movement that was established by his followers, and some of the most distinct mystical phenomena in the last few generations took shape within its context.

Hasidism has been portrayed, in scholarly works and in literature, as a redeeming social movement, representing a refreshing new pietism that replaced the single-minded immersion in talmudic, legalistic study. No wonder that such presentations, most notably by Martin Buber, described Hasidism in a manner that appealed to nonorthodox Jews and to Christians. It seemed to represent the denial of those aspects of Judaism that the nonorthodox and non-Jews detested, and made Hasidism accessible to spiritually inclined, socially and humanistically motivated people in the late nineteenth and twentieth century. In brief, Hasidism was conceived as a "less Jewish" and more human and humane phenomenon. In this context, the term *mysticism* in its more benign connotations was appropriate: It expressed the image of Hasidism as emphasizing the spiritual rather than the legal, the internal rather than the external aspects of worship.

One condition was necessary if one wished to preserve such an attitude toward Hasidism: It must come to an end in the beginning of the nineteenth century, somewhere around 1815. It must be conceived as a movement that flourished in the early modern times, and then replaced by Enlightenment, Reform, Emancipation, Assimilation, Socialism, and Zionism. If it is allowed to continue to exist in the later nineteenth and twentieth century, notwithstanding the early twenty-first century, it must be recognized as a power that fiercely opposed Enlightenment, Jewish integration in modernity, Socialism, and especially Zionism, and become the most strictly orthodox element in Judaism, rejecting and denying the study of mathematics and English, throwing stones at cars traveling on the sabbath in Jerusalem, and voting in the Israeli parliament against the Oslo agreements with the Palestinians. Indeed, many histories of Hasidism stop at 1815 including S. Dubnow,[44] and even Gershom Scholem's portrayal of the movement in the concluding chapter in *Major Trends in Jewish Mysticism* reads more like a eulogy for a lost past than a confrontation with contemporary religious-mystical phenomenon.[45] Almost all of Buber's monographs are dedicated to the Besht, the Great Maggid, Rabbi Dov Baer of Mezeritch who died in 1772, and Rabbi Nahman of Bratzlav who died in 1811, and his masterpiece, *Gog und Magog*, ends in 1815. Many tales in his *Tales of the Hasidim* quote Hasidic teachers who lived later, but they are denied any historical context, and are described as ancient sages who do not participate in later events.[46]

Hasidism, however, did not perish in 1815, but continued and continues to flourish, despite cataclysmic events and catastrophes that could destroy anything—the pogroms in eastern Europe after 1880, the First World War, the Russian Revolution and civil war, the persecutions by Stalin's regime, and above all, the Holocaust, which decimated it and seemed to have put an end to its physical existence. When the movement was uprooted from its places of origin in southern Russia, the Ukraine and eastern Poland, it moved west, and reestablished itself in Warsaw, Romania, and Hungary. When the Holocaust destroyed these new centers, contemporary Hasidism crossed the seas and built new habitats around New York and in Jerusalem and Bnei Brak in Israel. They still preserve the names of the old towns in Eastern Europe as identifying their communities, while becoming integrated in a world of satellite television, videotapes, software, and diamond commerce. It grew very fast since the 1950s, and can be regarded today as the most dynamic social groups in contemporary Judaism, its influence growing not only in Israel but also in New York and in American politics.

What is the source of this unbelievable regenerative power? The answer cannot be sought only in the teachings of the Besht and his direct disciples. It has to be found in the forces that held it together for two and a half centuries and continue to be active and dominant today. This cannot be attributed to a specific religious idea; attempts to identify Hasidism as a whole by a certain body of ideas have all failed.[47] The answer can be found in its new concept of leadership, the establishment of mystical leadership, as a hereditary power inherent in the families of the founders. These leaders, the Zaddikim, are conceived as intermediaries between man and God, being themselves entities that are essentially divine in nature, the incarnation of the kabbalistic sefirah, the ninth one, called yesod or zaddik in the classical texts of the kabbalah.

Hasidism is meaningful not only in its encouragement of the mystical element in the kabbalah, but also in its designation of a class of leaders that is characterized by mystical contacts with both its community and the divine realms—the Zaddik, the leader of a Hasidic community. The early teachers of Hasidism, in the two generations following the Besht, were charismatic leaders whose influence over their followers was the result of their own spiritual power. But very soon Hasidism was transformed into a dynastic system, in which dozens of families of Zaddikim directed the lives of the families of their adherents generation after generation. The Zaddik was understood in Hasidism as intermediary between his community and God, and as a representative of the divine on earth, essentially different from ordinary human beings. They are endowed with mystical powers by heredity, and they are bonded with their adherence in a connection that cannot be described by any other term but *mystical*. Here we find, for the first time, a class of Jewish leaders who are conceived—independent of their personal character and inclination—as mystics. It is ironic that Judaism had to wait until the postenlightenment period in order to produce a class of mystical leaders who lead segments of it in the postmodern era.

One of the best-known contemporary expressions of Hasidism has been the fierce messianic outburst surrounding the leader of Habad, Lubavitch Hasidism, which came to believe that its recent leader, Rabbi Menakhem Mendel Shneersohn, was the messiah; this movement peaked in the late 1980s and early 1990s and did not perish when he died in 1996. It is wrong, however, to assume that this Hasidic sect, one of the largest, was inclined toward messianism from its beginnings in the late eighteenth century. Quite to the contrary, the first teachers of Lubavitch, the founder, Rabbi Shneur Zalman of Liadi, his great disciple Rabbi Ahraon ha-Levi of Stroszila, and Rabbi Shneur's son and heir, Rabbi Dov Baer, developed the most intense and radical mystical worldview in modern Judaism.[48] According to them, all existence is an illusion, a deception; what is real only seems to be so, and reality itself can be achieved only by complete withdrawal and rejection of sensual and intellectual perceptions into the realm of the *ayin*, nothingness, which is the true being. They showed the way for an individual to sever all contacts with the world and immerse himself in the pure spirituality of the divine realm. This mysticism negates historical activity, and does not encourage messianism. A legend that prevailed in Habad circles insisted, however, that there will be seven successive leaders in the Lubavitch dynasty, and the seventh will be childless and he will be the messiah. Rabbi Menakhem Mendel Shneersohn, the seventh in this line, was thus expected to redeem the world. It should be noted that his extensive writings, or at least those that were published to date, lack any experiential element, nor did he or any of his followers publish anything that could be regarded as a record of a mystical experience.

C. Contemporary Judaism

The twentieth century may be described as a period of decline of Jewish mystical creativity, yet the urge for a direct, metalinguistic approach to God manifested itself in numerous ways and directions. Traditional kabbalistic writing is most prominently represented by the great *Commentary on the Zohar* by Rabbi Ashlag, in nearly thirty volumes. Based on the teachings of Isaac Luria, it was written in the first half of the twentieth century. One should not ignore the unprecedented surge in the printing of kabbalistic works, many of them never published before, like the great *Commentary on the Zohar* by Rabbi Moshe Cordovero, written in Safed in the middle of the sixteenth century, also in numerous large volumes. Some circles of kabbalists continued to flourish in Jerusalem in the first half of the twentieth century, though they did not publish any distinct, unique new approaches to the classical kabbalistic subjects.

Hasidism remained the main representative of the living tradition of kabbalah and mysticism, even though no prominent figures in either of them emerged in this period. Hasidism expressed its spiritual power by its resurgence after disasters, by the adherence to the traditional leaders, by preserving its traditions in a fast-changing world.

A new mixture of kabbalistic traditions, worship of leaders, and especially magic took shape in Israel in the last few decades. Parallel to the Western New Age, Israelis, especially those of Asian origins, developed new reverence to "kabbalistic" leaders, who were in most cases magicians and writers of amulets. Numerous "gurus" are presently operating in Israel, healing spiritual and physical ailments and offering ways of confronting the hardships of modern existence; they are routinely called "kabbalists," even though there is hardly any element of the authentic traditions of the kabbalah in their teachings. Celebrations are held at the tombs of old sages, in Safed and Netivot, attracting sometimes tens of thousands of adherents; as usual in such circumstances, this popular quest for heroes, saints, and healers is sometimes commercialized and used or abused by impostors. On the whole, the situation is not different from the contemporary surge of interest in magic, astrology, and gurus that characterizes contemporary Western culture.

Modern Hebrew literature, which followed the Enlightenment and Zionism, was initially posited as an opposition to mysticism, kabbalah, and traditional life in general. Some important works of the Hebrew writers of the first half of the nineteenth century represented attacks on traditional way of life in general and Hasidism in particular. This, however, was replaced by the end of that century by a complex mixture of nostalgia and criticism, expressed in the classical works of Mendele Mocher Sefarim, Hayim Nachman Bialik, Michah Yosef

Beryzchevski, and Shmuel Yosef Agnon, among many others. None of the modern Hebrew writers can be described by any stretch of the term as inclined toward mysticism. They were, however, deeply immersed in Jewish traditional literature, including the kabbalah, so that they often used terms and phrases derived from such sources. In a few cases they did express experiences that can be described as mystical; this is especially true concerning Bialik, whose views concerning the nature of language and the meaning of poetry were very close to those current among mystics; an example, the poem Heziz va-Met, is included in the selection below.

The emerging Jewish community in the Land of Israel produced a vibrant, dynamic literature in Hebrew, both in poetry and prose, which was regarded as central to the emerging Jewish culture in the Holy Land, and therefore was highly respected and even revered. This attitude did not change when the State of Israel was established in 1948; rather, despite deep changes in social and cultural circumstances, Hebrew literature preserved its dynamism and its centrality in Israeli culture. The number of poets and novelists publishing in Israel far surpasses the norms of other countries, and their works are read with more dedication and attention than is customary in most contemporary cultures. Even the current revolutionary, and sometimes destructive, postmodern and post-Zionist cultural trends did not diminish the energy and the impact expressed by contemporary Hebrew writers.

Israeli literature is withdrawing very fast from direct, meaningful contact with the traditional Jewish literature, including the Bible, the Talmud, and the kabbalah. Following the transformation of Hebrew into a spoken, "normal" language, the reliance on the literary sources is diminishing. It is very rare, therefore, to find in contemporary Hebrew creative writing elements that represent a direct continuation of the past, including past mystics. Yet there is a distinct mystical aspect in current Israeli culture that should not be ignored in this anthology. It can be explained in part by the impact of secondary sources, especially the works of Martin Buber, Gershom Scholem, and Isaiah Tishby, which had and have wide readership in Israel and have become part of the intellectual discourse. Tishby's translation of parts of the Zohar in Hebrew,[49] Scholem's monograph on Shabbatai Zevi, and Buber's *Tales of the Hasidim* integrated sections of the mystical tradition within contemporary culture. The influence of Western trends, imported from Europe and America, revering Hindu and Buddhist mystics, also encouraged some writers—especially poets—to turn to what they regarded as the Jewish counterparts of such expressions. In several cases one can discern authentic, original expressions of mystical experiences in the works of Israeli poets, often completely detached from older traditions. This is not a central characteristic of contemporary Israeli literature, yet mystics seldom view themselves as standing in the center of a culture. It is sufficient proof, however, to the fact that the varieties of Jewish mysticism have not been exhausted.

VII. The Christian Kabbalah

Since the sixteenth century, the term *kabbalah* (in different spellings, including cabala, for example) has become a common word in European languages. It denotes a secret lore that was preserved by the Jews, which is closely associated with magical powers. It brings to mind methodologies like numerology and the mysterious powers of the alphabet, and it also has become a reference to a secret society, a group of rebels (*cabal*). It has spread in the last generation and became a central term in the various manifestations of the New Age, and numerous groups and schools in the United States and Europe teach something they call kabbalah as a remedy for all modern ailments, spiritual and physical. It seems to be occupying today the place that Zen Buddhism held a few decades ago, it is closely associated with astrology and alchemy, and it is believed to contain the power to bring peace of mind and fortify contemporary men and women for a successful life. The roots of this phenomenon, which is radically different from the Hebrew kabbalah, lie in a unique religious phenomenon of the late fifteenth century and the beginning of the sixteenth.

The school of humanists in Florence that was led by Marcilio Ficino was the origin of this movement. Ficino, a protégé of the great Medici house, was the translator of Plato's works from Greek to Latin, but his most important contribution to European culture in early modern times was the translation into Latin of the Hermetic corpus, a collection of treatises that was believed to have been authored by the legendary Hermes Trismegistus, who was a contemporary of Moses in

Egypt and whose writings were believed to have been the source of Greek esoteric tradition, most often associated with Pythagoras. Today it is believed that the Hermetic treatises originated in Egypt in late antiquity, reflecting the last stages of Egyptian Hellenistic culture, probably influenced also by Gnosticism, before it was taken over by Christianity. Ficino and his disciples became deeply committed to assembling and analyzing the "mysteries of the East"—Egyptian hieroglyphs, Coptic and Arabic scripts, ancient alchemy and astrology, and all the manifestations of magic old and new. They believed that these mysterious sources included in them the early, true philosophy, which is the real source of Christian truth.

The leading figure in this school after Ficino was a young Italian count, Giovanni Pico della Mirandola, who at a very young age distinguished himself in the knowledge of languages, courageous writing, and charismatic personality. He learned Hebrew, and became fascinated by the kabbalah as presented to him by several Jewish scholars and Jewish converts to Christianity (though there were Jewish scholars who tried to dissuade him from this field, like his teacher of Aristotle's philosophy, Rabbi Eliyahu del Medigo, who later wrote a Hebrew philosophical treatise against the kabbalah, identifying the *Zohar* as a medieval work). Among his teachers were Rabbi Johannan Alemano, a known kabbalist, and Flavius Mithridates (known by several other names as well), a Jewish convert who translated for Pico from the Hebrew numerous treatises of kabbalah and writings of the Kalonymus circle of esoterics.[50] Pico's studies, summarized in his famous *Nine Hundred Theses*, led him to the conclusion that the truth of Christianity can be best demonstrated by kabbalah and magic.[51] This and other statements caused Pico to be severely criticized by the church. He died very young (1494), but his intellectual legacy had great impact on subsequent generations of humanists and esotericists. He himself summed up his attitude by saying: Truth can be better gleaned from what is not understood than from what is understood.

As far as the kabbalah is concerned, the most important disciple of Pico was the German theologian Johannes Reuchlin, who published in 1494 his first treatise on the subject—*De Verbo Mirifico*—but his masterpiece was published many years later—in 1517, *De Arte Kabbalistica*.[52] This work served as a basis for the numerous treatises that followed in

the next two centuries, which constitute the body of speculative literature known as the Christian kabbalah.

Reuchlin acquired an impressive knowledge of the Hebrew language (he wrote several treatises on the language and its grammar) as
well as a meaningful knowledge of postbiblical Hebrew literature,
including the Talmud and midrash, Jewish medieval philosophy and
Hebrew commentaries on the Bible. The term *kabbalah* in his works
refers to all this vast body of literature and thought, and not to the particular esoterical tradition that we identify as kabbalah proper. In this
Reuchlin accepted the claim of the medieval Jewish kabbalists themselves, that the kabbalah is a secret tradition inseparable in its origin and
transmission from the oral law and talmudic-midrashic hermeneutics.
Reuchlin is not the first to identify Maimonides, for instance, as a kabbalist: Jewish esotericists did that since the thirteenth century. Needless
to say, Reuchlin (like Pico) did not differentiate between the Rhineland
esotericists and the Kalonymus school and kabbalists of Spain,
Provence, and Italy. Thus, the library that Reuchlin used to describe the
Hebrew kabbalah was very different in scope and character from that of
actual works of the medieval kabbalists in the Jewish tradition.

De Arte Kabbalistica is a narrative of a three-day discussion of
secret lore between a Christian, a Muslim, and a Jewish scholar, who
meet in an inn. The Jewish scholar, Simon, is presented as the leader
and the most knowledgeable among the three. Reuchlin described him
as a scion of the family of Rabbi Shimeon bar Yohai, the author of the
Zohar. It is very difficult to find in medieval and early modern Christian
literature a more respectful presentation of a Jew, as well as a positive
depiction of the Talmud, which traditionally was portrayed as the root
of all evil, including in this particular period. Reuchlin was denounced
for this, and throughout the rest of his life he had to defend himself
from accusations of heresy.[53] The central message of the work is the
ultimate unity of the messages of ancient philosophy, represented by
Pythagoras, the ancient kabbalah, and the esoteric truth of Christianity.
Reuchlin, like all other Christian kabbalists, was first and foremost a
Christian theologian, completely dedicated to his religion, who
believed that he has found a new, potent source that unveils hitherto-
unknown levels of Christian truth that make his faith stronger and
closer to God.

Reuchlin, like the many Christian kabbalists who followed him, did not derive from the Hebrew sources the elements that were paramount in the world of the Hebrew kabbalists, namely the emanation of the divine manifestations from the Godhead, the juxtaposition of divine powers of good and evil, the meaning of the prayers and commandments in the struggle between them, nor in the intricacies of the inner relationships within the divine realm between the masculine and feminine powers. Instead, Reuchlin was fascinated by midrashic methodologies, those of gematria, notaricon, and temurah, and the commentaries on the forms of the Hebrew letters and their meanings. It can be said that what Reuchlin discovered in the postbiblical Jewish traditions was the semiotic, rather than semantic, usage of language, something that was lacking in Christian sources that dealt almost exclusively with the semantics of the divine message. This included also the traditions of divine names, unknown in Christianity and the vast treasury of angelology and angel's names, including the magical possibilities inherent in these powerful, mysterious names. Most of these elements are not essentially connected with the Hebrew kabbalah: They represent talmudic-midrashic methodologies and esoteric traditions, many of which developed without any dependence on the kabbalah; some kabbalists used them extensively, while others ignored them. As a result, the Christian kabbalah is different, in content and form and its basic conceptions, from the Hebrew esoteric tradition designated by that name.

In the Christian kabbalah, the balance between magic and mysticism was completely changed. The Christian kabbalists can hardly be described as mystics. They did not seek experience of God, but rather knowledge of his secrets in esoteric methodologies. We have very few, if any, examples of experiential or visionary material in this vast literature. It is presented as a subject of study, like ancient languages, deciphering the Egyptian hieroglyphs, astrology, and alchemy, and especially magic, rather than a means to spiritual proximity to God. Later Christian kabbalists identified all these esoteric sciences with the kabbalah, and only a few of them returned to the Hebrew sources to glean new information (especially influential was Knorr von Rosenroth, author of the *Kabbalah Denudata*, in two volumes, Sulzbach 1677–1684).

The main purpose of the sixteenth- and seventeenth-century Christian kabbalists was to demonstrate the *harmonia mundi*, the identity of structure between man and his soul, the cosmos and its scientific laws, and God himself. In this, the kabbalah was helpful, and special significance was given to the Sefer Yezira, which was regarded as an early source of the kabbalah. In this they were in close contact with their Jewish sources, which strongly held the view of the intricate similarity of structure and interdependence in the spiritual significance of all realms of existence, from the most elevated divine realms to the humblest creatures on earth. Yet the Christian kabbalah was destined to develop these ideas into another channel in which the Hebrew sources seldom led: modern experimental science.[54] Several of the greatest figures of European thought in the late seventeenth century and the beginning of the eighteenth represent the transition from magic, *harmonia mundi*, and Christian kabbalah to modern science, the most prominent among them being Giordano Bruno, Leibniz, and Newton.

Christian kabbalah continued its existence in European esotericism throughout the eighteenth, nineteenth, and twentieth centuries, and seems to be surging again in the beginning of the twenty-first century. The "traditionalism" of Molitor influenced Gershom Scholem, according to his own testimony, in his early studies of the kabbalah, while he rejected the usage of this doctrine by Karl Gustav Jung. A new "scientific" awakening of this concept is found in the articles of Simo Parpola, who maintains that the tetragrammaton, and its kabbalistic interpretations, were the source of some symbols in ancient Assyrian writings, as well as that of Greek philosophy, monotheism, and culminating in Christianity.[55] Kabbalah has become a meaningful component of the various New Age sects and views that began to spread several decades ago and seem to be a dominant force in the emerging culture of the new century. It is being united with astrology and alchemy, with Zen Buddhism and Hinduism, as well as with the multitude of schools of "alternative medicine" that are becoming a new dominant religion. Circles studying "kabbalah" have spread throughout the Western world from Los Angeles to Berlin; hundreds of books of New Age lore are published including *kabbalah* in their titles, and thousands of such locations are spread throughout the Internet. Nothing of the authentic Hebrew kabbalah was retained during this process.[56] Needless to say, most of the perpetrators of this phenomenon have no knowledge of Hebrew and no access to the original sources of the kabbalah.[57]

1 THE REVELATION OF THE SECRET OF THE WORLD

This is one of the earliest texts of Hebrew mysticism. It is a complex expression of a dramatic mystical-historical experience; it can be understood as the mystics' own description of the beginning of Jewish mysticism in late antiquity.

The work in which this section is included is known as *Hekhalot Rabbati*, "The Greater Book of Divine Palaces," and its core is a detailed narrative presenting the ascension of Rabbi Ishamel to the seventh palace, in the seventh heaven, and his successful vision of the "king in his beauty" on the throne of glory. The story of the ascension, however, is integrated within a complex fictional tale that includes apocalyptic and martyriorological elements, which reach their peak together in a description of an assembly of the mystics in the temple in Jerusalem, when their leader, Rabbi Nehunia ben ha-Kanah, reveals "the secret of the world"—the instructions for the mystical procedure of ascent to and descent from the holy chariot.

The treatise *Hekhalot Rabbati* includes the main part of the story, but some of the details are found in another, closely related work, known in Hebrew literature as "The Story of the Ten Martyrs."[1] According to the combined narrative, the emperor of Rome, called here Lupinus or Lupianus, became aware of the biblical verse that condemns to death anyone who kidnaps a person and sells him as a slave.[2] He realized immediately that the ten brothers of Joseph, the sons of the Patriarch Jacob, committed just this crime and had never been punished. He decided to act in order to fulfill the demands of justice, and to execute, in place of the ten brothers, ten great scholars of that time. Their names are given, and they are all prominent Tanaim (sages of the Mishnah) of the second century, several of them known to have been martyred by the Emperor Hadrian around 135–138, in the context of the Bar Kochba rebellion.

In *Hekhalot Rabbati*, chapters 4 and 5, there is the description of the reaction of the circle of mystics, "the descenders to the chariot" to the news of this Roman decree, which condemned many of them to death. Their leader, Rabbi Nehunia ben Ha-Kanah, sends Rabbi Ishamel to the divine realm to inquire whether this decree is just a human decision of the emperor—if it was such, the mystics have no difficulty in overcoming it by their magical powers—or whether it is a divine decree that has to be obeyed. Rabbi Ishmael ascends and finds that it was a divine one, the result of a long and difficult process of negotiations between God and the celestial representative of Rome, the archenemy of Israel, who is given here the name of Samael.[3] Samael insisted that justice demands that the ten sages will be executed. This cannot be denied by the celestial court, but in return Samael is required to agree that the city of Rome and its emperor will be cruelly destroyed. Samael accepted the condition, and the text includes a detailed apocalyptic description of the process in which clouds of pestilence will rain destruction over Rome for many months, until "a person may say to another: you can have Rome and all that is in it for one penny, and he will answer: it is not worth it." The text includes also a cruel description of the demise of the emperor, Lupianus.[4]

When Rabbi Ishamel returns to the circle of mystics and recounts what he learned in the celestial court, Rabbi Nehunia declares a day of rejoicing, orders that a feast will be presented, an orchestra of musicians plays and sings, to celebrate the imminent destruction of evil Rome; the sacrifice of ten sages seems to be an appropriate one for the achievement of this great redemptive moment, the deliverence of the world from the yoke of Rome. In the narrative text "The Story of the Ten Martyrs," this is followed by ten chapters, each describing in cruel, graphic terms the tortures that each of the ten martyrs underwent before his death. This has become one of the most important literary expressions of Jewish martyriology, and had great influence in the Middle Ages.

Rabbi Ishmael, according the narrative, then assembles, in the "third great hallway of the House of God" in Jerusalem,[5] all the members of the rabbinic courts of the time, and they sit there, surrounded by celestial torches of fire, and then Rabbi Nehunia reveals to them "the secret of the world"—the procedure of the ascension to the chariot, which from now on becomes "like a person who has a ladder in his home"—one of the earliest, if not the first, mystical reference to the mystical experience as the ascent by a spiritual ladder.

This unique assembly, which combined the meeting of all great mystics, a background of martyriology and apocalypse, a combination of disaster and messianic hope, and the revelation of great ancient secrets that have been hidden until now, is the first such event in the history of Hebrew mystical literature, but not the last. Several medieval and early modern Jewish mystics used this format for expressing such experiences. One prominent example is the Zoharic Idras,[6] and later— groups of mystics in Safed and in the early Hasidic movement in the eighteenth century.[7]

✶Rabbi Ishmael said: When Rabbi Nehunia ben ha-Kanah saw that evil Rome had decided to obliterate the great [sages] of Israel, he stood up and revealed the secret of the world.

The characteristic befitting one who is worthy to observe the King and the throne, His glory and His beauty, the holy beasts and the angels of power, the wheels of the divine presence, the terrifying lightening and the terrible *hashmal*,[8] the burning lava encircling the throne, the bridges[9] and the flames which burst out between the bridges, the dust and smoke and the fragrance which arise from the dust (= smoke) which was covering and enshrouding all the chambers of the palace of the *aravot* firmament,[10] and the fog of his burning coals, and Soria,[11] the prince of the divine countenance, the servant of Totrochiel[12] Lord God, the proud.

What is this like? Like a man who has a ladder in his house, for everyone who is pure and clean of worship of idols, and of fornication and of blood-shedding and wicked gossip and swearing in vain, and desecration of the holy name, and of false pride and hatred without reason, and observes all the commandments and prohibitions.

Rabbi Ishmael said: Rabbi Nehunia ben ha-Kanah told me: Ben

settling up who is worthy to behold structure and God in his perfection

Geim,[13] happy he is, and happy is the soul of anyone who is pure and clean of these eight characteristics, which are despised by Totrochiel and his servant Soria. [He can] descend and observe the hidden pride and the power which is beyond understanding, a numinous pride and a brilliant force, when they rush in front of His throne of glory three times every day in the celestial realm since the day the world was created until now, in praise, as Totrochiel Lord God behaves in it in that realm [#198–200].

Rabbi Ishmael said: When my ears heard this warning, my strength left me. I said to him [to Rabbi Nehunia]: If it is so, there is no end [to these demands], because there is no living person who is clean and pure of these eight [evil] characteristics. He said to me: Ben Geim, if not, go and bring before me all the great men of this company, all the leaders of the academy (yeshivah), and I shall state before them the secrets and mysteries which are hidden and esoteric, and the structure on which the perfection of the world and its beauty stand, and the goodness of the earth and the heaven, for all the wings of the earth and the cosmos and the wings of the supreme firmaments are tied within it. And the way of the celestial ladder, whose first edge is on the earth and its second edge on the right leg of the throne of glory [#201].

Rabbi Ishmael said: Immediately I stood up and assembled all the members of the greater and the smaller sanhedrin[14] to the great entrance-hall, the third one, of the House of God,[15] and he [Rabbi Nehunia] sits on the bench of pure marble which my [Ishmael's] father, Elisha, gave to me, at the wish of my mother, who brought to him as a part of the matrimonial agreement.

There came Raban Shimon ben Gamliel and Rabbi Eliezer the Great, and Rabbi Lazar ben Damah and Rabbi Eliezer ben Shamua and Yohanan ben Dhavai and Hanania ben Hachinai and Jonathan ben Uzziel and Rabbi Akivah and Rabbi Judah ben Bava.[16] We all came and set before him, and all the multitude of the fellows standing on their feet, for they were seeing lamps of fire and torches of light which separated them from him. Rabbi Nehunia ben ha-Kanah was sitting and arranging before them [i.e., teaching them] all the matters of the chariot, descending and ascending, how the descender descends and how the ascender ascends [#202–203].

When a person wished to descend to the chariot he would call

upon Soria the Prince of the Countenance, and would invoke him one
hundred and twelve times in the name of Totrosiai, Lord God, who was
called Totrosiai Zortak . . . [17] He should not add to the one hundred and
twelve times nor subtract from them, for if he adds or omits he will pay
with his life. But his mouth should pronounce [holy] names and the
fingers of his hand counting one hundred and twelve. Immediately he
descends and governs the chariot [#204–205].

Rabbi Ishmael said: Rabbi Nehunia ben ha-Kanah, my teacher,
told me this: Totrosiai, Lord God of Israel, is sitting in seven palaces, a
chamber within a chamber. In the gate of each palace there are eight
guardians . . . four to the right side of the gate and four to the left. These
are the names of the guardians of the first palace . . . at the gate of the
seventh palace there stand, somberly, all the powerful heroes, strong
and tough, terrible and frightening, taller than mountains, brighter
than hills, their bows drawn in front of them, their swords bright in their
hands, lightening erupting from their eyes, flames burning from their
noses and torches erupting from their mouth, wearing helmets and covered by armour, spears hanging on their arms. Their horses are the
horses of darkness, of the land of death, horses of fire, of hail, of blood,
of iron, of fog; horses which when mounted stand over troughs of fire,
full of burning coals and eating burning coals from them, a hundred
cubits in every mouthful; the measure of each mouth is like three times
that of the troughs of Caesarea. Beside them flow rivers of fire which
the horses drink, like the flow of the water in the river Kidron which
hold all the rain-water of Jerusalem. And there was a cloud above their
heads and the heads of their horses. This is the characteristic distinguishing the guardians of the gate of the seventh palace and the horses
in front of every [other] palace.

And all the matters [of the procedure] of the descenders to the
chariot who were ascending without any harm [were observed], and
after seeing all this they would descend in peace and would come and
stand and testify to the terrible sights, things which cannot be found in
any palace of any earthly king. [They would] praise and bless and beau-
tify . . . and give honor and greatness to Tortosiai, Lord God of Israel,
who would be happy with the descenders to the chariot, and would be
sitting and waiting for every single one from the people of Israel, when
is he going to descend.[18] In unique pride and unequaled power, the

pride of the numinous and the power of great light which come before the throne of glory three times every day in heaven from the day the world was created until now, in praise [#213–216].

Totrosiai Lord God of Israel—in the measure that he waits for the redemption and the time of deliverance which is kept for Israel after the destruction of the Second Temple, the last one—waits and hopes for that time when the descender will descend, when he will see the heavenly pride, when the end, the redemption, will be heard, when eye will see what no eye has ever seen, when he will ascend and speak to the seed of his beloved Abraham [#218].

Rabbi Ishmael said: When you come and stand at the gate of the first palace, take the two seals[19] in your two hands, one that of Totrosiai Lord God and one of Soria the Prince of the Countenance, and show [the first] to the [guardians] who are standing on the right, and that of Soria show to those who are standing on the left. Immediately, the Prince Rahaviel who is in charge of the gate of the first palace and stands to the right of the threshold and the Prince Topiel who stands to the left of the threshold, they together immediately take hold of you, one on the right and one on the left, and they lead you and hand you, after warning you, to the Prince Tagriel, who is in charge of the gate of the second palace and is stationed to the right of the threshold and the Prince Matpiel who is stationed to the left of the threshold, together with him [#219].

This procedure is repeated at the gate of each of the next five palaces, though the names on the seals differ in each case. The process is interrupted at the gate of the sixth palace:

Because the guardians of the sixth palace usually destroy the descenders to the chariot, and not the descenders to the chariot without permission. [Superior powers] used to order them [to stop it], beat them up and burn them up and put other [guardians] to replace them. Yet those who came instead of the first ones behave in the same way, they are not afraid, and they do not tell themselves: Why are we getting burned, what pleasure do we derive from destroying the descenders to the chariot and not the descenders to the chariot without permission. And this is still the characteristic of the guardians of the sixth palace[20] [#224].

2 VISIONS OF RABBI AKIBAH AND RABBI ISHMAEL

 ershom Scholem published one of the most important texts of the ancient Jewish mystics as an appendix to his book, *Jewish Gnosticism, Merkabah Mysticism and Talmudic Tradition*.[1] The treatise did not have any title in the manuscripts, and Scholem suggested that it may be identified as *Maaseh Merkavah* ("The Work of the Chariot"), relying on medieval quotations. It is an anthology of the hymns and the visions of the "descenders to the chariot," presented by Rabbi Akibah and Rabbi Ishmael. They differ in the most meaningful way from the religious literature created at that time (third and fourth centuries) in mainstream Judaism, which was characterized by the midrashic format that relied on interpretation of verses and the authority of previous sages as source of authority. Here we find a literature that substitutes individual experience to any traditional authority. At the same time, the authors of these texts developed a unique concept of language, which had meaningful impact on subsequent Jewish mysticism.

Rabbi Akibah said:
Who may be able to think about the seven palaces and to envision the heavens above the heavens, and to observe the chambers inside the chambers and to claim: I have seen the chamber of God?

In the first palace there stand four thousands of ten thousands[2] chariots of fire, and forty thousands of ten thousands pyres of fire[3] are scattered among them.

In the second palace there stand a hundred thousands chariots of fire, and forty thousands of ten thousands pyres of fire are scattered among them.

In the third palace there stand . . . [4]

In the fourth palace there stand a thousand of thousands of thousands of ten thousands of chariots of fire and two thousands of ten thousands of pyres of fire are scattered among them.

In the fifth palace there stand four thousands of thousands of ten thousands chariots of fire, and two thousands of thousands of ten thousands pyres of fire are scattered among them.

In the [sixth] seventh palace [5] there stand forty thousand thousands of ten thousands chariots of fire and two thousand thousands of ten thousands pyres of fire are scattered among them.

In the seventh palace there stand a hundred thousand thousands of ten thousands chariots of fire and two thousands thousands of ten thousands pyres of fire are scattered among them.

In the first palace they say "holy, holy, holy," and the pyres of fire scatter and then re-assemble into the second palace and they say "holy, holy, holy" and the pyres of fire scatter and then re-assemble to the third palace and they say "holy holy holy" in the third palace, chariots of fire say "blessed is the name of the glory of his kingdom for ever and ever [6] from the place of his house of residence [shekhinah]. [7] And the pyres of fire are re-assembled to the fourth palace and say "blessed is the name of the glory of his kingdom for ever and ever." In the fourth palace chariots of fire say "blessed is God who lives and exists for ever and for ever and ever, overpowering above all the chariot. And the pyres of fire are assembled to the fifth palace and say" blessed is God, living and existing [for ever]. In the fifth palace chariots of fire say: "blessed is his sacred kingdom from the place of the house of his residence." And the pyres of fire are assembled to the sixth palace and say: "blessed is his sacred kingdom from the place of his house of residence." In the sixth palace chariots of fire say: "Blessed is God, master of all the power, the creator of power and the governor of every chariot. And pyres of fire assemble to the seventh palace and say: "Blessed is God, master of all the power, etc. In the seventh palace chariots of fire say: "blessed the king of kings of kings God, the master of all power, who is like the living and existing God, whose praise is in the heavens of heavens, the sanctity of his kingdom in the heavens of heavens above, his power in chambers within chambers, holiness on this side and holiness on this side, and their singing flows, always stating the name of Nehoria YHY God of Israel and they say: Blessed blessed is the name of the glory of his kingdom for ever and ever from the place of the house of his residence."

Concerning the language of these early Jewish mystics, this textualization of a supernal vision is a typical example. We do not find in these ancient texts declarations concerning the limitations of language and the denial of the accuracy and clarity of the descriptions. On the other hand, it is evident, I believe, that close reading of these sentences obligates us to regard these visions not as direct, full, and informative, but rather an indirect use of language to convey some intimations of a supreme phenomenon that cannot be expressed by semantic means. The text is carefully structured in all its components, and the language used is not free but encapsulated in a series of key phrases that cannot be regarded as semantic and nothing else. The numbers—always expressed in terms of "thousands of thousands of ten thousands" cannot be regarded as information, but an indirect indication of a metalinguistic vision. The transformation of Ezekiel's unique, complex, multilayered description of the chariot has been transformed here into a blurred chaos of billions and trillions of "chariots." What are these chariots? Actually, we have no idea. Among them are scattered other bodies of fire; we have no idea what is the relationship between chariots and pyres of fire, even though both terms are repeated in every sentence. They are distinguished from each other by using slightly different phrases of praise to God, but they are actually the same phrases, sung by the two groups in the various palaces like a canon, repetitive yet slightly different in order. Any attempt to reconstruct what did Rabbi Akibah "really" see when he ascended to the divine realms on this occasion will be fruitless and counterproductive. We may analyze the history of the phrases used, and speculate concerning their impact on listeners and readers, but what "really" happened when the myriads of these fiery entities scattered and reassembled and voiced the sections of celestial prayer of sanctification is beyond any textual analysis.[8] All we can know is that the dominant component of the vision was a vast landscape of dynamic elements of fire, which serve as the celestial choir reciting God's praise and sanctifying him.

The rhetorical devices used by the writer both express and invoke ecstasy. The phrases are repetitive, the structure—the seven palaces, the transition from one to another twice in this brief text, every sentence moving up from one to another, the avoidance of complexity of language and insisting on minor changes from one stanza to another—all these denote the ecstasy engulfing the speaker that is transmitted to his listeners.

This should be compared to another dominant literary device used by the ancient Jewish mystics, the recital of long lists of synonyms. In some cases we find in these texts series of words and phrases, twenty to forty items long (sometimes arranged alphabetically), which, on the one hand, convey the numinousity of the experience of envisioning the supreme entity, and on the other demonstrate the inability of language, even when exhausted by the lists of synonyms, to actually express anything semantic concerning its nature. The strings of words do not add meanings but denote the feebleness and inadequacy of language when confronted with such phenomena, so distant from the semantic realms. Series of such synonyms have become a component of Jewish hymns; some of the Hekhalot hymns were accepted into the regular prayer book, and others have been written in the same manner.

At the core of this anthology is a narrative that describes how Rabbi Ishmael acquired the knowledge of the secret of "The Prince of the Torah," a mnemonic-magical series of names and formulas, including some esoteric, bizarre names of God and angels. The narrative is scattered in several paragraphs in the text, and it is difficult to reconstruct the story. It seems that when Rabbi Ishmael was thirteen years old—the age in which a boy achieves religious responsibility and independence—he complained to his teacher, Rabbi Nehunia ben ha-Kanah, that he cannot absorb his Torah studies and constantly forgets what he learned. Rabbi Nehunia then instructs him, in detail, how to use this secret formula that employs the "prince of the Torah," sometimes called Yefehfia, and as a result the user retains all that he learns. From some sections in this work it is evident that the secret is not confined to this mnemonic purpose, but leads the user to a profound mastery of the secrets of the universe and he acquires the ability to invoke supernal powers and use them for a variety of needs. The difference between knowledge of the Torah and identification with it and being elevated with it is not a complete one, so that there are both mystical and magical aspects to this practice. As we find often in this literature, this unique knowledge and power that Rabbi Ishmael acquired in this supernatural way evoked the jealousy of some celestial powers, and the following exchange is recorded:

Rabbi Ishmael said: Zevudiel, the angel of the countenance, said to me: Ben Geim, what is the merit (or: right) of your father and your mother that enabled you to master this secret which all the rest of the world did not have the merit to acquire, only I and Rabbi Akibah had the merit to use it.[9]

Rabbi Ishmael said: Shakedhoziah angel of the countenance said to me: Ben Geim, do not be proud and see yourself elevated above all your colleagues, and do not claim to be the only one who has merited this, because this did not come because of your power and force but as a result of the power of your father in heaven. But you are happy in this world and you shall fare well in the next world and you shall be happy and fare well for ever and ever and ever, and this is true also for all people who support you and pray like you, morning and evening.

Rabbi Ishmael said: When I heard this from Shakedhozia angel of countenance I stood up, gathering all my strength, and asserted myself and stood up and gave sanctity in front of the king of the universe and I said: YVY my God, you shall be sanctified for ever, you shall rise proudly over the holy beasts and the chariots of your power, you shall be glorified and blessed, there is none like you. You shall be sanctified for there are no deeds like yours, the heavens of the heavens pronounce your justice, the most terrifying [angels] are recounting your glory. The celestial seraphim and the ones below bow before you, for you are great and terrible. There is no dishonesty and no forgetting before your throne of glory. Blessed are you, YHVH, the true creator of all creatures.

Rabbi Ishmael said: When my Rabbi, Rabbi Nehunia ben ha-Kanah, heard that I have stood facing heaven and identified every single angel who is in every single palace. He said to me: Why did you identify the angels who are positioned in the gates of each palace? I told him: I did not do it in order to praise myself, but in order to praise the king of the universe. Rabbi Ishmael said: My rabbi, Rabbi Nehunia ben ha-Kanah told me: The true torah which Aharon the priest acquired is what was your support, and [because of it] you did not suffer as a result [of disclosing] this secret. But if you wish to make use of this secret you should fortify yourself with eight prayers which I shall recite. At that time he arranged before me the prayers, each one including twelve letters from the name of the living, eternally existing God,[10] the revered God who is sanctified and who is inhabiting all the vistas of the celestial realms. Rabbi Ishmael said: Since Rabbi Nehunia ben ha-Kanah arranged before me these prayers, I have been praying every day by the names in each of them, when ascending and when descending, and all the limbs of my body were comforted (583–586).

It is evident that the secret names, prayers, and formulas that Rabbi Nehunia taught Rabbi Ishamel were not just mnemonic magic assisting in the process of learning; they included secrets that facilitated the mystical processes of ascent and descent to the divine world. The following paragraphs in the text present these eight prayers, thus making the text of ma'aseh merkavah into a manual that the reader may use in order to achieve the same powers by which Rabbi Ishmael was endowed. The great secret described so reverently in the text is presented in clear, unambiguous terms to every reader of this treatise. We may conclude that while this work may be esoteric in nature, and not intended to be read by a wide public, it is not so to anyone who managed to get hold of it. The great mysteries that were revealed to Rabbi Ishmael in such unique circumstances are now open to every reader of the treatise.

THE DEIFICATION OF ENOCH

ne of the important methodological norms of the analysis of mystical texts is the assumption that when a mystic describes somebody else's supreme spiritual achievement, he may be actually reporting his own endeavor, or at least presenting an ideal toward which he aspires. Thus, for instance, when revelations to biblical prophets are described in detail, one wonders whether the reporting mystic is not portraying the visions he himself has had, or expects to experience in the future. This cannot be accepted as a universal law; sometimes mystics express marvel at achievements that they do not dare to hope to share, yet the question of the relevance of the description of past mystical elevations and visions to the mystic's present and future is a haunting one. The following text is an extreme example of such a problem. It may be regarded as the most dramatic and far-reaching description of deification of a human being found in Hebrew mystical works, yet it is very difficult to assess its implications concerning the actual aspirations of the school of mystics from among which it emerged.

This text presents the mystical autobiography of the biblical Enoch, son of Jared, who was taken by God to heaven (Gen. 5:24), and his transformation into the celestial power Metatron, who is described here as "the little YHVH," a divine entity second only to God himself. Is the author just commenting on the biblical text, describing an event that occured in ancient times and can never be repeated, or is it a paradigmatic one, representing the extreme spiritual achievement toward which a mystic may aspire?

This mystical autobiography constitutes the first part of a work that was very well known in the early Middle Ages, in a treatise called *Sefer Hekhalot*, "The Book of Divine Palaces." It was published in a detailed critical edition, an extensive introduction and commentary and English translation by Hugo Odeberg in 1928.[1] Odeberg studied the subject in the framework of biblical and postbiblical studies, so he gave the book a new title: "Third Enoch or the Hebrew Book of Enoch," joining it to the apocryphal works of First Enoch (the Ethiopic one) and Second Enoch (the Slavonic one). It was thus accepted as a late contribution to the biblical apocrypha and psdeuepigrapha. In this framework it was retranslated into English by Prof. Philip Alexander of Manchester, with a new introduction and commentary, and included in the new edition of this corpus edited by James Charlesworth.

This work belongs to the later stratum of Hekhalot mystical literature, written probably several centuries after Hekhalot Rabbati. The absence of Greek influences and other reasons seem to indicate that it was written in Babylonia, between the seventh and the ninth centuries. Most of the text—from chapter 17 to the end (chapter 48)—is dedicated to the presentation of the structure of the divine realms and the great divine powers that govern them, being the most detailed treatise on this subject in ancient Jewish mystical literature. The first part begins with a brief description of the ascension of Rabbi Ishamel to the chariot, in a manner familiar from *Hekhalot Rabbati* and other older texts, but without going into details, as if it were a common, well-known practice. Some of the angels surrounding the Throne of Glory object to Rabbi Ishmael's presence among them, and he is protected by Metatron, "The Prince of the Countainance." During the discussion Rabbi Ishamel hears the other angels refer to Metatron as "the youth" (*na'ar*); surprised that such a great power is called by this undistinguished apellation, Rabbi Ishamel inquires for the reason. Responding to this question, Metatron recounts his biography, and the next ten chapters are told by him, in the first person.

Metatron, according to this narrative, was originally Enoch, son of Jared, who was called by God to heaven to serve as a witness to the evildoings of people before the deluge, thus justifying the ferocious divine punishment that they received. He is a latecomer to the divine realms, and therefore he is called "a youth." The text gives no reason why God did not preserve him as a witness and nothing more, but continued to transform him, step by step, into the greatest divine power besides him. He is endowed with superhuman intellectual qualities, the knowledge of all languages including those of animals and birds. His body begins its transformation, his limbs turn into fire, he grows numerous wings and in each of them many eyes, which burn like the sun. He is given a throne and a chariot with horses of fire, and is clothed, like God, by a garment of light. God gives him a crown, on which "the letters by which the heaven and earth were created" are engraved, and the name of God— YHVH.[2] He was given the task of sitting and judging the nations, thus mastering all the attributes of God himself. Because of this, when Elisha ben Avuya, one of the four sages who entered the *pardes* (Tosefta Hagiga 2:4), saw Metatron, he proclaimed: Are there two powers in heaven?, becoming the talmudic paradigmatic heretic.[3] To prevent such a mistake being repeated, God sent another divine power, Anafiel, to punish Metatron with sixty lashes of fire, "so that everyone will know who is the master and who is the slave." The last words in this description—Anafiel making Metatron stand up on his feet—indicate the Jewish belief that angels have no joints, therefore they cannot sit down. When Elisha ben Avuya saw Metatron sitting on a throne, he had to conclude that this was no angel but a divine power (whereas the reason for his ability to sit was that originally he had been a human being, Enoch). After receiving his punishment, Metatron is forbidden to sit down.

There is no earlier text that identified Metatron with Enoch, and until evidence to the contrary are presented, we have to assume that this is the work of the author of this treatise. Why did he describe the great divine power as a transformation of a human being? Why did he insist that Metatron be endowed with all the regalia of God himself? A probable explanation is that the concept of "two powers in heaven," the lesser of them being the creator, the demiurge (*yotzer bereshit*), identified with Metatron, was prevalent in some Jewish circles, and this treatise is intended to refute this, by describing Metatron as a transformation of a human being who was born several generations after the creation so that he could not participate in this process. This necessitated describing him as endowed by all the external attributes of God, so that Elisha's mistake is an understandable one.[4] This might be the theological-historical reason for the emergence of this myth. Yet the devotion to detail that is demonstrated by the author in the description of the transformation may attest to a possible identification of Enoch with the paradigmatic mystic. If Metatron evolved from a human being—even if that was a biblical figure—maybe other human beings may aspire to share a similar illustrious fate. Talmudic and Midrashic literature ignored the figure of Enoch, and the verse in Genesis indicating his elevation to heaven while still alive was interpreted as referring to his death. The author of this work, while presenting a conservative view opposing the existence of a divine demiurge, expressed a radical position by endowing Enoch not only with everlasting life but also with the achievement of almost complete deification.

Ishmael Enters the Seventh Palace

"Enoch walked with God. Then he vanished because God took him." (Gen. 5:24)

Rabbi Ishmael said: When I ascended to the height to behold the vision of the chariot, I entered six palaces, one inside the other, and when I reached the door of the seventh palace I paused in prayer before the Holy One, blessed be he; I looked up and said: "Lord of the Universe, grant, I beseech you, that the merit of Aaron, son of Amram, lover of peace and pursuer of peace, who received on Mount Sinai the crown of priesthood in the presence of your glory, may avail for me now, so that Prince Qaspi'el, and the angels with him, may not prevail over me and cast me from heaven." At once the Holy One, blessed be he, summoned to my aid his servant, the angel Metatron, Prince of the Divine Presence. He flew out to meet me with great alacrity, to save me from their power. He grasped me with his hand before their eyes and said to me, "Come in peace into the presence of the high and exalted King to behold the likeness of the chariot." Then I entered the seventh palace and he led me to the camp of the Shekhinah and presented me before the throne of glory so that I might behold the chariot. But as soon as the princes of the chariot looked at me and the fiery seraphim fixed their gaze on me, I shrank back trembling and fell down, stunned by the radiant appearance of their eyes and the bright vision of their faces, until the Holy One, blessed be he, rebuked them and said, "My servants, my seraphim, my cherubim, and my ophanim, hide your eyes from Ishmael my beloved son and honored friend, so that he does not shrink and tremble so." At once Metatron, Prince of the Divine Presence, came and revived me and raised me to my feet, but still I had not strength enough to sing a hymn before the glorious throne of the glorious King, the mightiest of kings, the most splendid of potentates, until an hour had passed. But after an hour the Holy One, blessed be he, opened to me gates of might, gates of speech, gates of song, gates of shekhinah, gates of peace, gates of wisdom, gates of strength, gates of might, gates of speech, gates of song, gates of sanctifying praise, gates of chant. He enlightened my eyes and my heart to utter psalm, praise, jubilation, thanksgiving, song, glory, majesty, laud, and strength. And when I opened my mouth and sang praises before the throne of glory the holy creatures below the throne of glory and above the throne responded after me, saying,

Holy, holy, holy,

and,

Blessed be the glory of the Lord in his dwelling place.

Metatron Vouches for Ishmael

R. Ishmael said: Then the eagles of the chariot, the flaming ophanim and the cherubim of devouring fire, asked Metatron, "Youth, why have you allowed one born of woman to come in and behold the chariot? From what nation is he? From what tribe? What is his character?" Metatron replied, "He is of the nation of Israel, whom the Holy One, blessed be he, chose from the seventy nations to be his people. He is of the tribe of Levi, which presents the offering to his name. He is of the family of Aaron, whom the Holy One, blessed be he, chose to minister in his presence and on whose head he himself placed the priestly crown on Sinai." At once they began to say, "This one is certainly worthy to behold the chariot, as it is written,

Happy is the nation of whom this is true,

happy is the nation whose God is the Lord."

Ishmael Questions Metatron

R. Ishmael said: Then I questioned the angel Metatron, Prince of the Divine Presence. I said to him, "What is your name?" He answered, "I have seventy names, corresponding to the seventy nations of the world, and all of them are based on the name of the King of the kings of kings; however, my King calls me 'Youth.'"

Metatron Is Enoch

R. Ishmael said: I said to Metatron, "Why, are you called by the name of your Creator with seventy names? You are greater than all the princes, more exalted than all the angels, more beloved than all the ministers, more honored than all the hosts, and elevated over all potentates in sovereignty, greatness, and glory: why, then, do they call you 'Youth' in the heavenly heights?" He answered, "Because I am Enoch, the son of Jared. When the generation of the Flood sinned and turned to evil deeds, and said to God, 'Go away! We do not choose to learn your ways,' the Holy One, blessed be he, took me from their midst to be a witness against them in the heavenly height to all who should come into the world, so that they should not say, 'The Merciful One is cruel! Did *all* those multitudes of people sin? And even if *they* sinned, what sin did their wives, their sons, and their daughters commit? And what of their horses, their mules, their beasts, their cattle, and all the birds of the world which the Holy One destroyed with them in the waters of the Flood—what sin did *they* commit that they should have perished as well?' Therefore the Holy One, blessed be he, brought me up in their lifetime, before their very eyes, to the heavenly height, to be a witness against them to future generations. And the Holy One, blessed be he, appointed me in the height as a prince and a ruler among the ministering angels."

"Then three of the ministering angels, Uzzah, 'Azzah, and 'Aza'el, came and laid charges against me in the heavenly height." They said before the Holy One, blessed be he, "Lord of the Universe, did not the primeval ones give you good advice when they said, Do not create man!" The Holy One, blessed be he, replied, "I have made and will sustain him; I will carry and deliver him." When they saw me they said before him, "Lord of the Universe, what right has this one to ascend to the height of heights? Is he not descended from those who perished in the waters of the Flood? What right has he to be in heaven?" Again the Holy One, blessed be he, replied, and said to them, "What right have you to interrupt me? I have chosen this one in preference to all of you, to be a prince and a ruler over you in the heavenly heights." At once they all arose and went to meet me and prostrated themselves before me, saying, "Happy are you, and happy your parents, because your Creator has favored you." Because I am young in their company and a mere youth among them in days and months and years—therefore they call me 'Youth.'

God Removes the Shekhinah

R. Ishmael said: Metatron, Prince of the Divine Presence, said to me:

From the day that the Holy One, blessed be he, banished the first man from the garden of Eden, the Shekhinah resided on a cherub beneath the tree of life. The ministering angels used to muster and come down from heaven in companies, and in bands and cohorts from heaven, to execute his will in all the earth. The first man and his generation dwelt at the gate of the garden of Eden so that they might gaze at the bright image of the Shekhinah, or the brilliance of the Shekhinah radiated from one end of the world to the other, 365,000 times more brightly than the sun; anyone who gazed at the brightness of the Shekhinah was not troubled by flies or gnats, by sickness or pain; malicious demons were not able to harm him, and even the angels had no power over him. When the Holy One, blessed be he, went out and in from the garden to Eden, and from Eden to the garden, from the garden to heaven, and from heaven to the garden of Eden, all gazed at the bright image of his Shekhinah and were unharmed, until the coming of the generation of Enosh, who was the chief of all the idolators in the world. What did the men of Enosh's generation do? They roamed the world from end to end, and each of them amassed silver, gold, precious stones, and pearls in mountainous heaps and piles. In the four quarters of the world they fashioned them into idols, and in each quarter they set up idols about 1,000 parasangs in height. They brought down the sun, the moon, the stars and the constellations and stationed them before the idols, to their right and to their left, to serve them in the way they served the Holy One, blessed be he, as it is written, "All the array of heaven stood in his presence, to his right and to his left." How was it that they had the strength to bring them down? It was only because

'Uzzah, 'Azzah, and 'Aza'el taught them sorceries that they brought them down and employed them, for otherwise they would not have been able to bring them down.

Thereupon the ministering angels conspired to bring a complaint before the Holy One, blessed be he. They said in his presence, "Lord of the Universe, what business have you with men, as it is written, 'What is man (Enosh) that you should spare a thought for him?' It does not say here, 'What is Adam?' but, 'What is Enosh?' because Enosh is the chief of the idolators. Why did you leave the heaven of heavens above, the abode of your glory, the high and exalted throne which is in the height of 'Arabot, and come and lodge with men who worship idols? Now you are on the earth, and the idols are on the earth; what is your business among the idolatrous inhabitants of the earth?" Immediately the Holy One, blessed be he, took up his shekhinah from the earth, from their midst. Then the ministering angels came, and the cohorts of the hosts, and the armies of 'Arabot, one thousand companies strong, and myriads of hosts. They took trumpets and seized horns and surrounded the shekhinah with psalms and songs, and it ascended to the heavenly heights, as it is written,

God went up to the sound of horns,

the Lord went up with a fanfare of trumpets.

The Angels Object to Enoch's Elevation

R. Ishmael said: The angel Metatron, Prince of the Divine Presence, said to me: When the Holy One, blessed be he, desired to bring me up to the height, he sent me Prince 'Anapi'el YHWH and he took me from their midst, before their very eyes, and he conveyed me in great glory on a fiery chariot, with fiery horses and glorious attendants, and he brought me up with the shekhinah to the heavenly heights. As soon as I reached the heavenly heights, the holy creatures, the ophanim, the seraphim, the cherubim, the wheels of the chariot and the ministers of consuming fire, smelled my odor 365,000 myriads of parasangs off; they said, "What is this smell of one born of a woman? Why does a white drop ascend on high and serve among those who cleave the flames?" The Holy One, blessed be he, replied and said to them, "My ministers, my hosts, my cherubim, my ophanim, and my seraphim, do not be displeased at this, for all mankind has rejected me and my great kingdom and has gone off and worshiped idols. So I have taken up my Shekhinah from their midst and brought it up to the height. And this one whom I have removed from them is the choicest of them all and worth them all in faith, righteousness, and fitting conduct. This one whom I have taken is my sole reward from my whole world under heaven."

On the Wings of the Shekhinah

R. Ishmael said: The angel Metatron, Prince of the Divine Presence, said to me: when the Holy One, blessed be he, removed me from the generation of the Flood, he bore me up on the stormy wings of the Shekhinah to the highest heaven and brought me into the great palaces in the height of the heaven of 'Arabot, where the glorious throne of the Shekhinah is found, and the chariot, the cohorts of wrath, the hosts of fury, the fiery shin'anim, the blazing cherubim, the smoldering ophanim, the ministers of flame, the lightning hashmallim and the flashing seraphim. He stationed me there to serve the throne of glory day by day.

The Heavenly Treasuries

R. Ishmael said: Metatron, Prince of the Divine Presence, said to me: Before the Holy One, blessed be he, set me to serve the throne of glory, he opened for me

    300,000 gates of understanding,
    300,000 gates of prudence,
    300,000 gates of life,
    300,000 gates of grace and favor,
    300,000 gates of love,
    300,000 gates of Torah,
    300,000 gates of humility,
    300,000 gates of sustenance,
    300,000 gates of mercy,
    300,000 gates of reverence.

The Holy One, blessed be he, bestowed upon me wisdom heaped upon wisdom, understanding upon understanding, prudence upon prudence, knowledge upon knowledge, mercy upon mercy, Torah upon Torah, love upon love, grace upon grace, beauty upon beauty, humility upon humility, might upon might, strength upon strength, power upon power, splendor upon splendor, loveliness upon loveliness, comeliness upon comeliness; and I was honored and adorned with all these excellent, praiseworthy qualities more than all the denizens of the heights.

Enoch Is Enlarged

R. Ishmael said: Metatron, Prince of the Divine Presence, said to me: In addition to all these qualities, the Holy One, blessed be he, laid his hand on me and blessed me with 1,365,000 blessings. I was enlarged and increased in size till I matched the world in length and breadth. He made to grow on me 72 wings, 36 on one side and 36 on the other, and each single wing covered the entire world. He fixed in me 365,000 eyes and each eye was like the Great Light. There was no sort of splendor, brilliance, brightness, or beauty in the luminaries of the world that he failed to fix in me.

Enoch's Throne

R. Ishmael said: Metatron, Prince of Divine Presence, said to me: After all this, the Holy One, blessed be he, made for me a throne like the throne of glory, and he spread over it a coverlet of splendor, brilliance, brightness, beauty, loveliness, and grace, like the coverlet of the throne of glory, in which all the varied splendor of the luminaries that are in the world is set. He placed it at the door of the seventh palace and sat me down upon it. And the herald went out into every heaven and announced concerning me: "I have appointed Metatron my servant as a prince and a ruler over all the denizens of the heights, apart from the eight great, honored, and terrible princes who are called YHWH by the name of their King. Any angel and any prince who has anything to say in my presence should go before him and speak to him. Whatever he says to you in my name you must observe and do, because I have committed to him the Prince of Wisdom and the Prince of Understanding, to teach him the wisdom of those above and of those below, the wisdom of this world and of the world to come. Moreover I have put him in charge of all the stores of the palaces of 'Arabot, and all the treasuries that are in the heavenly heights."

God Reveals Secrets to Enoch

R. Ishmael said: The angel Metatron, Prince of the Divine Presence, said to me: The Holy One, blessed be he, revealed to me from that time onward all the mysteries of wisdom, all the depths of the perfect Torah and all the thoughts of men's hearts. All the mysteries of the world and all the orders of nature stand revealed before me as they stand revealed before the Creator. From that time onward I looked and beheld deep secrets and wonderful mysteries. Before a man thinks in secret, I see his thought; before he acts, I see his act. There is nothing in heaven above or deep within the earth concealed from me.

Enoch's Robe, Crown, and Name

R. Ishmael said: Metatron, Prince of the Divine Presence, said to me: Out of the love which he had for me, more than for all the denizens of the heights, the Holy One, blessed be he, fashioned for me a majestic robe, in which all kinds of luminaries were set, and he clothed me in it. He fashioned for me a glorious cloak in which brightness, brilliance, splendor, and luster of every kind were fixed, and he wrapped me in it. He fashioned for me a kingly crown in which 49 refulgent stones were placed, each like the sun's orb, and its brilliance shone into the four quarters of the heaven of 'Arabot, into the seven heavens, and into the four quarters of the world. He set it upon my head and he called me, "The lesser YHWH" in the presence of his whole household in the height, as it is written, *My name is in him* (Exod. 23:21)."

The Crown Is Inscribed

R. Ishmael said: The angel Metatron, Prince of the Divine Presence, the glory of highest heaven, said to me: Out of the abundant love and great compassion wherewith the Holy One, blessed be he, loved and cherished me more than all the denizens of the heights, he wrote with

his finger, as with a pen of flame, upon the crown which was on my
head

> the letters by which heaven and earth were created;
> the letters by which seas and rivers were created;
> the letters by which mountains and hills were created;
> the letters by which stars and constellations, lightning
> and wind, thunder and thunderclaps, snow and hail,
> hurricane and tempest were created;
> the letters by which all the necessities of the world and
> all the orders of creation were created.

Each letter flashed time after time like lightnings, time after time
like torches, time after time like flames, time after time like the rising
of the sun, moon, and stars.

Enoch Receives Homage

R. Ishmael said: The angel Metatron, Prince of the Divine Presence,
said to me: When the Holy One, blessed be he, placed his crown upon
my head, all the princes of kingdoms who are in the height of the
heaven of 'Arabot and all the legions of every heaven trembled at me.
Even the princes of the *'elim*, the princes of the *'er'ellim* and the princes
of the *tapsarim*, who are greater than all the ministering angels that
serve before the throne of glory, trembled and shrank from me when
they saw me. Even Samma'el, the Prince of the Accusers, who is greater
than all the princes of kingdoms that are in the height, was afraid and
shuddered at me. Even the angel of fire, the angel of hail, the angel of
wind, the angel of lightning, the angel of whirlwind, the angel of thunder, the angel of snow, the angel of rain, the angel of day, the angel of
night, the angel of the sun, the angel of the moon, the angel of the stars,
the angel of the constellations, who guide the world by their direction,
trembled and shrank back in alarm from me when they saw me.

Enoch Is Transformed into Fire

R. Ishmael said: The angel Metatron, Prince of the Divine Presence,
the glory of highest heaven, said to me: When the Holy One, blessed

be he, took me to serve the throne of the glory, the wheels of the chariot and all the needs of the Shekhinah, at once my flesh turned to
flame, my sinews to blazing fire, my bones to juniper coals, my eye-
lashes to lightning flashes, my eyeballs to fiery torches, the hairs of my
head to hot flames, all my limbs to wings of burning fire, and the substance of my body to blazing fire. On my right—those who cleave
flames of fire—on my left—burning brands, round about me swept
wind, tempest, and storm; and the roar of earthquake upon earthquake
was before and behind me.

Metatron Dethroned

R. Ishmael said: The angel Metatron, Prince of the Divine Presence,
the glory of highest heaven, said to me: At first I sat upon a great throne
at the door of the seventh palace, and I judged all the denizens of the
heights on the authority of the Holy One, blessed be he. I assigned
greatness, royalty, rank, sovereignty, glory, praise, diadem, crown, and
honor to all the princes of kingdoms, when I sat in the heavenly court.
The princes of kingdoms stood beside me, to my right and to my left,
by authority of the Holy One, blessed be he.

But when Aher came to behold the vision of the chariot and set
eyes upon me, he was afraid and trembled before me. His soul was
alarmed to the point of leaving him because of his fear, dread and terror of me. when he saw me seated upon a throne like a king, with ministering angels standing beside me as servants and all the princes of the
kingdoms crowned with crowns surrounding me. Then he opened his
mouth and said, "There are indeed two powers in heaven."
Immediately a divine voice came out from the presence of the
Shekhinah and said: *Come back to me, apostates sons* (Jer. 3:22)—apart
from Aher." Then Anapiel YHVH, the honored, glorified, beloved,
wonderful, terrible and dreadful Prince came at the command of the
Holy One blessed be he, and struck me with sixty lashes of fire, and
made me stand on my feet.

TO SEE WITHOUT EYES, TO HEAR WITHOUT EARS

R abbi Bahya Ibn Paquda's book, *The Duties of the Heart*, written in Arabic in the eleventh century and translated into Hebrew by Judah Ibn Tibbon in Provence late in the twelfth century, is the manifest of Jewish spirituality in the Middle Ages. It is one of the most influential works of medieval Judaism, which has been quoted in equal reverence in the sixteenth century and the twentieth. Its contents can easily be described as antinomian and heretical, yet it was accepted wholeheartedly by nearly a millennium of orthodox Judaism.

Very little is known about Rabbi Bahya. The exact time and place of his life are not known; it is surmised that he flourished in Saragosa, in Spain, in the second half of the eleventh century.[1] Besides his book, we have two liturgical poems composed by him, but no knowledge concerning his other works, nor concerning his teachers or disciples. The outstanding fact that clearly emerges from the study of his book is his close relationship to contemporary Islamic thinkers, mainly Sufis; many of the stories, anecdotes, and epigrams that he included in his work can be traced to writings of Muslim ascetics and mystics. Indeed, it has been pointed out that the original work in Arabic could easily be read as a typical Sufi book, if one disregards the frequent use of verses quoted from the Hebrew bible. Seldom have Jewish and Arabic thought come so close to each other as in Bahya's spiritualistic teachings.[2] It seems that there was an early phase of Jewish mystical expression in Spain governed by the Arabs before the kabbalah began to develop in Christian Spain late in the twelfth century.[3]

The contents and structure of *The Duties of the Heart* can be understood as an alternative Ten Commandments: God gave to Moses the Ten Commandments of the body, and Bahya gives to Judaism the ten commandments of the heart. In the introduction to the work Rabbi Bahya complained that he found many books dealing with the physical aspect of religious practice, and none concerning the spiritual one. He states that God created human beings composed of body and soul, and therefore a person must worship God with both body and soul; how is it that the Jewish manuals of worship deal only with the physical? *The Duties of the Heart* is the answer. In this work the spiritual aspect of religious life is presented, in the form of ten chapters, each dedicated to a central and essential commandment that concerns the heart and the spirit.

A most meaningful element in the teachings of this work is the definition of a "duty of the heart" as opposed to a "duty of the limbs." Rabbi Bahya made use of a talmudic phrase that defined "worship of the heart" as relating to prayer.[4] Yet he did not include prayer in his list of the spiritual duties, even though he used this phrase as a basis for his terminology. According to Jewish law, a prayer should be articulated by the mouth; it may be said silently, but the lips have to form the words of the prayer. For Rabbi Bahya, this was enough to deny the prayer a place among the duties of the heart: Limbs participate in its performance, therefore it cannot be regarded as spiritual. Similarly, the study of the Torah, which is the central intellectual commandment in Judaism, is not included, because eyes and ears participate in the process of learning. Only obligations in which the body does not participate at all can be included in the list of the ten duties of the heart. The dualist concept of conflict between body and soul reached its maximal expression in Rabbi Bahya's concept of worship. Any physical participation contaminates and defiles the purity of spiritual adherence to God. His response to the question, therefore, why should a person perform the "duties of the limbs" at all is that carrying out the physical commandments is accompanied by spiritual intention, and this component is the one that gives religious value to the ritual. The question whether this intention cannot be separated from the deed and be expressed without any physical action, thus making the actual performance superfluous, is not addressed by Bahya.

The author is faced with the question: If the duties of the heart are so important, why is it that most of the scriptures are dedicated to the physical commandments and narratives concerning history and politics? His response is presented by two parables. One is, that when a guest comes to a person's home, riding on a horse, the host presents the horse with a large heap of hay, while the guest himself is presented with a small plate of good food. Most of the Bible is dedicated, therefore, to the "horse"—the body, while only scattered verses deal with the real food of the soul. Rabbi Bahya does not hesitate to equate the vast literature of the halakhah, Jewish law, to hay given to animals. In the other parable, scriptures are described as a gift of silk threads that a king gave to his servants in order to test them. The stupid servants used it all to enjoy themselves in worldly things, while the wise ones separated the good threads from the inferior ones, from which they wove beautiful clothes that they wore when seeing the king, and sold the rest for money. The nonspiritual material in the Bible—the laws, narratives, history—is just a test designed by God to identify the wise ones among his worshippers. They get rid of it, and use the spiritual verses alone to connect them with God.

"Spirituality" in Rabbi Bahya's world included both emotional and intellectual elements, without distinguishing between the two. Thus, the first spiritual duty is the intellectual recognition of the unity of God, presented in the first chapter of the book in the usual rationalistic manner that prevailed in Arabic and Jewish philosophy of the period. The reader is required to follow and internalize the logical arguments that prove that God is one and he is the creator of the universe. The last chapter—the tenth—is dedicated to the love of God, which is described in emotional terms, and is presented as the pinnacle of religious devotion. Other chapters are dedicated to the examination of God's greatness in the creation and direction of the world, to a person's spiritual detachment from the physical pleasures of the world, to self-examination and the struggle to subdue one's physical desires, to repentance (which is presented as purely internal process, performed within one's heart exclusively). Rabbi Bahya's response to people who complain about the evil found in the world is presented by another parable: A king built for his servants a beautiful palace, which includes everything they wish for in food, drink, and furniture of the most exquisite quality. They, however, are blind, so they do not find the food, destroy the furniture, and then complain that the king did not give them proper accommodations. He does not respond to the question why did God create his servants blind.

As a spiritualist and rationalist, Bahya demands that each person discover and understand divine precepts on his own, not relying on tradition. Followers of tradition are described by the famous medieval parable of a convoy of blind people unthinkingly following a leader, who may or may not be blind himself. If so, why did God give people scriptures? Rabbi Bahya answers that this is for the benefit of people who cannot perceive truth on their own, like little children, sick people, and women. It is testimony to the power of this work—and the Jewish thirst for spiritualistic literature—that the book was so widely accepted and admired despite the denigration of the religious significance of the Torah expressed in this book.

Bahya presented in this work a spiritualistic way of life, especially that of inner life, which should, according to him, be separated from everyday, earthly and material concerns. His attitude seems to approach that of mystics when he denies all sensual perceptions as relevant to true worship, and points the way to a metasensual approach to God. He did not develop this direction in a systematic, comprehensive way, but the inclination toward mystical perception is clearly apparent in the following paragraphs, which are translated from the third chapter of *Duties of the Heart*, which presents a series of considerations that a person should adopt when considering his relationship to God.

To See Without Eyes, To Hear Without Ears

The Tenth ["account"]: The account to a person with his own soul concerning the observance of God over his external and hidden aspects, and that He observes him and remembers all his deeds, and all that passes in his heart (= thoughts), thoughts which are good and ones which are bad. He should always be apprehensive from Him and endeavoring to improve and correct his external [behaviour] and his hidden [thoughts], towards God, blessed be He. He should be in control of it. If a person were observing him constantly and watches his movements, would it be right for him to do anything which that person who watches him hates?

This is even more true if that person has given him good things and treated him charitably. This is even more so if that person is his master. This is even more so if that person is his Creator who observes him. Therefore, how much has a person to be ashamed and self-conscious before Him, and to be careful not to transgress His wishes, and to hasten to worship Him, and to yield to His will and his love.

Furthermore, it is known among us that when we go out to meet our kings and princes and the leaders of our age we put on our best clothes and adorn ourselves, because they may observe our exterior, as it is said: *Though none might enter the king's gate clothed with sackcloth* (Esther 4:2); and it is said: *Then Par'o sent and called Yosef and they brought him hastily out of the dungeon and he shaved himself and changed his garments* (Gen. 41:14). In this way we are required to adorn ourselves when we worship our God, our creator, in our external and internal, hidden aspects, before God, because of His constant, unchanging observance over us. If we imagined that kings may watch our hidden, secret aspects in the same way that they observe our visible bodies, we would not hesitate to adorn the hidden parts as they would have liked it.

It is obvious that the majority of people who study the sciences and teach them do not do that but for the reason to use them to aggrandize themselves in the eyes of the kings. This is also true concerning [religious] teachings, because the people of a country are commanded to follow the religion of their king. What one does for an earthly king is more necessary and more fitting to do for God, blessed be He, who deserves such reverence much more. It is our obligation to adorn both our exterior and our interior with the rituals, in our hearts as well as our limbs, because He observes them both and sees them constantly, and nothing should distract us from this, as the verse says: *I, the Lord, search the heart, I try the inward parts* (Jer. 17:10), and it says: *The eyes of the Lord are in every place, watching the evil and the good* (Prov. 15:3), *The eyes of the Lord they rove to and fro through the whole earth* (Zech. 4:10). The verse also says concerning the reverence of the Creator who observes all: *Be not rash with thy mouth, and let not thy heart be hasty to utter anything before God, for God is in heaven and thou upon earth* (Eccl. 5:1), and it says: *The Lord looked down from heaven upon the children of men* (Ps. 14:2).

When the believer ponders this idea constantly, and returns frequently to it, and considers it in his soul, then the Creator, blessed be He, is constantly present with him, in his innermost essence. He will observe Him with the eye of his mind, and will always be fearful of Him and will elevate Him. He will constantly examine His employs, ponders His ways in leading his creatures, ways which testify to His greatness and His highness and His wisdom and His power. And when the worshipper is dedicated to this, the Creator will allow him to rest from his melancholy, and will calm his heart from his fear, and will open for him the gates of His knowledge, and will reveal to him the secrets of His wisdom, and will pay attention to guiding him and directing him, and will not forsake him to be bound by his own self and his own ability, as it is said in the Psalm *The Lord is my shepherd, I shall not want* (Ps. 23), until its end.

This worshipper will be elevated to the highest station of the pious and in the highest degree of the degrees of the righteous. He then shall see without an eye, and will hear without an ear, and will speak without a tongue and will feel things without senses, and will understand them without logic, and will not be repelled by anything, and will not love nor choose anything which is not the choice of the Creator. He will adjust his will to the will of the Creator, and his love to His love, and what he loves will be what is beloved by Him, and will abhore what is abhored by Him. About such people the wise one (= Solomon) has said: *Happy is the man who hearkens to me, watching daily at my gates* (Prov. 8:34), and he said also: *For whoever finds me finds life and obtains favour of the Lord* (Prov. 35).

GOD AND THE UNIVERSE

S olomon Ibn Gabirol was one of the outstanding figures
of the Jewish "Golden Age" in Spain, within the framework of the peak of Arab-Islamic civilization in the High
Middle Ages. He is one of the greatest poets in Hebrew
literature, and one of the most important Jewish philosophers. His great poem, A *Kingly Crown*, is his one work
that unites his unusual talents as a poet and philosopher.

The problem of the relationship between neo-
Platonic philosophy and mysticism has haunted scholarship in the history of Christian medieval philosophy and
mysticism. William Inge,[1] one of the founders of the
modern study of Christian mysticism, declared clearly
that he does not have any valid criterion that could distinguish between neo-Platonism and mysticism. Some
of the most important works of Christian mysticism can
be characterized as treatises in neo-Platonic philosophy:
This is true concerning the Pseudo-Dionysian corpus of
treatises,[2] the Greek writings, probably from the sixth
century, which belong to the handful of most influential
works in Christian mysticism, as well as concerning the
writings of Scotus Eriugena, especially his *De divisione
naturae*.[3] Neo-Platonist philosophers often denied the
real existence of anything material, identifying "material" with "absence" and "nonexistence"; the relationship between spirit and matter, according to them, is like
that between light and darkness. Matter is just the
absence of spirit, as darkness has no substance — it is just
the absence of light. "Light," identified with spirit, is
conceived as the emanation of divine light, which is the
only source of existence. There is no wonder, therefore,

that the boundary between mysticism and such a philosophy is so difficult to define.[4]

Solomon Ibn Gabirol was born in Malaga, Spain, in 1021, lived
most of his life in Saragosa, and died in Valencia in his early or mid-
thirties.[5] His major philosophical treatise was known among Christian
philosophers in the Middle Ages in a translation entitled *Fons Vitae*,
written by "Avicebron," whose identity was unknown until the nineteenth century. This work, in its twelfth-century Spanish and Latin
translations from the Arabic, exerted meaningful influence on
medieval debate concerning the nature of divine will and the powers of
angels, as well as other theological subjects. Its readers regarded the
author as an Islamic philosopher. The Jewish identity of the author was
discovered only when Solomon Munk published in 1845 his finding of
a portion of the work in a Hebrew translation made by Shem Tov
Falaqueira in the thirteenth century.[6] Such confusion is testimony to
the absence of any identifying Jewish sources and ideas in the work; it
is universal religious philosophy that is not related necessarily to any of
the three scriptural religions.[7] Gabirol developed in this work the concept of the divine will, which serves as a bridge between philosophy and
religion. On the other hand, Gabirol wrote many liturgical poems,
some of which were included in the Jewish prayer book and made his
name one of the most revered in a religious-spiritual Jewish context.
His secular poetry, which followed the conventions of Arabic poetry of
the period, is regarded as the most lyrical and sensitive in Hebrew
medieval poetry. This lyrical poetry expresses forcefully the poet's
enmity toward the ephemeral, illusory nature of human life and the
pleasures of the world, a craving for solitude and transcendence of
worldly boundaries, in a manner often reminiscent of Sufi conventions.

In several poems Gabirol used the ancient Hebrew *Sefer Yezira*
("The Book of Creation") as a primary source, paraphrasing its enigmatic phrases and integrating them into his own worldview.[8] He also
used—though in a more selective way—mystical traditions derived
from the Hekhalot and Merkavah texts. These Jewish sources were integrated with contemporary science, philosphy, astronomy, and Sufi mysticism that dominated the Arabic culture in Spain at that time.[9]

Keter Malchut, "The Kingly Crown," is Gabirol's most famous
work. It is comprised of forty stanzas, divided into three parts: The first

describes the nature of God and his praise (stanzas 1–9), describing his unity, eternity, and infinite power, his wisdom, and identifying his essence with that of infinite light; the emanated divine will as the source of existence and the creation. The second part (stanzas 10–32), which is the most extensive and detailed, is a description of the creation, the earth and its elements, and especially the ten spheres encircling the earth, from the lowest—the lunar sphere—to the spheres of the intellect, the throne of glory and the archangels, the source of souls. The third part (stanzas 33–40) is a prayer, expressing the lowliness and corruption of man, the misery of human life, beseeching God's mercy and forgiveness. The poem was translated into English by the renowned scholar of Arabic and Islam, Bernard Lewis, and the selection includes the first part, stanzas 1–9, and the second half of the second part, stanzas 23–32.[10]

The Praises of God

I

Thine are the greatness and the strength and the splendour and
   the glory and the majesty.
Thine O God is the Kingdom and the rising above all things and
   the richness and the honour.
Thine are the higher and the lower creatures, and they bear witness that they perish and Thou dost endure.
Thine is the might whose secret our thoughts are wearied of seeking, for Thou art so much stronger than we.
Thine is the mystery of power, the secret and the foundation.

Thine is the name that is hidden from the wise, the strength that
   sustains the world over the void, the power to bring to light
   all that is hidden.
Thine is the mercy that rules over Thy creatures and the goodness preserved for those who fear Thee.
Thine are the secrets that no mind or thought can encompass,
   and the life over which decay has no rule, and the throne
   that is higher than all height, and the habitation that is hidden at the pinnacle of mystery.

Thine is the existence from the shadow of whose light every being
was made to be, and we said "Under His shadow we shall
live."

Thine are the two worlds between which Thou didst set a limit,
the first for works and the second for requital.

Thine is the reward which Thou hast set aside for the righteous
and hidden, and Thou sawest that it was good, and hast kept
it hidden.

II

Thou art One, the beginning of all computation, the base of all
construction.

Thou art One, and in the mystery of Thy Oneness the wise of
heart are astonished, for they know not what it is.

Thou art One, and Thy Oneness neither diminishes nor
increases, neither lacks nor exceeds.

Thou art One, but not as the One that is counted or owned, for
number and change cannot reach Thee, nor attribute, nor
form.

Thou art One, but my mind is too feeble to set Thee a law or a
limit, and therefore I say: "I will take heed to my ways, that I
sin not with my tongue."

Thou art One, and Thou art exalted high above abasement and
falling—not like a man, who falls when he is alone.

III

Thou art, but the hearing of ears and the seeing of eyes cannot
reach Thee, and how and why and where have no rule over
Thee.

Thou art, but for Thine own essence, and for no other with
Thyself.

Thou art, and before all time was Thou wert, and without place
Thou didst dwell.

Thou art, and thy secret is hidden and who can reach it—"far off,
and exceeding deep, who can find it out?"

IV

Thou livest, but not from determined time or known epoch.

Thou livest, but not with soul or breath, for Thou art soul of the soul.

Thou livest, but not as the life of man that is like vanity, its end in moths and worms.

Thou livest, and whoever attains Thy secret will find eternal delight—"and eat, and live for ever."

V

Thou art great, and beside Thy greatness all greatness is subdued and all merit is shortcoming.

Thou art great above all thought and sublime above the highest heaven.

Thou art great above all greatness, "exalted above all blessing and praise."

VI

Thou art mighty, and there is none among all Thy creatures that can equal Thy works and Thy mighty deeds.

Thou art mighty, and Thine is the perfect might that knows neither change nor vicissitude.

Thou art mighty, and from the greatness of Thy power Thou forgivest in the moment of Thy wrath and softenest Thine anger for sinners.

Thou art mighty, and Thy pity covers all Thy creatures—it is the mighty one which was of old.

VII

Thou art the supreme light, and the eyes of the pure of soul shall see Thee, and clouds of sin shall hide Thee from the eyes of sinners.

Thou art the light hidden in this world and revealed in the world of beauty, "In the mount of the Lord it shall be seen."

Thou art the eternal light, and the inward eye yearns for Thee and is astonished—she shall see but the utmost part of them, and shall not see them all.

VIII

Thou art the God of Gods and Lord of Lords, Master of heavenly
and of earthly beings.

Thou art God, and all creatures are Thy witnesses, and in honour
of this Name every created thing is bound to serve Thee.

Thou art God, and all creatures are Thy slaves and worshippers,
and Thy glory is not diminished by those who worship others
than Thee, for the goal of all of them is to attain to Thee.

But they are as blind men who turn to seek the king's highway,
and they stray from the road.

One sinks in the pit of destruction, another stumbles into an abyss.

All of them believing that they have reached their desire, yet they
have toiled in vain.

But Thy servants are as clear-sighted ones who follow the straight
path,

They do not stray to right or left until they reach the palace of the
king.

Thou art God, who supportest all creatures with Thy Godhead
and sustainest all beings with Thy Oneness.

Thou art God, and there is no separation between Thy Godhead
and Thy Oneness, Thy pre-existence and Thine eternity.

For it is all one mystery, and though the name of each one be different "all go unto one place."

IX

Thou art wise; and wisdom, the source of life, flows from Thee,
and every man is too brutish to know Thy wisdom.

Thou art wise, pre-existent to all pre-existence, and wisdom was
with Thee as nurseling.

Thou art wise, and Thou didst not learn from any other than
Thyself, nor acquire wisdom from another.

Thou art wise, and from Thy wisdom Thou didst send forth a pre-
destined Will, and made it as an artisan and a craftsman,

To draw the stream of being from the void as the light is drawn
that comes from the eye,

To take from the source of light without a vessel, and to make all
without a tool, cut and hew and cleanse and purify.

That Will called to the void and it was cleft asunder, to existence
and it was set up, to the universe and it was spread out.
It measured the heavens with a span, and its hand coupled the
pavilion of the spheres,
And linked the curtains of all creatures with loops of potency; and
its strength reaches as far as the last and lowest creature—
"the uttermost edge of the curtain in the coupling."

The Wonders of Creation

X

Who can utter Thy mighty deeds when Thou madest the globe of
the earth divided in two, one part dry land and one part
water?
And Thou didst encompass the water with the sphere of air, the
air that turns and turns and rests on its turnings.
And Thou didst encompass the air with the sphere of fire.
But the foundation of these four elements is one, their source is
one,
And from it they come forth and renew themselves—"and from
thence it was parted, and became into four heads."

XI

Who can declare Thy greatness when Thou didst encompass
the sphere of fire with the sphere of firmament, in which is
the moon, which aspires and glows in the splendour of the
sun?
In twenty-nine days she turns about her orbit and goes up by her
own way.
Some of her mysteries are simple and some of them are deep; her
body is less than the earth, as is one part to thirty-nine.
By the will of her Creator she awakens month after month the
changes and events of the world, its good things and its
evil things—"to make known to the sons of men his mighty
acts."

XII

Who can tell Thy praises when Thou didst make the moon, the
measure for the computing of festivals and holy days and
epochs and signs for days and years?

Her kingdom is by night, until her term comes and her radiance
is darkened,

And she covers herself with a mantle of blackness, for her light is
from the light of the sun.

And on the fourteenth night, if both of them stand on the line of
the Dragon, and it comes between them,

Then the moon does not show her light and her lamp is
quenched,

That all the peoples of the earth may know that the heavenly bodies, though they be precious, have a Judge above them to cast
them down and raise them up.

But the moon lives again after her fall and shines after her
eclipse,

And when at the end of the month she joins with the sun,

If the Dragon rise between them, and both stand on the same
line,

Then the moon stands before the sun like a black cloud, and
hides his radiance from the eye of all his beholders,

So that all who see them may know that the Kingdom is not to
the host of the heavens and their legions,

But there is a Master above them, who darkens their luminaries,

"For He *that is* higher than the highest regardeth; and *these be*
higher than they."

And those who imagine that the sun is their god will at that time
be ashamed of their imaginings, for their words will be tested,

And they will know that the hand of God made this, and that the
Sun has no power, and that He who darkens his radiance
alone has sway,

He sends to him one of His Servants, as reward for his good
deeds,

To hide his light, destroy his idolatry, and remove him from being
king.

XIII

Who can reckon Thy deeds of justice when Thou didst encompass the firmament of the moon with a second sphere, without break or breach,
In which is the star called Mercury, which is as one twenty-two
  thousandth of the earth?
He traverses his orbit in ten days, moving swiftly,
And he awakens in the world quarrels and conflict, hatred and
  strife,
And gives strength to succeed, to gather riches, to acquire wealth
  and honour,
By the command of Him who created it to serve Him as a slave
  serves his master.
It is the star of understanding and of wisdom—"to give subtility to
  the simple, to the young man knowledge and discretion."

XIV

Who can understand Thy mysteries when Thou didst encompass
  the second sphere with a third sphere in which is Venus, like
  a queen among her hosts, and like a bride decked with her
  adornments?
In eleven months she turns about her orbit, and her body is as
  one thirty-seventh of the earth, according to those who know
  her secrets.
So also to the Scales and the Scorpion, set by his side; and the
  ninth that was made in the shape of an Archer whose might
  does not fail;
So were the Goat and the Pail created by Thy great strength,
And by him the last sign—"now the Lord had prepared a great fish."
These are the lofty signs, raised up in their heights—"twelve
  princes according to their nations."

XXIII

Who can search out Thy secrets when Thou didst bring forth,
  over the sphere of the signs, a sphere that is ninth in order,
Which encompasses all the spheres and their creatures, and they
  are enclosed within it,

And which leads all the stars of heaven and their orbits from east
to west, by the power of its movement?
Once every day it bows down in the west to the King who
enthroned it;
And all the creatures of the universe are in it as a grain of mustard
in the great sea, so great is it and so vast,
Yet it and its greatness are counted as naught and as nothing
before the greatness of its Creator and its King—"and they
are counted to him less than nothing."

XXIV

Who can understand the mysteries of Thy creatures when Thou
didst raise up over the ninth sphere the sphere of
Intelligence, "the temple before it," "and the tenth shall be
holy unto the Lord"?
That is the sphere exalted above all height, to which thought cannot attain,
There is the mystery, the canopy of Thy glory.
Thou didst cast it from the silver of truth, and from the gold of
intelligence Thou madest its covering,
On pillars of righteousness Thou didst set its orbit, and its existence derives from Thy power,
From Thee and to Thee is its purpose—"unto Thee *shall be* his
desire."

XXV

Who can fathom Thy thoughts when from the splendour of the
sphere of intelligence Thou madest the radiance of souls and
lofty spirits?
They are the messengers of Thy Will, the ministers of Thy countenance.
They are majestic in strength, mighty in dominion, in their hand
is the "flaming sword which turned every way."
They perform every task, wherever the spirit takes them,
They are all elemental forms, transcendent beings, servants of the
outer and inner courts, looking well to Thy ways,

From the holy place they go forth, and from the source of light
they are drawn,
Marshalled into companies, with signs on their flag traced by the
pen of a skillful scribe,
Some to command and some to minister,
Some of them are hosts that run and come, tireless and unwea-
ried, seeing and not seen,
Some are hewn of flames, some stormy winds, some are com-
pounded of water and of fire.
Some are fiery Seraphim, some leaping sparks, some comets,
some flashes of lightning,
And every company bows down before the Rider of the Heavens,
and at the peak of the universe they stand in thousands and
myriads,
Divided into watches by day and by night at the start of their vig-
ils, to make praises and songs to Him that is girded with
prowesses.
All of them, in fear and trembling, kneeling and bowing to Thee,
and saying: "We confess to Thee,
That Thou art our God, and Thou didst make us, not we ourselves, and we are all the work of Thy hand,
For Thou art our Lord and we are Thy servants, Thou art our
Creator and we Thy witnesses."

XXVI

Who can come to Thy dwelling-place, when Thou didst raise up
above the sphere of intelligence the throne of glory, in which
is the abode of mystery and majesty,
In which is the secret and the foundation, to which the intelligence reaches—and then stops short?
And above it Thou art raised up and exalted on the throne of Thy
might, and none shall come up with Thee.

XXVII

Who can do as Thy deeds, when under the throne of Thy glory
Thou madest a place for the spirits of Thy saints?

There is the abode of the pure souls, that are bound in the bundle of life.

Those who are tired and weary, there will they restore their strength.

There shall the weary be at rest, for they are deserving of repose.

In it there is delight without end or limitation, for that is the world-to-come.

There are stations and visions for the souls that stand by the mirrors assembled, to see the face of the Lord and to be seen,

Dwelling in the royal palaces, standing by the royal table,

Delighting in the sweetness of the fruit of the Intelligence, which yields royal dainties.

This is the repose and the inheritance, whose good and beauty are without limit, and "surely it floweth with milk and honey; and this is the fruit of it."

XXVIII

Who can reveal Thy mysteries, when in the heights Thou madest chambers and treasures, in which wonders are told, and the word of mighty deeds?

Some of them treasures of life for the righteous and pure,

Some of them treasures of salvation, for penitent sinners,

Some of them treasures of fire and rivers of sulphur, for the transgressors of the covenant,

And treasures of deep pits of unquenchable fire, "he that is abhorred of the Lord shall fall therein."

And treasures of storms and tempests, of freezing and frost,

And treasures of hail and ice and snow, drought and also heat and bursting floods,

Steam and rime and mist and cloud and darkness and gloom.

All of them didst Thou prepare, in their time, either for mercy or for judgment Thou didst ordain them, "O mighty God, Thou hast established them for correction."

XXIX

Who can contain Thy might, when from the abundance of Thy glory Thou didst create a pure radiance, hewn from the quarry of the Rock, and dug from the mine of Purity?

And on it Thou didst set a spirit of wisdom, and Thou didst call it the Soul.

Thou didst fashion it from the flames of fire of the Intelligence, and its spirit is as a fire burning in it.

Thou didst send it into the body to serve it and to guard it, and it is as a fire within, and yet it does not burn it.

From the fire of the spirit it was created, and went forth from nothingness to being, "because the Lord descended upon it in fire."

XXX

Who can reach Thy wisdom, when Thou gavest the soul the power of knowledge which inheres in her?

So that knowledge is her glory, and therefore decay has no rule over her, and she endures with the endurance of her foundation; this is her state and her secret.

The wise soul does not see death, but receives for her sin a punishment more bitter than death,

And if she be pure she shall obtain grace, and smile on the last day,

And if she be unclean, she shall stray amid a flood of anger and wrath,

All the days of her uncleanliness she shall sit alone, captive and moving to and fro; "she shall touch no hallowed thing, nor come into the sanctuary, until the days of her purifying be fulfilled."

XXXI

Who can requite Thy bounties, when thou gavest the soul to the body, to give it life, to teach and show it the path of life, to save it from evil?

Thou didst form man out of clay, and breathe into him a soul and set on him a spirit of wisdom, by which he is distinguished from a beast, and rises to a great height.

Thou didst set him enclosed in Thy world, while Thou from outside dost understand his deeds and see him,

And whatever he hides from Thee—from inside and from outside
Thou dost observe.

XXXII

Who can know the secret of Thine accomplishments, when Thou
madest for the body the means for Thy work?
Thou gavest him eyes to see Thy signs,
Ears, to hear Thy wonders,
Mind, to grasp some part of Thy mystery,
Mouth, to tell Thy praise,
Tongue, to relate Thy mighty deeds to every comer,
As I do to-day, I Thy servant, the son of Thy handmaid,
I tell, according to the shortness of my tongue, one tiny part of
Thy greatness.
Behold, these are the ends of Thy ways—and how splendid are
their beginnings, "for they are life unto those that find them."
By them, all those who hear them can recognize Thee, even if
they do not see the face of Thy splendour.
Whoever does not hear Thy power, how can he recognize Thy
Godhead?
How can Thy truth enter into his heart, how can he bend his
thoughts to Thy service?
Therefore Thy servant found it in his heart to speak before his
God,
To tell one tiny part of the heads of His praises.
Perhaps thereby his sins may be overlooked, "for wherewith
should he reconcile himself unto his master? Should it not
be with the heads . . . ?"

6 ADDRESSING AN EMANATED GODHEAD

The anonymous text entitled *Pesaq ha-Yira'ah veha-Emunah*, "A Decision Concerning the Fear of God and Faith," is one of the earliest exoteric medieval statements in which the concept of the multilayered divine world is used for instruction concerning prayer, thus making the recognition of a mystical *pleroma* a ritualistic norm in Jewish religious culture. It is not an individual expression of adherance and communion with the divine world, but a declaration that the only correct way to say a blessing or a prayer is one that recognizes the multiple character of the divine realm. It is very close in this to the text of the "Gate of the Intention of the Early Kabbalists," though the visual and experiental element is less pronounced here, while the normative, theological one is put in the center. Yet both these texts—and many others from this period—represent the transition from the traditional concept of prayer to the medieval-modern one, in which the awareness of God to whom the prayer is directed has become complex and dynamic, radically different from the traditional concepts.

The group of esoterics and mystics that are represented by this text is unique in its spiritual characteristics.[1] It flourished in the Rhineland and northern France from the last decades of the twelfth century to the middle of the thirteenth, and we have about a dozen treatises that they authored. Most of these treatises are anonymous. The only known author from this group was Rabbi Elehanan ben Yakar, who flourished in London and in northern France in the first half of the thirteenth century and wrote two commentaries on the *Sefer Yezira*, and a theological treatise, *Sod ha-Sodot* ("Secret of Secrets"), dealing with the process of the creation. Their main spiritual source is a pseudepigraphical text, called *Barayta of Joseph Ben Uzziel,* which is a paraphrase of the *Sefer Yezira.* The person to whom this treatise is attributed, Joseph ben Uzziel, is described as an ancient figure of strange ancestry: He is claimed to be the son of Ben Sira (Ecclesiasticus), who was, according to legend, the son of the prophet Jeremiah.[2] The name "Joseph ben Uzziel" is not known from any other source but the narratives attributed to Ben Sira, which were written probably in the ninth century in Babylonia. The main subject in this basic treatise as well as in most of the other works of this group is cosmogony and cosmology, based to a very large extent on exegesis of the ancient *Sefer Yezira.*

This circle is known by the name "the unique cherub circle" because of the key figure presented in its theology: a "unique cherub," a divine power emanated from God, who resides on the throne of glory, and who serves as the divine power to be revealed to prophets and to mystics.[3] These writers insist that the divine glory, the secondary, emanated divine power, cannot be described in anthropomorphic terms, and therefore it cannot be envisioned by prophets and mystics. All visions, and all anthropomorphic descriptions in biblical and talmudic literature, refer to the Unique Cherub alone, who was emanated from God for this particular purpose, to serve as the humanlike representative of God. This circle thus believes in a triad of powers in the divine realm: the supreme God, who is the creator; the emanated divine glory, which has no dimensions and no boundaries, and the Unique Cherub, who can be revealed in seemingly physical attributes. Therefore, they insist, it is forbidden to direct prayers to the Cherub; prayers should be turned to the unlimited divine emanation, the divine glory. This is the main message of the text translated below.

The language of the ancient texts of the prayers is transformed in this new structure. It is interpreted as relating to the new theological concept of the existence of three powers in the divine realm, and the prayer has to be directed precisely according to the demands of the new, revolutionary concept of the structure of the divine world. Prayer is thus a declaration and an invocation, expressing the views and experiences of the esoterics and mystics who brought about this revolution.

All those who fear God have to direct their intention, when they say the blessing "blessed is God" and when they bow and express thanks and intend in their hearts—to His holiness alone, who is His glory, without image and form, only voice and speech. And so Isaiah said: *To whom then will you liken God, and what likeness compares with Him* (Isa. 40:18), but it is said: *Let us make man in Our image and after our likeness* (Gen. 1:26), and *the eyes of God* (Deut. 11:12, etc.) and also *upward from what had the appearance of his loins* (Ezek. 1:27),—all these metaphors do not refer to the place of His holiness and shekhinah, as I have explained that He, His holiness, does not have any form and image, only voice and wind and speech,[4] and he is filling the heaven and the earth, and there is no creature that knows the place of His holiness and His glory, not an angel nor a fiery angel nor all the hosts and armies [of angels] above, as it is said: Blessed is the glory of God from its place (Ezek. 3:12).

But all the written [= biblical] metaphors like *Let us make a man,* etc. as I interpreted it, refer to His *greatness,* which is his *kingdom,* that is in the East, and also the *measurement of the height* of Rabbi Ishmael refers to that *greatness* and *kingdom* of His. And it is called the *unique cherub,* which is emanated from His great fire, which is a fire that consumes fire. You know that, for He touched them with His little finger and the angels that were created of the fire were burned up when they said, *What is man that thou art mindful of him* (Ps. 8:5); so there is a fire that consumes fire: that is Him and His *holiness* and His *glory.*

From that great fire He emanated and created the *unique cherub,* and not from the same fire by from which the angels and the serafim and the celestial holy beasts and the *ere'elim* and the cherubim and all the hosts of the supreme world were created. And also all the heavens and the heavens of heavens that are nine in number were created from that fire that He derived from water, from the third part, as it is said: *He measured in the 'third' the soil of the earth* (Isa. 40:12). And that *unique cherub* that was created from His great fire that he emanated from His *holiness* and not from the fire from which the celestial hosts were created, so that his station will not be comparable to theirs.

For him [= the *unique cherub*] He created an image and a form and a human form, and eyes, and hands and *from his hips upward* (Ezek. 1:27), and on his forehead it is engraved *Yah Akhatriel,* and phylacteries on his head, and it is written about him: *who like your people Israel one nation on earth* (2 Sam. 7:23), and he has the *shiur komah* of Rabbi Ishamel, and in his image man was created, and he sits on the throne of glory, and he is is above all the proud ones, which are the four kings of earth—eagle, lion, bull and man, who are [stationed] on the four sides of the throne, to indicate that he is the king above all the kings. And also the cherubs below, over the ark [in the Temple] and the *shekhinah* with them, for the *unique cherub* is above on the throne of glory, his greatness is not from him but from His holiness, which is in the west, and this is why there are cherubs below who serve His holiness.

The unique cherub, sitting on his throne of glory, has a *pargod* of colored *hashmal*, whose name is Ishael, and its [color] is like light blue, and this is the *pargod* which surrounds the throne of glory on three sides, except the west, were His *holiness* in the west shines over His *greatness* in the east over the throne of glory. This is [the meaning of] *blessed is the glory of God*, the glory of God is His *holiness, from his place* (Ezek. 3:12), he goes and shines over His *greatness* and His *kingdom*. And to this glory we say the blessing: *Blessed is the glory of God from his place*.

And that *kingdom* of His, which is His *holiness*, is called in the *Sefer Yezira* the world of the *modi*, and it is one of the four worlds which are ten *sefirot*: the world of the *modi*, the world of *ravrevanut* (= great power?), the world of mada (= knowledge, intellect), and the world of the *nefesh* (= soul, spirit). The meaning of modi is derived from the word 'praise,' for God has created that *unique cherub* as a fixed place enabling all the celestial princes to praise and worship their Creator.

His greatness is elevated over all the peoples and is uplifted. "Uplifted" includes the letters of the word "he is not," in order to say that His holiness does not have any form or image. This is why the triple blessing is concluded by the term "the holy God" and not "the great God," as has been explained, because it is wrong to say a blessing or to intend, in every ritual of the Creator, only to His holiness which is without form or image. "For thou art a great and holy king," "great" is His *greatness* and His *kingdom* and it is the *unique cherub*, and "holy" is His *holiness* in the west, and this is our faith. This is [the meaning] of what we say [in prayer] "and the holy beasts will sing," etc., the face of every beast and ophan and cherub, to the cherub, that is, to the *unique cherub* that is the world of modi, "they turn their faces and bow."

A secret. We have studied in the *Barayta of Joseph ben Uzziel*, who revealed it from the mouth of Jeremiah the prophet, and should not be revealed but to the humble and esoteric. This is from the book of Rabbi Avigdor ha-Zarfati, and this is also from his book:

And God of Hosts is exalted in justice (Isa. 5:16). When He judges the nations of the world He is elevated in His world and He rises up on His throne and His name is sanctified in His heights, as it is said: *So I will show my greatness and my holiness* (Ezek. 38:23), etc. Another interpretion: In the treatise of celestial palaces [it is written]: *And the God of hosts is exalted in justice*, etc.—this is because the throne of glory is not situated equally (= straight, even), but one side is high and one side is low. When the Holy One Blessed be He sits on the chair in the measure of justice, then He is elevated, sitting and ascending on the high side, as it is said: *God has risen in the voice of shofar* (Ps. 47:6). [The name] *Elohim* indicates the measure of justice and then He rises when He hears the cry of Israel, Lord is the measure of mercy, the voice of *shofar* [means] that when they pray loudly they improve their deeds, and then it is transformed to the measure of mercy; it is as if the glory descends to the lower side of the throne. And then it is called YHVH, because YHVH in *etbash* is MZPZ,[5] which is, in *gematria*, "with mercy." This is the name of His holiness [which is] without a form or image, only voice and wind and speech, and he is like the lights in the west, and this is [the meaning of] *for I am holy, I the Lord* (Lev. 20:26).

This cannot be disclosed but to the humble and esoteric: [In the] *Barayta of Joseph ben Uzziel:* And they saw the God of Israel (Exod. 24:10)—this proves that they saw the Shekhinah, *and there was under His feet like a pavement of sapphire stone* (Exod. 24:10), under the throne of glory. Our sages of blessed memory said: Anyone who translates this verse literally, that is, *and they saw the glorious God of Israel*, is a liar, and anyone who adds to it, [like] *they saw the angels of the Lord God of Israel*, is committing infamy and curses God, for he makes the glory into an angel.[6] It should be: *And they saw the glory of the God of Israel.* Ibn Ezra: *And a vision, not in riddles* (Num. 12:8), this means that he was envisioning in a bright glass (or: mirror)—could it be the vision of the shekhinah? The Bible says that man shall not see me and live, neither man nor the holy beasts,[7] they do not see the face of the shekhinah, they even do not know its place, as it is said, *Blessed is the glory of God from its place* (Ezek. 3:12). As our sages of blessed memory said, man is a microcosmos,[8] meaning that in the same way that God blessed be He fills up all the universe and in His spirit established the worlds, the lower world and the upper world, so the soul establishes the body and leads it in any direction it wishes. And what our sages of blessed memory said, every place where [the Bible] says "and God," it is He and His court, meaning the [seventy nations?] because by it the wicked are punished, as it is said, *It is you who dries up the sea*, etc., *overcoming the serpent* (Isa. 51:9).

THE VOICE OF GOD OVER THE WATER

THE WORSHIP OF THE HOLY NAME

The secret power of the holy names of God, and first and foremost that of the tetragrammton, the name comprising four letters, is a central theme in Jewish religion, esoteric speculations, mysticism, and magic. It is forbidden to pronounce it, and it represents a main avenue of establishing contact between the divine realm, the universe, and humanity. Since late antiquity Jewish magicians, mystics, and esoterics studied the secret powers of the name, and formulated more and more secret names of an increasing complexity, to which they wrote detailed commentaries. They added to the tetragrammaton names comprising twelve letters, then forty-two letters, and the ultimate holy name in prekabbalistic and kabbalistic traditions comprised seventy-two groups of three letters each, known as the name of *ayin-bet*, seventy-two.

The structure of this name denotes the source of the belief in the divine force immanent in the holy names. It is derived from three consecutive biblical verses, Exod. 14:19–21, each of which comprised exactly seventy-two letters. The mystic or magician writes the letters of the first verse in their scriptural order, and then the letters of the second verse below them, in an inverse order, starting with the last one and ending with the first. Then, below these two rows he writes the letters of the third verse in their regular order. The name is then derived from reading the three rows vertically, thus receiving seventy-two groups of three letters each.[1]

The result of this procedure is the transformation of the section of the biblical narrative concerning the events surrounding the deliverence of the Israelites from Egypt into a meaningless array of random letters, which do not have any semantic message. When presented in this way, the verses cannot be read as coherent linguistic expression, but as a mysterious, intriguing assemblage of units that then can be interpreted by each exegete in any way he wishes. This is a deliberate denial of the biblical verses as including a specific content, and conceiving them as obscure hints of hidden divine secrets, which cannot be expressed by communicative language (it can be described as the transformation of the semantic into the semiotic representation of divine truth).

The denial of communicative meaning is characteristic of every name. It does not denote anything semantic, but directly points at a person, disregarding any possible connection to linguistic message. Girls named Belle are not more or less beautiful than ones called Jane. The names of God denote the divine entity directly, without the mediation of linguistic meaning, and therefore they are conceived as containing the direct flow of divine power. The more mysterious and nonsemantic their structure, the closer they are understood to contain a divine essence, a source of spiritual energy. Magicians may use these names to achieve their earthly purposes, while mystics may use them as avenues for approaching the divine realms.

Kabbalists in the thirteenth century extended the concept of secret, powerful divine names to include scriptures as a whole. The verses in Exod. 14:19–21 are remarkable because of the singular phenomenon of containing an identical number of letters, a fact that was understood as a divine hint at a hidden secret in them. The great Catalonian kabbalist, Rabbi Moshe ben Nahman (known as Nachmanides), went a step further and described the whole Torah as a series of hidden, secret names of God.[2] Another step was taken by kabbalists who defined the Torah as a whole as one name of God, indivisible into particular components. These are all expressions of the denial of the mediation of semantic language and the quest for the direct expression of divine power, in scriptures and in existence as a whole.

Expressions of such reverence to the holy name are found in many Jewish mystical works. The example presented here is taken from one of the most detailed Jewish works dedicated to this subject—*Sefer ha-Shem*, "The Book of the Holy Name," written by Rabbi Eleazar of

Worms around 1220. This work, which is one of the few major works in Jewish mysticism and esotericism that has never been printed (it is found in manuscript British Library 737 and several others), is a part of Rabbi Eleazar's presentation of the central themes of the secret traditions that he received from his forefathers, which he called "the Secrets of Secrets" (*Sodey Razaya*).[3] The *Book of the Name*, a three-hundred-page treatise, includes commentaries on several names, but mainly on the tetragrammton. It begins with a brief introduction, which describes the secret ceremony in which a rabbi transmits the traditions concerning the name to a disciple. This ritual has to be performed when the two participants are immersed in water, and it includes several biblical verses referring to God's name's presence in waters and seas.[4]

Rabbi Eleazar's work is not the first source that describes such a ceremony. We have a short treatise that is mainly concerned with magical traditions, *Sefer ha-Malbush*, "The Book of the Garment," which describes the ritual in a similar way, and adds another that is not found in Rabbi Eleazar's version: The name is to be worn like a mantle. The treatise includes detailed instructions on how to cut the mantle from the parchment of a deer; it must also include a head cover, but it can be without sleeves. The holy name—given in the work—is to be written on the mantle and the hat, and after seven days of fasting and self-purification the practioner has to go to a water source and put it on while immersed in the water. The author promises to the wearer of such a name infinite powers and divine protection.[5] The magical element, dominant in *Sefer ha-Malbush*, is almost completely absent from Rabbi Eleazar's version, in which the knowledge of divine secrets is the paramount motive.

Reading these texts one cannot avoid the realization that the knowledge of the secret divine name was not purely intellectual but included a mystical element of a sense of elevation, excitement, and a feeling of touching, however remotely, the hidden essence of God, which is partly revealed to the adherent by the nonsemantic, mysterious, and complex esoteric name of God. The recital of the biblical verses, all of which have similar phrases, is haunting and hypnotic. All of them include the term "thy name," and the first series emphasizes his power in and over water, and the second sequence—singing and rejoicing, while praising the name.

YHVH is God's unique name, it is a dignified and terrible name. We shall explain its meaning inasmuch as it is possible to express and to know the glorious and supernal name of God and its numinosity. May the merciful God forgive us for expounding it. It is known and obvious before Him that I am writing only to make known His glory and worship. The name cannot be transmitted but to humble people who never act out of anger, those who constantly fear and worship God and perform His commandments.

The Name may not be transmitted but over water, as it is said: *The voice of the Lord is upon the waters* (Ps. 29:3). Before the Rabbi teaches his disciple [these secrets], they should bathe in the water and immerse themselves in the ritual bath of forty measures,[6] and then they should put on white garments. On the day of the transmission they should fast, and then they should stand in the water, the water reaching to their ankles. Then the Rabbi should open his mouth and recite with deep devotion and say:

Blessed art thou, our God, the king of the universe, the Lord God of Israel. Thou art one and thy name is one. You have commanded us to keep your name hidden, because it is so terrifying. Blessed art thou and blessed is your glorious name forever, the numinous name of the Lord our God. *The voice of the Lord is upon the waters.* Blessed art thou our Lord who reveals His secret to those who worship him, the One who knows all secrets.

The Rabbi and the disciple should then look at the water and should say: *The floods have lifted up, O Lord, the floods have lifted up their voice, the floods lift up their roaring. The Lord on high is mightier than the noise of many waters, than the mighty waves of the sea* (Ps. 93:3–4). *The voice of the Lord is upon the waters; the God of glory thunders, the Lord is upon many waters* (Ps. 29:3–4). *The waters saw thee O God, the waters saw thee, they were afraid, the depth also trembled* (Ps. 77:17). *Thy way was in the sea, and thy path in the great waters and thy footsteps were not known* (Ps. 77:20). Then they should go to a place where there is water, either in the synagogue or in the house of Torah study, and they shall have [before them] water in a pure container, and the Rabbi should say:

Blessed art thou the Lord our God the king of the universe, who sanctified us by his commandments and gave us his orders, and separated us from all the nations and handed us his mysteries and gave us the understanding of his great and awesome name. Blessed art thou Lord who reveals his secrets to Israel. They then should say, in pleasant voice and fear and deep intention: *Look upon me and be gracious unto me, as is thy wont towards those who love thy name* (Ps. 119:132); *Therefore will I give thanks to thee, O Lord, among the nations and sing praises to thy name* (Ps. 18:50). *I will praise the Lord according to his righteousness and will sing praise to the name of the Lord most high* (Ps. 7:18). *I will be glad and rejoice in thee, I will sing to thy name* (Ps. 9:3). *So will I sing praise to thy name for ever, as I perform my vows day by day* (Ps. 61:9). *Sing to the glory of his name, make his praise glorious* (Ps. 66:2). *All the earth will worship thee, and shall sing to thee, they shall sing to thy name, sela.* (Ps. 61:4). *Sing to God, sing praises to his name, extol him who rides upon the clouds, Ya is his name, and rejoice before him* (Ps. 68:5). *It is a good thing to give thanks to the Lord, and to sing praise to thy name, O most high* (Ps. 92:2). *Haleluya for the Lord is good, sing praises for his name for it is pleasant* (Ps. 135:4). Blessed is the glorious name of his kingship forever and ever. *Blessed be the name of the Lord from this time forth and forever more* (Ps. 113:2). Blessed is the Lord forever, Amen.

THE ROKEAH

THE DEVOTION IN PRAYER

T he analysis of the writings of Rabbi Eleazar ben Judah of Worms (c. 1160–c. 1230) points clearly to the irrelevance of the term *mysticism* when applied to Jewish writers of esoterical and spiritual works. A very good case can be presented to justify designating him as a mystic, while other characteristics of his religious works place him in opposition to some of the most important mystical trends of his time. He wrote one of the most important strictly esoteric works of medieval Jewish spirituality—*Sefer ha-Shem*, "The Book of the Holy Name" (a portion of his introduction to this work is presented in the following section in this anthology), and at the same time he did more to popularize the secret traditions of the Kalonymus family, the most important group of mystics, esoterics, and pietists in medieval Germany.

Rabbi Eleazar was the son of one of the great scholars of this family, Rabbi Judah ben Kalonymus, from whom he received the traditions of the Rhineland Jewry in the realms of law, poetry, pietism, and esoteric theology. He was also the most prominent disciple of the major spiritual leader of the time, Rabbi Judah ben Samuel, "the pious." Some of the theological treatises written by Rabbi Eleazar are summaries and paraphrases of Rabbi Judah's works. The great collection of theological works that Rabbi Eleazar authored, the five-volume *Sodey Razaya* ("Secrets of Secrets"), was written after the death of Rabbi Judah (in 1217), and intended to preserve for future generations the teachings of his rabbi.[1] Eleazar was loyal to his teacher's views concerning many theological subjects, but in others he was in complete opposition to him. One of them concerned the mystical nature of prayers. Rabbi Judah wrote an extensive, six-volume commentary on the prayers (which has been lost; numerous quotations from it reached us), which was dedicated to demonstrating the inherent, mystical structure of the ancient texts, which reflected, according to Rabbi Judah, the inherent mystical harmony between the text and the structure of the universe, of man and of the other sacred texts, especially the scriptures. Rabbi Judah used mainly numerical methods in order to demonstrate this divine harmony. Rabbi Eleazar also wrote an extensive commentary on the prayers, in which he included the main ideas and attitudes of his teacher. But he presented this concept of mystical harmony as one of several possible ways of understanding the prayers, not as the overwhelming, dominant one. In this way he transformed Rabbi Judah's mystical vision into one more midrashic, exegetical aspect that can be found in the prayers besides many others. It is obvious that Rabbi Eleazar did not adhere to his teacher's monistic, all-absorbing mystical concept of the prayers, and especially the significance of the numerical structures that Rabbi Judah found within them.

Rabbi Eleazar, like most of the other disciples of Rabbi Judah the Pious, did not share the social-religious vision of Rabbi Judah, which included an attempt to establish a sect of devoted pietists who shall live in separate communities, reject from among them "ordinary" worshippers, and concentrate on achieving a perfect religious and social status. The pietistic ideals are presented in Rabbi Eleazar's works as an individual endeavor, a perfection that every person should aspire to achieve alone, while Rabbi Judah attempted to establish structured communities, led most probably by himself, which will express these ideals.[2] Rabbi Eleazar's moderate attitude prevailed, and it is possible that this was the reason for Rabbi Judah's migration from the Rhineland to Regensburg; he probably sought more loyal adherents farther to the east.

We should not conclude, however, that Rabbi Eleazar was moderate in every aspect of spiritual life. One of the boldest expressions of the erotic nature of the love of God is found in Eleazar's description of the love of God, presented in his brief ethical introduction to the large collection of his theological works, *Sodey Razaya*:

> The Root of Love [of God]: It is to love God when the soul is overflowing with love, and is bound with the bonds of love in

great happiness. This happiness drives away from a person's heart the pleasures of the body and the enjoyment of worldly things. This great love and joy overcomes his heart and makes him think constantly how he could fulfill the wish of God. The enjoyment of his children and wife become like nothing compared with the immense love of God. [What he feels is] more than like a young man who did not have sexual intercourse with a woman for a long time, and he craves her and desires her and his heart is burning to be with her, and because of his great love and desire when he has intercourse with her his semen shoots from him like an arrow and his enjoyment is supreme. All this is like nothing compared with the following of God's will, and making others worthy, and sanctify himself and surrender himself to God in his love . . . and the love of heaven is in his heart like a fire inherent in a burning coal,[3] and he becomes oblivious of women and he does not pay attention to worldly affairs and insignificant things and devotes all his energy to fulfill the will of God and will sing songs of praise expressing the joy of the love of God.[4]

This description of ecstatic love of God, which is expressed in the strongest erotic terms, stands out among the usually sombre, even tragic, descriptions of worship that prevail in the discussions of pietism in the writings of the Kalonymus school. It proves that Rabbi Eleazar did not deny the elements of joy, singing, fulfilment, and ecstasy from the highest rungs of the ladder of spiritual worship.

While this and other descriptions are found in esoteric works, the following text is translated from Rabbi Eleazar's most exoteric book, his work on religious law entitled *Sefer ha-Rokeach*.[5] This work presents a code of *halakhah*, following the Kalonymus family tradition. Rabbi Eleazar added to it two introductory chapters, one dedicated to the norms of pietism and the other to the rules of repentance.[6] The chapter on pietism includes the following theological presentation of the concept and practice of prayer: It adds to the traditional text and ritual a series of instructions for contemplation, directing the worshiper toward spiritual elevation by the deep realization of the greatness and magnificence of the God whom he is addressing. It is an expression of the insufficiency of the minimal following of the legal demands when a deeper and more meaningful religious experience is sought. Rabbi

Eleazar used for this presentation elements derived from ancient Jewish esoteric and mystical traditions—those of the *Sefer Yezira* ("The Book of Creation," which was attributed to Abraham the Patriarch), from the writings of the Hekhalot mystics, and from the poetic paraphrase of Rav Saadia Gaon's theological work, *Emunot ve-Deot* ("Beliefs and Ideas," written in Arabic in the first half of the tenth century in Babylonia; the Hebrew paraphrase was written in Byzantium in the end of the eleventh century). To these Rabbi Eleazar added the particular ideas of the school to which he belonged, mainly concerning the separate power in the divine world, the *kavod* (divine glory, the revealed divine power). Rabbi Eleazar's instructions include several paragraphs which paraphrase the ancient texts, *Sefer Yezira* and Hekhalot, and he thus includes these hitherto marginal expressions in the normative ritual of prayer. It is difficult to draw the line here between mysticism and spirituality, but there is no doubt that this and similar texts express a new attitude towards prayer and the spiritual aspect of religious life.

The Principle of the Sanctity of the Unity of God and His Name and the Secrets of the Chariot

You should sanctify himself even in what is permitted [by the law] and in everything; this will benefit you. You should sanctify yourself, and your thoughts, and you should ponder who do you worship and who do you trust, who is observing you and who knows all your deeds, and to whom you shall return in repentance . . .

We, your servants, . . . [7] are obligated to know your unity, to recognize your glory. You are one alone and we are your witnesses, there is none but you. Your venerated Name indicates your [other] names: Your name YHVH—HYH, HVH, YHYH in your grandeur.[8] It is the truth that you are the First and the Last alone, it is you who was before the universe was created in your consultations, you are since the world was created in your beauty, you are in the present world in your hosts, and you shall be in the next world with your beloved [worshippers]. From eternity to eternity you are in your majesty, and all the universes are in your hands, your love is full of all that is good, silence is your praise and your charity testifies for you. You cannot be compared to your creatures, there is no image which can be compared to you. No one perceived and knew your secrets, nobody approached you, you observe everything in front of you. I am bowing to your beloved, celebrated [name], YHVH is our God YHVH is one, I shall declare your unity.

Everyone who has a wise heart should acquire at least some knowledge of a small part of the truth of his unity, the unity of name and the secret of the creator.[9] No one has the power to investigate and know what he is; no living thing has ever observed him, neither an angel or a seraph nor a prophet, for everything is created and he created everything. He is the creator and the one who shaped everything, he is one and there is no second to him, and no one observed him, therefore he cannot be compared to any image or vision, for anything which has an image is finite, but the creator is infinite, he does not have an edge neither up nor down and in the four directions,[10] and no beginning nor end to his wisdom and his abilities. However, the force of his employs he revealed to his people, in order to make known his powers and the glory and the grandeur of his kingship.

Is it not that all his creatures pray to him at the same time, in one moment, each of them exposing his heart and recounting his troubles, and he responds to each and every one of them?[11] You should know then that he is close to all those who call upon him, and the wise one, whose eyes are open, should understand that.

My son, listen to my words and do not spend your energy in an attempt to understand his nature, for there is no way to know the essence of the creator, who is not created; he was, he is, and he will be, and what image can be attributed to him and to what can he be compared and found equal,[12] for the image of all those which were created is not found in the creator, and all the forms of those which were made are not to be found in their maker, and all the shapes which exist are not to be found in the one who brought them into being. If all the creatures will congregate together, all the wise and knowledgable and famous, they cannot fathom all his essence. This is why his name is YHVH. But we should know in our wisdom together that YHVH our God is one, the God of Abraham, the God of Isaac, the God of Jacob, the unique one, whom we love and to whom we bow and worship in reverence. Therefore, my soul craved for you at night and I have remembered you in my bed at all times, always thinking of you.[13] When

Abram came, who was [later called] Abraham, and witnessed the [evil generation] of the "division" (*haplaga*), he pondered how everything was in the beginning before everything, and he was then forty-eight years old, and studied this alone for three years, until God told him: do it with Shem the son of Noah, for a wise son makes his father in heaven happy,[14] so Abraham contemplated his creator who made him, and how he created the world, and he wrote a treatise which he called The Book of Creation . . .[15]

. . . I have imagined God in front of me always,[16] I shall speak with him in my dream. He is one and united, and created the whole universe by his will and his wish, his soul wished and he made it[17] and nothing is which he did not wish, by the word of God the heavens were made. The creator does not need a place and an abode, for he existed before everything, and no walls or logs hinder him, for he would not create anything which is inimical to him. The creator who made everything is more spiritual than anything spiritual, wonderful and hidden, obscured from all. No creature is equal to the creator, and no measurement is relevant to him, neither breadth nor width, nor image nor physical shape nor a connection to anything nor limbs nor shadow nor light nor shape nor image nor a turn. According to his will, he makes his voice heard to his Glory, which blesses [him] and presents itself in any image necessary.

His name is YHVH. [The letters] *yod he vav he* have the numerical value of [the words] "he is one."[18] Similarly, in ETBS [it is] MZPZ, which has the numerical value of "the creator exists in everything."[19] The creator does not have any image and form,[20] [he is not subject] to any accident, no physical attributes, he is not combined with anything nor part of anything, and he does not need anything, neither a place or an abode, and he is not connected to a particular place and he fulfills all the heavens and earth and the sea and the air and all the universes. There is no relevance to him in [descriptions] which include standing or sitting or walking or relying.[21] He is alive in his power and his ability for ever.[22] There is no movement relevant to him and no action and no effort; he creates everything effortlessly, and brings forth without toil all the kinds of creatures. No eye can observe or discern him. He is the creator and existed before there was any abode and preceded the existence of everything. He is "first" before everything, living and existing, great and powerful and terrible, a king who is glorified and praised, and there can be no addition to him nor any diminishing. His existence is infinite, no one can reach his secrets and come to the end of his being, his greatness is beyond any number and his wisdom infinite.[23]

. . . The maker of all is the creator;[24] you should believe in his divinity for the creator is one and shows his Glory[25] according to his will and wish. This is the wonderous form, which is elevated and brilliant, bright . . . "and the spectacle of the Glory is like the consuming fire" (Exod. 24:17) and it is called the shekhinah.[26] Sometimes it is envisioned without a form, just a great light without an image of anything created, and [the prophet] hears the utterance and sees the wonderous vision and says "I have seen God,"[27] including his Glory. When it is envisioned by [the prophet's] eyes, it seems to be 236 thousands of ten thousands parasangs, according to the verse "our master is large and powerful"[28] the numerical value of which is 236.[29]

God shows in the vision of his glory his divine will, which reflects his decisions. Moses had seen more of the great splendour of the glory than other prophets. In the images of the vision God shows the prophets what he wishes, and he gives the glory a shape reflecting the nature of his decisions.[30] It may be a human image or any other image. It is seen in the divine glory, united with the hosts of God [= the angels]. Then the divine speech comes forward from the divine glory.

DIVINE WILL CLOTHED IN HUMAN WILL

THE INTENTION OF PRAYER IN EARLY KABBALAH

The ritual of prayer—so central in the religious life of all three scriptural religions—is the most intense expression of the paradoxical status of the mystics within the framework of traditional worship. Prayer is conceived, on the one hand, as the closest point of contact between the worshipper and God in religion. During prayer the believer expresses his love to God, and believes that his pain and joy, his needs and his accomplishments are being presented before the throne of glory. When standing in prayer, the worshipper is an individual who has been given by his religious structure the opportunity to address God directly. On the other hand, prayer is the most traditional part of worship. The circumstances of prayer, the place and the time, are strictly regulated. The time of prayer is shared with the whole community and its religious leadership. And, above all, the text of the prayer is fixed by tradition, word for word, and any deviation from the sacred text is at least frowned upon, if not worse. How can the individuality of the worshipper express itself within this highly structured ritual?

If this is a serious problem for all worshippers, it is doubly so for the mystic, who craves a full bilateral relationship between himself and God. The experience he seeks is unique, separated from tradition and from communal ritual. How can he find an expression of his visionary, intensely individual state of spiritual elevation within the rigid structure of ancient, repetitive texts and the presence of the whole community besides him?

This paradox led, in the three religions, to the development of various solutions, which tried to combine the religious ritual of prayer with the unique experience of the mystic. Several Christian mystics developed the concept of the "silent prayer," in which a mystic may add to the traditional ritual a hidden expression of his own spirituality.[1] Others went further and suggested a nonverbal prayer, which ignores the sacred text and creates a bond between the mystic and the divine by purely spiritual elevation.[2] Others spiritualized the whole ritual and replaced physical participation by mystical contemplation,[3] and many other ways, each of which had numerous variations and emphases. In Judaism, the main avenue of living within this paradox was expressed by the concept of kawwana, the spiritual intention that accompanies the traditional prayer but finds within it unlimited vistas of meaning, which are not shared by the community that adheres to the traditional norms. It was accompanied by new interpretations of ancient texts and ideas, which strived to find the roots of new concepts in old traditional sources.

It should be emphasized that the term *kawwana*, which became common in Jewish spirituality since the thirteenth century,[4] does not have a fixed meaning. Many kabbalists and mystics used it in different ways, and its significance has to be determined by its context in the spiritual world of each writer.

The textual foundation for the kabbalistic concept of the prayers has been laid down in the book Bahir, the earliest work of the kabbalah that was written in the last years of the twelfth century. In an exegesis of the Kedushah (the trisaggion), one of the peaks of traditional prayer, the author found the reflection of the complex structure of the divine world,[5] and made possible the understanding—never expressed clearly in this work—that the contemplation of this esoteric meaning should be inserted into the daily ritual prayer. Later kabbalists amplified this concept, and in the Gerona circle we find already detailed commentary on the prayers in which each word—sometimes each letter—of the prayers is identified with a particular aspect of the divine world, and this relationship has to be expressed in the ritual of prayer.[6] One of the earliest documents criticizing the kabbalistic worldview in the thirteenth century emphasizes the author's opposition to the identification of different targets for different prayers in the divine world, as done by the kabbalists.[7] The view that the ritual of prayer brings the worshipper into contact with the various powers in the divine pleroma became central in the Zohar,[8] and even more so in the Lurianic kabbalah in the late sixteenth century. Prayer accompanied by mystical "intentions," relating parts of the text to different aspects in the divine world, became one of the most prominent characteristics of kabbalists, separating them from other worshippers.

Gershom Scholem published a brief treatise,[9] entitled *Sha'ar ha-Kawwanna la-Mekubalim ha-Rishonom*, "The Gate of Intention of the Early Kabbalists," which is undoubtedly one of the earliest texts in which a kabbalist tried to bridge the chasm between traditional prayer and a mystical one. He suggested that the author may have been Rabbi Azriel of Gerona, in the early decades of the thirteenth century, but no conclusive proof for that attribution has been found. It is better to regard it as an anonymous text, expressing one of several trends that were prevalent in the circles of the early kabbalists concerning mystical expression in the ritual of prayer.

The author of this text did not emphasize the exegetical element; instead, he instructed his reader concerning his state of mind and his emotions during prayer. His starting point seems to have been the old tradition, found in the Mishnah, that "the early Hasidim" used to wait in contemplation an hour before starting the ritual prayer.[10] The writer interpreted this period as one in which the worshipper-mystic has to transform himself, to shed his material body and become purely spiritual, immersed in divine light surrounding him and becoming himself light rather than matter. When in this state, the mystic envisions the components of the spiritual world as pillars of light, of different colors, surrounding him. The mystical goal of this prayer is a very ambitious one—it is to reach the realm of the infinite, unbound Godhead beyond the limited manifestations of the divine realm, and be united with it—"so that the higher will is clothed in his will." Such radical expressions of spiritual union with the highest divine power are very rare in kabbalistic literature. It should be also noticed that the author did not use kabbalistic terminology extensively, and most of the sentences can be understood without reference to the particular set of symbols employed by the early kabbalists.[11]

He who resolves upon something in his mind with a perfect firmness, for him it becomes the essential thing. Therefore if you pray and pronounce the benedictions or otherwise truly wish to direct the *kawwanah* to something, imagine that you are light and that everything around you is light, light from every direction and every side; and in the light a throne of light, and, on it, a "brilliant light," and opposite it a throne and, on it, a "good light." And if you stand between them and desire vengeance, turn to the "brilliance"; and if you desire love, turn to the "good," and what comes from your lips should be turned towards its face. And turn toward the right, and you will find "shining light," toward the left and you will find an aura, which is the "radiant light." And between them and above them the light of the *kabhod*, and around it the light of life. And above it the crown of light that crowns the desires of the thoughts, that lights up the path of the representations and illuminates the brilliance of the visions. And this illumination is unfathomable and infinite, and from its perfect glory proceed grace and benediction, peace and life for those who observe the path of its unification. But to those who deviate from its path comes the light that is hidden and transformed from one thing into its opposite, [and it sometimes appears to him] as a chastisement and [sometimes] as right guidance, everything according to the *kawwanah* of him who knows how to accomplish it in the right manner: through cleaving, *debhequth*, to the thought and the will that emanates in its full force from the unfathomable. For according to the intensity of the *kawwanah*, with which it draws strength to itself through its will, and will through its knowledge, and representation through its thought, and power through its reaching [to the primordial source of the will] and firmness through its contemplation, if no other reflection or desire is mixed in it, and if it grows in intensity through the power that guides it, in order to draw to itself the current that proceeds from *'en-sof*[12] —[according to the measure of such an intensity of the *kawwanah*] every thing and every act is accomplished according to its spirit and its will, if only it knows to embrace the limits of the finite things and of the will that inhabits their thought from the principle from which they derive. Then, it must elevate itself above them through the power of its *kawwanah* and go into the depths in order to destroy the [ordinary] path from its very principle and to pave a new way according to his own will: through the power of his *kawwanah*, which stems from the perfect glory of the withdrawing light, which has neither figure nor image, neither measure nor size, neither evaluation nor limit, neither end nor foundation nor number, and which is in no respect finite.

And he who elevates himself in such a manner, from word to word, through the power of his intention, until he arrives at 'en-sof, must direct his *kawwanah* in a manner corresponding to his perfection, so that the higher will is clothed in his will,[13] and not only so that his will is clothed in the higher will. For the effluence [of the emanation proceeding from the divine will] is like the inexhaustible source that is never interrupted only if, in approaching the higher will, it carefully watches that the higher will is clothed in the will of its aspiration. Then, when the higher will and the lower will, in their indistinctness and in their *debhequth* to the [divine] unity, become one, the effluence pours forth according to the measure of its perfection. But the perfection of the lower will cannot take place if it approaches [the higher will] for its own need, but only if it approaches it [the higher will] and if it clothes itself in the will through which enough of the nondistinctness is manifested, which is [otherwise] concealed in the most hidden mystery. And if it approaches it in this manner, the higher will also approaches it and grants to its power firmness and to its will the impulse to perfect and execute everything, even if it be according to the will of its soul, in which the higher will has no part. And this is what the verse [Prov. 11:27] says: "He who earnestly seeks what is good pursues what is pleasing [literally: the will]." For as far as the will clings to an object that corresponds to the higher will, the impulse [of the divine will] is clothed in it and is attracted, following its own [human] will, toward every object for which it exerts itself with the power of its *kawwanah*. And it draws down the effluence, which crowns the secrets of the things and essences through the path of the *hokhmah* and with the spirit of the *binah* and with the firmness of *da'ath*.[14] And in the measure that it is clothed with the spirit and explains its *kawwanah* through its words and fixes a visible sign through its actions, it draws the effluence from power to power and from cause to cause, until its actions are concluded in the sense of its will.

In this manner the ancients used to spend some time in meditation, before prayer, and to divert all other thoughts and to determine the paths of their *kawwanah* [during the subsequent prayer] and the power that was to be applied to its direction. And similarly [also] some

time during prayer, in order to realize the *kawwa ah* in the articulated speech. And similarly some time after prayer, in order to meditate on how they could also direct the power of the *kawwanah*, which came to its conclusion in the speech, in the paths of visible action. And since they were truly pious men, Hasidim, their Torah became action and their work was blessed. And this is the path among the paths of prophecy, upon which he who makes himself familiar with it will be capable of rising to the rank of prophecy.

ABRAHAM ABULAFIA

AN APOCALYPTIC VISION

braham Abulafia (c. 1240–1292) is one of the best-
known Jewish mystics. He has fascinated readers and
scholars who studied his writings (most of them still in
manuscript) since the first half of the nineteenth century. Some scholars even tried to attribute to him the
authorship of the *Zohar,* despite the obvious difference
between his teachings and those of the classics of Jewish
mysticism. Nearly thirty of his treatises survived, but
many others were lost.[1] He wandered from country to
country in Europe and the East, seeking disciples, and
developed a unique kind of mysticism that fascinated
several Jewish esoterics and mystics in his own lifetime
and in later centuries. He opposed—and sometimes
even ridiculed—the kabbalistic system of the sefirot,
developed mainly by the kabbalistic center in Gerona,
and substituted it with a system inspired by the ancient
Sefer Yezira, based on the combinations of the Hebrew
alphabet, numerical analysis, and the study of the holy
names of God. He was influenced deeply by the works
of Rabbi Judah the Pious of Regensburg, Rabbi Eleazar
of Worms, and Iyyun ("Contemplation"), a circle of
Jewish mystics in the early thirteenth century. It is possible that he was also influenced by Muslim Sufis and
other contemporary schools of esoterics and mystics. His
main attraction may have been his detailed instructions
concerning the intellectual, spiritual, and physical steps
that lead to an immersion in mystical visions and spiritual contemplation. Abulafia was convinced that his
mysticism was a continuation and elevation of the rationalistic philosophy of Moses Maimonides: He wrote a

commentary on the *Guide to the Perplexed*, and believed that he had discovered the intrinsic mystical core of Maimonidean philosophy. While Maimonides did not encourage a quest for prophetic qualities, Abulafia insisted that his teachings, based on his own interpretation of the *Guide*, can and should lead the mystic to the heights of prophecy.

The main message of Abulafia's mystical system is intensely individualistic, leading the mystic toward approach to God and even to union with him. Such an attitude usually develops into a spiritual life, which is detached from society and history. Yet Abraham Abulafia—especially in his last years—became dedicated to messianic-apocalyptic visions, which he defined as "prophetic." He wrote many treatises describing his prophetic visions, most of which did not reach us. *Sefer ha-Ot* ("The Book of the Sign") is the exception, and the following text is a translation of the concluding chapter of that book.[2] He wrote this work in 1288, a few years after he initiated a peculiar messianic adventure in which he sought an audience with the pope in order to bring forth the redemption. The pope, Nicholas III, died on that night (1280), and Abulafia was arrested and held in prison for a month by the College of Franciscans and then released.

It is impossible to understand the details of this apocalyptic vision, which includes elements from the visions of Daniel and other traditional apocalypses. There are, undoubtedly, some references to the political-military situation that Abulafia saw and envisioned, combined with his own literary and mystical inclinations. It is a demonstration of the multileveled mystical experiences of Abulafia, moving from those involving letters and numbers to those dealing with knights and duels. The ecstatic and the prophetic, the contemplative and the messianic, are combined in the tormented soul of this lonely visionary.

A new vision my God has revealed to me in the name, renewing his spirit over me. On the fourth day of the seventh month, which is the first month of the beginning of the eighteenth year in which I have been seeing visions. I was envisioning, and saw a person come from the west, followed by a great army, and the number of the fighters in his army was twenty-two thousands. That man, the leader of the army, was endowed with glory and glamour, the valour of his heart sounding the whole land and exiting the hearts of the soldiers following him, who had strong arms, mounted knights and soldiers almost infinite in number. On his forehead there was a sign, written in blood and ink on the two sides, and the image of the sign like a stick which in the middle between two poles and deciding between them; this is a very sublime and esoteric sign.[3] The color of the blood was black, and then turned to red, and the color of the ink was red, and turned to black, and the image of the sign which was in the middle, deciding between the two pictures, was white. These are the wonders revealed in the sign engraved on the forehead of the person whom I have envisioned coming forward, and the whole army was moving following his command.

When I saw his face in the vision I was frightened and my heart was pounding as if it were jumping out of its place. I wanted to speak, to call upon God to help me, but I did not have the strength to do it. When the person observed how strong was my fear he opened his mouth and spoke to me, and I responded to him. When I was speaking my strength returned to me, as if I were a different man, and I opened my eyes and looked at him. I saw a sign engraved on his forehead;[4] the man called this sign deadly poison, but I called it the elixir of life, because I turned him from death to life.

When the person saw the transformation which I have accomplished in honor of the God of Israel, he became very happy and blessed me an eternal blessing and opened his mouth turning to me and declared loudly: Happy is the righteous plant and happy are his parents and teachers and happy are the people who follow him and obey him, and blessed is the Lord God of Israel, his God, who has blessed him. His blessing is eternal, because it is the source from which everything came to be; it is surrounded by charity and beauty, and in it are justice and judgment. It shoots arrows of mercy and its sword reaches the blood of one's heart. Your heart is like a flower in the Garden of Eden, a plant rooted in the celestial realms, for you have won my war and transformed the blood of my forehead and its colors, and understood all my experience and my thoughts. The sign, the ink of which you have glorified, will sanctify you. You shall become sacred by sign and by miracle and by this grand and sacred name which is: YHVA YHVH YAVH again and again. This terrible and numinous name will assist you, and the sign on the forehead will inform you; it will sustain your spirit from the depth of your heart, and will hand to you the golden sceptre which can provide you with eternal life. This will be your proof: On the day in which I shall do battle with the people of the earth, I shall reveal to your ears and you shall see by your eyes and your heart shall understand the wondrous sign which is engraved clearly on my forehead.

These are the teachings of the sign and its laws. From one epoch to another it changes, and from one generation to the other it is transformed. It fights the wars of the heavens and takes the spoils of the sword. It turns death into life. It turns into life the death of God's people, the righteous, the ones who know His secrets and those who love the esoteric paths of His wonders. It was engraved like philacteries on the top of the head with the power of black ink and that of red blood, ascending and descending from measure to measure. The letters YH were engraved on every measure, serving like its roof, and hidden within it is the unique source according to which the powers of the sign are periodically revealed and hidden. . . .

The soul of everyone who is alive and conscious moves from the tent of mud to the tent of blood, and from the dwelling-place of blood it moves to the tabernacle at the heart of the heavens, and there it dwells all its life. The secret of its life and its hidden breath hang on fate, a time for this and a time for that, and it is decided by the sign on my forehead. This is until one of them reaches the power of kingdom; until then, they do not cease fighting each with his brother, and when one achieves kingdom a servant falls by the hand of a servant. This is because the divine power enforces new decrees throughout the world, by the power of eternity and of anger and the force of fate and the epoch, and according to the decisive power of the sign on my forehead.

The Rock of Israel, the judge of all measures, enforces the measures until those who are supreme now will be brought down, and until the downtrodden will be supreme in the celestial realms. The horn of the kingdom and the bugle of the powers blow, and the master of fate leads the sound from one end of the cosmos to the other. A terrible wind and a spirit which burns the hearts is invoked in the inner chambers of Knowledge to take revenge from this side and that side, revenge for bloodshed and fornication. A terrible and honorable Name brings forth redemption to the earth, and takes revenge from those who had forgotten it; it is renewed at the time of trial and the day of memory, at the moment of triumph. The Torah and its commandments are dressed in the garments of revenge and shoot forth the arrows of judgment into the hearts which are the targets for the messages of ideas, and they pronounce good news for those who remember the names.

When I heard this blessing from that person who came to fight the wars of the Lord God the God of Israel, a blessing which is peppered with wisdom and mixed with intelligence and surrounded by understanding my heart rejoiced with the person, feeling eternal happiness. I bowed before him and gave praise to the Lord God who sent him to revive my soul and strengthen my spirit and awaken my heart from the sleep of death. I observed the sign on the forehead and understood it, and then my heart became aware when I was looking at it and my spirit became alive with it eternal life, and it teachings moved me to speak and compose this *book of the sign*. The person then vanished from my eyes after he had spoken to me, and continued to wage war, ever stronger, until he has overcome every foe. The hearts of all those who were powerful and their forces melted when they heard about his employs. All the kings and heroes of all camps have returned empty-handed and lost their hope, and all their armies and servants ran away because of their fright.

At that time I endeavored and risked my life, I, Brekhyahu son of Salviel, the servant of the Lord God of Israel and I beseeched him to inform me what will be the fate of our nation during these wars. I then raised my eyes and saw three knights running after each other and pursuing each other, each distant from the other by the range of an arrow-shot, and each of them encouraging each other to stand and fight. I saw the first one rushing towards the second one, who ran away from him, and while running he shot at him a sharp arrow. The arrow landed in front of him and hit a crawling stone which moved from one side to the other and then stuck to his foot. The man then screamed with great pain and said: Oh my Lord, God of my fathers, I am going to die because of this poisoned arrow. Even when he was speaking his foot was swelling as if full of air, and the pain increased in all parts of his body until all his limbs were swollen as if nourished by yeast. When I heard his cry I became moved by pity towards him, and I ran and approached him and whispered in his ear; immediately the pain in all his limbs ceased because of my whisper. When the first knight, who was injured in his leg by the arrow, observed that the other knight's pain was relieved by my whisper, he attacked him, running towards him and hitting him with his spear; he stuck it in his abdomen and spilled his intestines on the ground, until he collapsed and died. When the third knight saw that the first one killed the second, he attacked him with his sword and hit him with it once and a second time and a third time, ten blows, until the tenth one killed him. I then approached that knight, addressed him and blessed him: May God be with you, hero. I then asked him to explain to me the meaning of the fight which I observed in this vision.

The knight then made me see an old man sitting on a throne, like a judge. He was wearing light-blue and crimson cloths. The knight told me: Ask that man who is sitting on the mountain of judgment and he will reveal to you what are these wars and what will be their result, for he is from your people. I ascended the mountain of judgment and approached the old man; I kneeled before him and fell down on my face before his feet. He then put his hand over me and made me stand on my feet in front of him. He said to me: Approach in peace, peace be unto you and to all those who love you. You have been saved from the war, and you have won all my wars. Now you should know and understand that I have been expecting you many years, until you finally came, and now I shall reveal to you the meaning of the wars you have witnessed:

The three knights who were pursuing each other are three kings who will reign in three ends of the earth, who will have conflicting views. They will conduct wars against each other, and while they were fighting one battle after another they will exchange messengers between them and each will reject the others' messages, which will be like arrows piercing their hearts. The crawling stone which you have observed is a frightened thought which draws like a magnet pulls iron in its unique force. This will have an impact on the kingdom, and will cause the heart of the second king to die inside him. When his heart dies the wise men of his people will give him advice which will support and encourage him; this is the whisper to his ear which you have delivered, which healed the injury of the arrow-thought which struck him. The sight you have seen of the knight falling and being hit again and again, these are the bitter messages which he received, indicating the loss of his kingdom, and he then died. The sight of the third knight beating the first and overcoming him after hitting him ten blows, he is the Eastern king who will win the fight with the Southern one, by the name of God, after the Northern king has died. This is why you have been instructed to ask him for explanation of the struggle you have envisioned. He referred you to me, because we are sons of the people of Israel, and he is not. He is a messenger sent by God to fight for us and overcome our enemies. These three kings have representatives in the celestial realm, their names identical and from them they derive their power. One of the names is Kadriel, the second is Magdiel and the third is Alfiel, and the name of the knight you have seen in the beginning of the vision is Toriel. My name is Yahoel, who consented to speak with you several years ago . . . There is a fifth knight, who is my Messiah, who will reign after the time of the four kingdoms. This is the interpretation which is clear to everyone; the hidden meaning is known only to those who have secret understanding.

THE MYSTICAL IMMERSION IN NAMES AND LETTERS

When Gerson Scholem wrote his most influential book, *Major Trends in Jewish Mysticism*, he used a minimum of translated quotations. There are very few paragraph-length translated statements in the whole volume. The chapters of the book were based on public lectures, and he preferred to paraphrase ideas and present them in his own language rather than present extensive texts in translation. The only exception to that rule is the following testimony, which, though a full eight pages long, was translated in an almost unabbreviated way and included in the book. Since the publication of that book (1941), there is no anthology or discussion of Jewish mysticism without a presentation of this text. This could be a very good reason not to include it in the present volume; such a decision, though desirable because of the cliché character that it has acquired, is impossible when a collection of Jewish mystical experiential texts is presented, because this one is arguably the most explicit and expressive one in nearly two thousand years of religious creative writing in Hebrew. At the time, this fact should serve as warning: This text is unique rather than a typical example. It fulfills the expectations of readers of Christian mystical texts, but it is a rare exception among Jewish ones.

The text is a part of an anonymous treatise entitled *Shaarey Zedek* ("Gates of Justice") that was written in 1295 probably in Spain by a disciple of Abraham Abulafia (though the author does not mention the name of the teacher to whom he refers), and it may be regarded as a presentation of Abulafia's concept of mysticism.

Scholem published the Hebrew text as one of his first studies written after he immigrated to Jerusalem,[1] using two manuscripts, one in Jerusalem and one in Leiden.

The author relates, in this spiritual autobiography, his way from inferior ways of searching for knowledge and elevation, those associated with Sufi self-negation and those related to rationalistic intellectual perfection to the true kabbalistic way, to which he was led by Abraham Abulafia. The ancient *Sefer Yezira*, "The Book of Creation,"[2] is regarded as the ultimate key to the secrets of the alphabet and the holy names, by which the soul is elevated into the mystical union with the divine secrets.

I, so and so, one of the lowliest, have probed my heart for ways of grace to bring about spiritual expansion and I have found three ways of progress to spiritualization: the vulgar, the philosophic, and the Kabbalistic way. The vulgar way is that which, so I learned, is practiced by Moslem ascetics. They employ all manner of devices to shut out from their souls all "natural forms," every image of the familiar, natural world. Then, they say, when a spiritual form, an image from the spiritual world, enters their soul, it is isolated in their imagination and intensifies the imagination to such a degree that they can determine beforehand that which is to happen to us. Upon inquiry, I learned that they summon the Name, ALLAH, as it is in the language of Ishmael. I investigated further and I found that, when they pronounce these letters, they direct their thought completely away from every possible "natural form," and the very letters ALLAH and their diverse powers work upon them. They are carried off into a trance without realizing how, since no Kabbalah has been transmitted to them. This removal of all natural forms and images from the soul is called with them *Effacement*.

The second way is the philosophic, and the student will experience extreme difficulty in attempting to drive it from his soul because of the great sweetness it holds for the human reason and the completeness with which that reason knows to embrace it. It consists in this: That the student forms a notion of some science, mathematics for instance, and then proceeds by analogy to some natural science and then goes on to theology. He then continues further to circle round this centre of his, because of the sweetness of that which arises in him as he progresses in these studies. The sweetness of this so delights him that he finds neither gate nor door to enable him to pass beyond the notions which have already been established in him. At best, he can perhaps enjoy a [contemplative] spinning out of his thoughts and to this he will abandon himself, retiring into seclusion in order that no one may disturb his thought until it proceed a little beyond the purely philosophic and turn as the flaming sword which turned every way. The true cause of all this is also to be found in his contemplation of the letters through which, as intermediaries, he ascertains things. The subject which impressed itself on his human reason dominates him and his power seems to him great in all the sciences, seeing that this is natural to him [i.e., thus to ascertain them]. He contends that given things are revealed to him by way of prophecy, although he does not realize the true cause, but rather thinks that this occurred to him merely because of the extension and enlargement of his human reason . . . But in reality it is the letters ascertained through thought and imagination, which influence him through their motion and which concentrate his thought on difficult themes, although he is not aware of this.

But if you put the difficult question to me: "Why do we nowadays pronounce letters and move them and try to produce effects with them without however noticing any effect being produced by them?"—the answer lies, as I am going to demonstrate with the help of *Shaddai*, in the third way of inducing spiritualization. And I, the humble so and so, am going to tell you what I experienced in this matter.

Know, friends, that from the beginning I felt a desire to study Torah and learned a little of it and of the rest of Scripture. But I found no one to guide me in the study of the Talmud, not so much because of the lack of teachers, but rather because of my longing for my home, and my love for father and mother. At last, however, God gave me strength to search for the Torah, I went out and sought and found, and for several years I stayed abroad studying Talmud. But the flame of the Torah kept glowing within me, though without my realizing it.

I returned to my native land and God brought me together with a Jewish philosopher with whom I studied some of Maimonides' "Guide of the Perplexed" and this only added to my desire. I acquired a little of the science of logic and a little of natural science, and this was very sweet to me for, as you know, "nature attracts nature." And God is my witness: If I had not previously acquired strength of faith by what little I had learned of the Torah and the Talmud, the impulse to keep many of the religious commands would have left me although the fire of pure intention was ablaze in my heart. But what this teacher communicated to me in the way of philosophy [on the meaning of the commandments], did not suffice me, until the Lord had me meet a godly man, a Kabbalist who taught me the general outlines of the Kabbalah. Nevertheless, in consequence of my smattering of natural science, the way of Kabbalah seemed all but impossible to me. It was then that my teacher said to me: "My son, why do you deny something you have not tried? Much rather would it befit you to make a trial of it. If you then should find that it is nothing to you—and if you are not perfect enough to find the fault with yourself—then you may say that there is nothing to it." But, in order to make things sweet to me until my reason might accept them and I might penetrate into them with eagerness, he used always to make me grasp in a natural way everything in which he instructed me. I reasoned thus within myself: There can only be gain here and no loss. I shall see; if I find something in all of this, that is sheer gain; and if not, that which I have already had will still be mine. So I gave in and he taught me the method of permutations and combinations of letters and the mysticism of numbers and the other "Paths of the book *Yetsirah*." In each path he had me wander for two weeks until each form had been engraven in my heart, and so he led me on for four months or so and then ordered me to "efface" everything.

He used to tell me: "My son, it is not the intention that you come to a stop with some finite or given form, even though it be of the highest order. Much rather is this the 'Path of the Names': The less understandable they are, the higher their order, until you arrive at the activity of a force which is no longer in your control, but rather your reason and your thought is in its control." I replied: "If that be so [that all mental and sense images must be effaced], why then do you, Sir, compose books in which the methods of the natural scientists are coupled with instruction in the holy Names?" He answered: "For you and the likes of you among the followers of philosophy, to allure your human intellect through natural means, so that perhaps this attraction may cause you to arrive at the knowledge of the Holy Name." And he produced books for me made up of [combinations of] letters and names and mystic numbers [*Gematrioth*], of which nobody will ever be able to understand anything for they are not composed in a way meant to be understood. He said to me: "This is the [undefiled] Path of the Names." And indeed, I would see none of it as my reason did not accept it. He said: "It was very stupid of me to have shown them to you."

In short, after two months had elapsed and my thought had disengaged itself [from everything material] and I had become aware of strange phenomena occurring within me, I set myself the task at night of combining letters with one another and of pondering over them in philosophical meditation, a little different from the way I do now, and so I continued for three nights without telling him. The third night, after midnight, I nodded off a little, quill in hand and paper on my knees. Then I noticed that the candle was about to go out. I rose to put it right, as oftentimes happens to a person awake. Then I saw that the light continued. I was greatly astonished, as though, after close examination, I saw that it issued from myself. I said: "I do not believe it." I walked to and fro all through the house and, behold, the light is with me; I lay on a couch and covered myself up, and behold, the light is with me all the while. I said: "This is truly a great sign and a new phenomenon which I have perceived."

receives an illumination

The next morning I communicated it to my teacher and I brought him the sheets which I had covered with combinations of letters. He congratulated me and said: "My son, if you would devote yourself to combining holy Names, still greater things would happen to you. And now, my son, admit that you are unable to bear not combining. Give half to this and half to that, that is, do combinations half of the night, and permutations half of the night." I practiced this method for about a week. During the second week the power of meditation became so strong in me that I could not manage to write down the combinations of letters [which automatically spurted out of my pen], and if there had been ten people present they would not have been able to write down so many combinations as came to me during the influx. When I came to the night in which this power was conferred on me, and midnight—when this power especially expands and gains strength whereas the body weakens—had passed, I set out to take up the Great Name of God, consisting of seventy-two names, permuting and combining it. But when I had done this for a little while, behold, the letters took on in my eyes the shape of great mountains, strong trembling seized me and I could summon no strength, my hair stood on end, and it was as if I were not in this world. At one I fell down, for I no longer felt the least strength in any of my limbs. And behold, something resembling speech emerged from my heart and came to my lips and forced them to move. I thought—perhaps this is, God forbid, a spirit of madness that has entered into me? But behold, I saw it uttering wisdom. I said: "This indeed the spirit of wisdom." After a little while my natural strength returned to me, I rose very much impaired and I still did not believe myself. Once more I took up the Name to do with it as before and, behold, it had exactly the same effect on me. Nevertheless I did not believe until I had tried it four or five times.

When I got up in the morning I told my teacher about it. He said to me: "And who was it that allowed you to touch the Name? Did I not tell you to permute only letters?" He spoke on: "What happened to you, represents indeed a high stage among the prophetic degrees." He wanted to free me of it for he saw that my face had changed. But I said to him: "In heaven's name, can you perhaps impart to me some power to enable me to bear this force emerging from my heart and to receive influx from it, for I wanted to draw this force towards me and receive influx from it, for it much resembles a spring filling a great basin with water. If a man [not being properly prepared for it] should open the dam, he would be drowned in its waters and his soul would desert him." He said to me: "My son, it is the Lord who must bestow such power upon you for such power is not within man's control."

That Sabbath night also the power was active in me in the same way. When, after two sleepless nights, I had passed day and night in meditating on the permutations or on the principles essential to a recognition of this true reality and to the annihilation of all extraneous thought—then I had two signs by which I knew that I was in the right receptive mood. The one sign was the intensification of natural thought on very profound objects of knowledge, a debility of the body and strengthening of the soul until I sat there, my self all soul. The second sign was that imagination grew strong within me and it seemed as though my forehead were going to burst. Then I knew that I was ready to receive the Name. I also that Sabbath night ventured at the great ineffable Name of God [the name JHWH]. But immediately that I touched it, it weakened me and a voice issued from me saying: "Thou shalt surely die and not live! Who brought thee to touch the Great Name?" And behold, immediately I fell prone and implored the Lord God saying: "Lord of the universe! I entered into this place only for the sake of Heaven, as Thy glory knoweth. What is my sin and what my transgression? I entered only to know Thee, for has not David already commanded Solomon: *Know the God of thy father and serve Him* (1 Chron. 28:9); and has not our master Moses, peace be upon him, revealed this to us in the Torah saying: *Show me now Thy way, that I may know Thee, that I may there find grace in Thy sight?*" And behold, I was still speaking and oil like the oil of the anointment anointed me from head to foot and very great joy seized me which for its spirituality and the sweetness of its rapture I cannot describe.

All this happened to your servant in his beginnings. And I do not, God forbid, relate this account from boastfulness in order to be thought great in the eyes of the mob, for I know full well that greatness with the mob is deficiency and inferiority with those searching for the true rank which differs from it in genus and in species as light from darkness.

Now, if some of our own philosophizers, sons of our people who feel themselves attracted towards the naturalistic way of knowledge and whose intellectual power in regard to the mysteries of the Torah is very weak, read this, they will laugh at me and say: See how he tries to attract our reason with windy talk and tales, with fanciful imaginations which have muddled his mind and which he takes at their face value because of his weak mental hold on natural science. Should however Kabbalists see this, such as have some grasp of this subject or even better such as have had things divulged to them in experiences of their own, they will rejoice and my words will win their favor. But their difficulty will be that I have disclosed all of this in detail. Nevertheless, God is my witness that my intention is *in majorem dei gloriam* and I would wish that every single one of our holy nation were even more excellent herein and purer than I. Perhaps it would then be possible to reveal things of which I do not as yet know . . . As for me, I cannot bear not to give generously to others what God has bestowed upon me. But since for this science there is no naturalistic evidence, its premises being as spiritual as are its inferences, I was forced to tell this story of the experience that befell me. Indeed, there is no proof in this science except experience itself . . . That is why I say, to the man who contests this path, that I can give him an experimental proof, namely, my own evidence of the spiritual results of my own experiences in the science of letters according to the book *Yetsirah*. I did not, to be sure, experience the corporeal [magic] effects [of such practices]; and even granting the possibility of such a form of experience, I for my part want none of it, for it is an inferior form, especially when measured by the perfection which the soul can attain spiritually. Indeed, it seems to me that he who attempts to secure these [magic] effects desecrates God's name, and it is this that our teachers hint at when they say: Since licence prevailed, the name of God has been taught only to the most reticent priests.

The third is the Kabbalistic way. It consists of an amalgamation in the soul of man of the principles of mathematical and of natural science, after he has first studied the literal meanings of the Torah and of the faith, in order thus through keen dialectics to train his mind and not in the manner of a simpleton to believe in everything. Of all this he stands in need only because he is held captive by the world of nature. For it is not seemly that a rational being held captive in prison should not search out every means, a hole or a small fissure, of escape. If today we had a prophet who showed us a mechanism for sharpening the natural reason and for discovering there subtle forms by which to divest ourselves of corporeality, we should not need all these natural sciences in addition to our Kabbalah which is derived from the basic principles or heads of chapters of the book *Yetsirah* concerning the letters [and their combinations] . . . For the prophet would impart to us the secrets of the combination of consonants and of the combination of vowels between them, the paths by which the secret and active powers emanate, and the reason that this emanation is sometimes hindered from above . . . All this he would convey to us directly whereas now we are forced to take circuitous routes and to move about restrainedly and go out and come in on the change that God may confront us. For as a matter of fact every attainment in this science of Kabbalah looked at from its point of view is only a chance, even though, for us, it be the very essence of our being.

This Kabbalistic way, or method, consists, first of all, in the cleansing of the body itself, for the bodily is symbolic of the spiritual. Next in the order of ascent is the cleansing of your bodily disposition and your spiritual propensities, especially that of anger, or your concern for anything whatsoever except the Name itself, be it even the care for your only beloved son; and this is the secret of the Scripture that "God tried Abraham." A further step in the order of ascent is the cleansing of one's soul from all other sciences which one has studied. The reason for this is that being naturalistic and limited, they contaminate the soul, and obstruct the passage through it of the divine forms. These forms are extremely subtle; and though even a minor form is something innately great in comparison with the naturalistic and the rational, it is nevertheless an unclean, thick veil in comparison with the subtlety of the spirit. On this account seclusion in a separate house is prescribed, and if this be a house in which no [outside] noise can be heard, the better. At the beginning it is advisable to decorate the house with fresh greens in order to cheer the vegetable soul which a man possesses side by side with his animal soul. Next, one should pray and sing psalms in a pleasant melodious voice, and [read] the Torah with fervor, in order to cheer the animal soul which a man possesses side by side with his rational soul. Next, one directs his imagination to intelligible things and to understanding how one thing proceeds from another. Next, one proceeds to the moving of letters which [in their combination] are unintelligible, thus to detach the soul [from the senses] and to cleanse it of all the forms formerly within it. In the same way one proceeds with the improvement of his [bodily] matter by meat and drink, and improves it [the body] by degrees. As to the moving of letters we shall deal with some methods in the chapter "Letters." Next, one reaches the stage of "skipping" as Scripture says, "and his banner over me was love." It consists of one's meditating, after all operations with the letters are over, on the essence of one's thought, and of abstracting from it every word, be it connected with a notion or not. In the performance of this "skipping" one must put the consonants which one is combining into a swift motion. This motion heats the thinking and so increases joy and desire, that craving for food and sleep or anything else is annihilated. In abstracting words from thought during contemplation, you force yourself so that you pass beyond the control of your natural mind and if you desire *not* to think, you cannot carry out your desire. You guide your thinking step by step, first by means of script and language and then by means of imagination. When, however, you pass beyond the control of your thinking, another exercise becomes necessary which consists in drawing thought gradually forth—during contemplation—from its source until through sheer force that stage is reached where you do not speak nor can you speak. And if sufficient strength remains to force one-self even further and draw it out still farther, then that which is within will manifest itself without, and through the power of sheer imagination will take on the form of a polished mirror. And this is "the flame of the circling sword," the rear revolving and becoming the fore. Whereupon one sees that his inmost being is something outside of himself. Such was the way of the *Urim* and *Tummim*, the priest's oracle of the Torah, in which, too, at first the letters shine from inside and the message they convey is not an immediate one nor arranged in order, but results only from the right combination of the letters. For a form, detached from its essence, is defective until it clothe itself in a form which can be conceived by imagination, and in this imaginable form the letters enter into a complete, orderly and understandable combination. And it seems to me that it is this form which the Kabbalists call "clothing," *malbush*.

THE BEGINNING

f it were necessary to choose only one short text as representing Jewish mysticism, instead of this whole volume, the following section from *Zohar* interpreting the first verse of Genesis, the beginning of the Bible, would be the obvious selection. It is at the same time both intensely unique and personal, and representative and typical. It is also, unfortunately, an example of the impossibility of translation. The English text—Goldstein's English translation of Isaiah Tishby's Hebrew one—does not convey the power and shades of meaning of the Aramaic original. A translation to the German made by Gershom Scholem (also translated to English) is no better.

The subject of this segment is the very beginning: the first appearance of something within the infinity of nothingness of the eternal, shapeless, and undescribable Godhead. This is the very beginning of differentiation, the shaping of a point that is destined to be the source of the divine world that will emanate from it. This is also the threshold of the appearance of language. Everything beyond this point is completely detached from any linguistic reference. Here, at this moment, language does its first tiny, indefinite, stuttering step at describing and telling. Every syllable used here is a "first," never pronounced before, and never having any meaning: In this process words first acquire their referential status. When there is nothing, language cannot refer to anything. When something begins to emerge, words begin to be formed to refer to them. The process described here could be viewed as the emergence of the divine out of nothing as well as the emergence of language out of nothing. Words take on specificity and distinction at the same time as the divine powers—potential entities only in this stage—aquire their characteristics. One of the most moving sentences here is the one describing, as an early result of the process of emanation, the process of the emergence of the letters of the alphabet, together with the signs of vowels (*neku-dot*)[1] and the musical signs (*teamim*), which in Hebrew are inseparable from the letters of the scriptures, comprising together an army marching and singing, parading existence from nothingness into existence.

God comes into being in these sentences, and at the same time his observer, the mystic, is also present for the first time. The early kabbalists used several terms to describe themselves, one of them being *maskilim*, a term taken from the eschatological-apocalyptic verse in Dan. 12:3, here awkwardly translated as "they that are wise." The author combines here his exegesis of Gen. 1:1 with the verse from Daniel. Yet this verse does not only refer to the mystic; it also introduces the book, the text being written—the *zohar*, its title taken from that very verse: "they that are wise (= *maskilim*) shall shine as the brightness (= *zohar*) of the firmament." The observed, the observer, the divine text (the *Torah*), and the mystical text, the *Zohar*, all make their first appearance in these few sentences. God and his language, the mystic and his language, all emerge together in this mystical moment seperating complete absence from the first hints of existence.

The complexity of this section is the result of the union achieved here between two intensely conflicting drives. One is the exegetical-homiletical: The author dives into the biblical texts, and derives and hints at new levels of meaning in every word. This section could be presented as a textbook example of profound midrashic interpretation. The combination of a verse from the Torah (Gen. 1:1) and a verse from the writings (Dan. 12:3) is exemplary. The term *zohar* as expressing the primeval light of creation, divine wisdom, kabbalistic wisdom, and at the same time a hint of a similarly sounding word, *zera*, meaning seed and semen, both in the meaning of the source of everything and the sexual process of procreation, and many other elements, make these sentences an intricate, sophisticated exercise in Jewish traditional midrashic hermeneutics.

A central image in this vision is the emergence and shaping of the holy names of God, which are the essence of the newly emanated divine manifestations. The author used here several phrases each having three components—the first three words of Genesis, the names of God in the prayer "Hear O Israel," and the three-word name given to Moses in the revelation in the desert (Exod. 3:14). The terms *heaven* and *earth* in the first verse of Genesis are also identified with divine names and divine powers, and ancient esoteric traditions concerning the esoteric names of God are interwoven into the homily.

Yet at the same time the writer of this passage is not a commentator or homilist but a *witness and participant*. This crucial aspect is hidden in the original text and impossible to demonstrate in the translated version. This is not a commentary only but an expression of an intense mystical experience, possibly the most profound experience of all: the mystic as observer and participant in the process of the divine coming into being, emerging from its infinite nothingness and acquiring differentiation, meaning and touching the referential power of language. The mystic witnesses the emergence of language and, together with God, he is the first to use it. He is not only commenting on a text: He shares the process in which both the text and the subject to which it refers come into being, and, in harmony with that, the mystic attempts to articulate an expression of his own of the process which is just happening, inventing words and images, and, I do not doubt that he feels that he failed miserably in achieving this purpose.

An example of the impossibility of translation—because of the limitations of expression—can be presented by analyzing the key phrase here, translated as "a spark of darkness," the first thing to be, the oxymoron concealing the potentiality of all divine and earthly subsequent existence. Scholem rendered this phrase as "dark light," using two of the most common words in language. Tishby coined a new Hebrew phrase—*ha-or ha-nechshach*, "the darkened light"—in his translation. The Aramaic original is: *bozina de-kardinuta*, the first word being a frequently used term for "light" or "spark," and the second is a completely unknown word, invented by the author. We are not even certain of its spelling: the letters *r* and *d* in the Hebrew alphabet are indistinguishable in Hebrew manuscripts. Some kabbalists read it as "kardinuta"— as did Scholem and Tishby—while other read it as "kadrinuta," opening many more possibilities of interpretation. The author invented a new word because his language did not include any term that may express whatever he was trying to express. The novelty and esoteric nature of the phrase is lost in the translations, which use existing words (though at least presenting them in an unusual oxymoronic way).

The prominent characteristic of mystical language—its insistence of denying itself—is obvious here. Almost every phrase is accompanied by a denial: "the secret of," "the hidden," "the unknown," etc., warning the reader not to accept any term or phrase literally. The words are just imprecise and vague attempts at hinting to the concealed meaning that cannot be expressed in words. On the one hand, therefore, nothing is actually stated here; on the other hand, a vast vision that combines hermeneutics of the sacred text, the ecstatic vision of the mystic, the orchestra of the alphabet and the holy names, the fusion of the various components of language, are united in a vast myth of the emergence of something out of nothing, the emanation of the divine manifestations that together are God the creator.

The Process of Emanation

In the beginning (Gen. 1:1)—At the very beginning the king made engravings in the supernal purity. A spark of blackness emerged in the sealed within the sealed, from the mystery of *En-Sof*, a mist within matter, implanted in a ring, no white, no black, no red, no yellow, no color at all. When he measured with the standard of measure, he made colors to provide light. Within the spark, in the innermost part, emerged a source, from which the colors are painted below, and it is sealed among the sealed things of the mystery of *En-Sof*. It penetrated, but did not penetrate, its air; it was not known at all, until from the pressure of its penetration—a single point shone, sealed, supernal. Beyond this point nothing is known, and so it is called *reshit* (beginning, genesis): the first word of all.

And they that are wise shall shine as the brightness (zohar) of the firmament; and they that turn the many to righteousness as the stars forever and ever (Dan. 12:3)—Zohar, sealed among the sealed things, made contact with its air, which touched, but did not touch, the point. Then the "beginning" (*reshit*) *extended* itself and made a palace for itself, for glory and praise. There it sowed the holy seed (*zera*) in order to beget offspring for the benefit of the world. This mystery is [in the verse] the *holy seed shall be its stock* (Isa. 6:13)—Zohar, which sowed seed in its own honor like the seed of the silk [worm], [that makes] fine purple fabric, is the one that covers itself within, and makes a palace for itself, which brings praise to it, and benefit to all. With this *reshit* the sealed one, which is not known, created this palace. This palace is called *Elohim*, and this mystery is [in the verse] *Bereshit* bara *Elohim* (Gen. 1:1). Zohar is that from which all the words were created, through the mystery of the expansion of the point of this concealed brightness. Since the word *bara* (He created) is used here, it is not surprising that it is written *And God created man in His image* (Gen. 1:27).

Zohar—this mystery is [in the word] *beresitl*: that which precedes all, whose name is *Ehyeh*,[2] a sacred name engraved in its extremities; *Elohim* engraved in the crown, *Asher*—a hidden and concealed palace, the beginning of the mystery of *reshit-Asher*, the head (*rosh*) that emerges from *reshit*. And when, after this, point and palace were established together, then *bereshit* comprised the supernal *reshit* according to the way of wisdom; for subsequently the form of the palace was changed, and it was called "a house"! (*bayit*), the supernal point was called "head" (*rosh*), comprised, one in the other, in the mystery of the word *bereshit*, when all [was] together in one unit before there was habitation in the house. When the seed was sown in order to prepare for habitation, then it was called *Elohim*, hidden and concealed. Zohar—hidden and stored away, until building [began] within it, in order to produce offspring, and the house stood as the process of the holy seed (*zohar= zera*) gathered momentum. But before it was impregnated, and before the process of habitation began, it was not called *Elohiin*, but everything was comprised within the generality of *bereshit*. Once it was established in the name of *Elohim*, then it produced the offspring from the seed that was sown in it. What was this seed? Engraved letters, the mystery of the Torah, which emerged from that point. The point sowed the seed of three vowels[3] in the palace: *holam, shuruk, hirek*, and they were comprised, one within the other, and became a single mystery: a voice that emerged in a single combination. When it emerged, its partner emerged with it, which comprised all the letters, as it is written: *et ha-shantayim* ("the heavens")—the voice and its partner." This voice, which is "the heavens," is the last *ehyeh*.[4] Zohar—which comprises all the letters and all the colors in the way that we have explained so far, YHVH *Elohenu* YHVH[5] —these are three levels that represent this supernal mystery.

Bereshit bara Elohim ("In the beginning God created"). *Bereshit*— a primeval mystery, *bara*—a concealed mystery, from which all extends; *Elohim*—a mystery that supports all below. *Et ha-shamayim* ("the heavens")—in order not to separate male and female, which are united together. *Et* ("the")—when He took all these letters, they comprised all the letters, beginning and end. Subsequently, the letter *he* was added in order to combine the letters with the *he*, and it was called *atah* ("you"), and of this it is said, *You gave life to them all* (Neh. 9:6). *Et*— the mystery of *Adonai*, and thus is it called; *ha-shamayim*—this is YHVH, the higher mystery. *Ve-et* ("and the")—the arrangement of male and female; *ve-et*—the mystery of *va*—YHVH and all is one. *Ha-arez* ("the earth")—this is Elohim, on the pattern of the upper world, so as to make fruits and herbs. This name is included in three places and thence the name extends on several sides.

Thus far the secret of the innermost mystery, which He engraved, built, and sustained in a concealed way, through the mystery of one verse. From now on: *bereshit*—*bara shit* ("created six").[6] He created six *from the one end of heaven unto the other* (Deut. 4:32), the six extremes that extend from the supernal mystery through the extension that He created from the primal point;[7] *bara*—extension from the point on high. And here was engraved the mystery of the forty-two-lettered name.[8]

"And they that are wise shall shine . . . " like the musical accents.[9] The letters and vowel-points follow them in their singing, and move at their behest, like an army at the behest of the king. The letters are the body, and the vowel-points are the spirit. All of them in their travels follow the accents, and stand in their place. When the singing of the accents moves, the letters and the vowel-points move after them, and when it stops, they do not move but remain in their stations. *"And they that are wise shall shine . . . "*—letters and vowel-points; "as the brightness"—the singing of the accents; "of the firmament"—the extension of the singing, like those which prolong and continue the singing; "and they that turn the many to righteousness"—these are the pauses among the accents, which stop their travels, as a result of which speech is heard. "Shall shine"—that is, the letters and the vowel-points, and they

will shine together on their travels, in a concealed mystery, on a journey by hidden paths. All extends from this. (Zohar I, 15a–15b)

The Chain of the Sefirot

And God said: Let there be light. And there was light (Gen. 1:3). From here we can begin to find hidden [mysteries], how the world was created in detail. Before this it was described in general, and it is given later in general once more; so that we have a generality, a particularity, and a generality. Up to this point, all depended on the air, in the mystery of *En-Sof*. When the force spread through the supernal palace [which is] the mystery of *Elohim*, it is described in terms of speech: "And God said." For in the preceding [verses] no actual "saying" is specified. And even though *bereshit* is a "saying," "and He said" is not written in connection with it. *Va-yomer* (And He said)—an object of inquiry and knowledge. *Va-yomer*—a power that was raised, and the raising was in silence, from the mystery of *En-Sof* through the mystery of Thought. "And God said"— now it begot that palace that was conceived from the holy seed, and it begot silence, and [the voice of) the newborn was heard outside. That which begot it begot it in silence, so that it could not be heard at all. When that which emerged emerged from it, a voice was formed that was heard outside. "Let there be light" (*yehi or*)—all that emerged through this mystery emerged. *Yehi* [this refers] to the mystery of father and mother which is *yah*[10] and it subsequently relates to the primal point, in order to be the beginning of the extension of another thing: "light."

"And there was light" (*va-yehi or*)—the light that had already existed.[11] This light is a sealed mystery: the expansion that extended itself and burst through from the secret mystery of the hidden supernal air. First of all, [the expansion] burst through, and produced a single hidden point from its own mystery, for thus did *En-Sof* burst out of its air and reveal a single point: *yod*.[12] Once that *yod* had extended itself, whatever remained of the mystery of the hidden air was light.[13] When the first point, *yod*, was discovered by it, it then appeared upon it, touching but not touching. Once it had extended itself it emerged as the light, a remnant of the air, "the light that had already existed." This [light] existed; it emerged, and removed itself, and was hidden, and one single point of it remained, and it has continuous contact, in a secret way, with this point, touching and not touching, illuminating it by means of the primal point, which had emerged from it. Therefore all hangs together; it illuminates on this side and on that. When it ascends everything ascends and is incorporated with it, and it reaches, and is concealed in, the place of *En-Sof*, and all is made one.

This point of light is "Light," and it expanded, and seven letters of the alphabet shone in it, but they did not solidify, and they were moist. Then darkness emerged, and another seven letters of the alphabet emerged, and they did not solidify, and remained moist. The firmament emerged, and dissipated the division between the two sides, and another eight letters emerged in it, making twenty-two in all. The seven letters on this side, and the seven letters on that side drew together, and were all engraved in the firmament, and they stayed moist. The firmament solidified, and the letters solidified, and they assumed their different shapes, and the Torah was engraved there in order to give light to the realms outside.

"Let there be light," which is *El gadol* (great God) is the mystery that emerged from the primal air. And there was the mystery of darkness, called *Elohim*. "Light"—where the left is included with the right, and then, from the mystery of El,[14] Elohim is made; right is included with left, and left with right.

And God saw the light that it was good (Gen. 1:4)—this is the central pillar.[15] *Ki lov* ("that it was good") illumines the regions above and the regions below, and all the remaining extremities, through the mystery of *YHVH*, the name that holds together all the extremities.

And God divided (Gen. 1:4), He broke up the controversy (= difference), so that all should be perfect.

And God called (Gen. 1:5), What does "and He called" mean? He called and summoned the perfect light, which stands in the center, to produce a light, which is the foundation (*Yesod*) of the world, and upon which worlds rest. And from that perfect light, the central pillar, there was drawn forth, from the right side, *Yesod*, the life of the worlds, which is "day."[16]

And the darkness He called night (Gen. 1:5)—He called and summoned that from the side of darkness there should be produced a female, the moon, which rules by night and is called "night," the mystery of *Adonai, Lord (Adon) of all the earth* (Josh. 3:1).

The right entered the perfect pillar that is in the center, which comprises the mystery of the left, and ascended aloft to the primal point, and it took and seized hold of the power of the three vowel-points: *holam, shuruk, hirek,* which are the holy seed—for there is no seed sown except through this mystery—and all was joined together through the central pillar, and it produced the foundation (*Yesod*) of the world, and it is therefore called "all" *kol*), for it holds all through the light of desire. The left flamed strongly and exuded odor. Throughout all levels it exuded odor, and from the fiery flame it produced the female, the moon; and this flame was darkened, because it came from darkness. And these two sides produced these two levels, one male and one female.

Yesod took hold of the central pillar through the additional light that it contains, for when this central pillar was perfected, and it made perfect peace throughout the extremities, an additional amount of light was immediately accorded it from above, and from all the extremities in an all-inclusive joy, and from this addition of joy the foundation of the worlds emerged, and it was called *Musaf* (addition). All the hosts emerged from here into the realms below, and holy spirits, and souls, through the mystery of YHVH *Zevaot, El Elohei ha-ruhot* ("God, the God of the spirits"—Num. 16:22). Night, *Adon kol ha-artz* ("Lord of all the earth"), is from the left side, from that Darkness. And since the desire of Darkness was to be included with the right, and its strength was weakened, Night spread out from it. When Night began to spread out, and before the act was completed, Darkness entered, and was included with the right, and the right took hold of it and Night was left in want. And just as it was the desire of Darkness to be included with Light, so it was the desire of Night to be included with Day. Darkness lacks Light and so it produced a level in want and without its own light. Darkness does not illumine unless it is included with Light. Night, which came from it, does not illumine unless it is included with Day. Night's lack cannot be made up except through *Musaf* (addition). What was added here was subtracted there. In *Musaf* there is the mystery of the supernal point, and the mystery of the central pillar with all the extremities, and, therefore, two letters were added to it, and from Night these two letters were subtracted, and so we have kara ("He called"). It is written *va-yikra* ("And [God] called"), and then *vav* and *yod* are subtracted, and it is then written *kara laylah* (He called "night"). Here is the mystery of the seventy-two-lettered name, the engraving of the supernal *Keter*. (Zohar I, 16b–17a)

13 RABBI SIMEON BAR YOHAI AND HIS SOCIETY OF MYSTICS

The visions of the *Zohar* are not limited to the dynamics of the inner life of the Godhead. The author of this work also envisioned a group of mystics, led by Rabbi Simeon bar Yohai, who observe, experience, discuss, and interpret the secrets revealed in this great work. It is impossible to separate in the *Zohar* "content," the theological-mystical message, from the narratives, which describe the circumstances in which the mysteries of the divine world were revealed. The same creative power, the same vivid imagination, are manifest in the narratives as well as in the descriptions of the divine powers. Isaiah Tishby, in his great selection of texts *The Wisdom of the Zohar*, dedicated the first chapter in his work to the presentation of some of the main narrative motifs in this work, most of them dealing with the stature and biography of the mystical leader Rabbi Simeon bar Yohai. Four such texts, woven together by Tishby, are presented in this chapter.

While the texts are fictitious and imaginary, they derive many elements from classical Jewish literature and especially early Hebrew mystical texts. The figures are those of second-century tanaim, sages of the Mishnah and the basic literary intention is to portray the circle of mystics as one similar to that which produced that great source of Jewish law. A central message of these narratives, expressed also in the texts below, is the insufficiency of knowledge of the revealed, obvious side of the Torah, which is identified as the halakhah, the laws governing behavior, ethics, and ritual, and the necessity of going beyond that into the esoteric, spiritual truth concerning the divine world. It is as if the *Zohar* wished to present the spiritual Mishnah, as transmitted by the same scholars who formulated the external, esoteric one. Rabbi Simeon bar Yohai and his son Eleazar are placed in the center of this group.

The dominant source from which the author of the *Zohar* derived his vision of the circle of mystics is *Hekhalot Rabbati*, "The Greater Book of Divine Palaces," a text that was written a millennium before the *Zohar*, in which the group of mystics, "the descenders to the chariot," is described (a section from that text is translated in this anthology, above pp. 51–52). The leader there is Rabbi Nehunia ben ha-Kanah, and the main figures are those of Rabbi Akibah and Rabbi Ishmael. The concept of the "assembly" (*idra*) is derived from the vision of Rabbi Nehunia teaching the other tanaim the secrets of the mystical ascent in that ancient text. Following these ancient sources, we find in the *Zohar*—and in the sections presented here—the clear influence of the experience of the Four Who Entered the Pardes, the classical Hebrew text that was interpreted as describing the mystical experience of ancient sages led by Rabbi Akibah, who "entered and emerged" safely from the hidden orchard of the divine realm.

The portions of the *Zohar* entitled "assembly," the *idras*, include some of the most radical descriptions of the divine realms, and were regarded as the most secret and most sacred parts of the work. The mystical revelations were integrated within the framework of the hagiographic narratives, an example of which is presented here.

The most important element that the author of the *Zohar* added to his ancient sources in his narrative is the elevation of the mystical leader Rabbi Simeon bar Yohai into a superhuman power, who holds all the secrets of the earthly and divine realms, and who, by his spiritual force, sustains the connections that bind them together. Rabbi Simeon in the *Zohar* is much more than a mystical leader; he is the representative of the divinity itself on earth. As he is asked when he experienced his last illness, "Can a man who is the pillar of the world be near death?" This question is based on a verse, Prov. 10:25, which declares the righteous, the *zaddik*, to be the pillar, or the foundation, of the world. The image of Rabbi Simeon in the *Zohar* is the beginning of a long process in which kabbalists extended the concept of the righteous-mystic and the representative of the divine in the world, whose powers extend upward and sustain the existence of the universe.

The texts express the great tension that characterizes the assemblies of the mystics, and especially the situation in the group when Rabbi Simeon's death becomes imminent: what can be revealed and what must be kept secret. Death is regarded as a result of revealing too much.[1] Rabbi Simeon's hesitations, and his colleagues' conflict between the wish to learn and the fear of the results, are major motifs in these narratives.

The Entry into the Great Assembly

It is taught that Rabbi Simeon said to the companions: How long shall we sit by a column that has but a single base? It is written, It is time to do something for the Lord. They have frustrated Your Torah (Ps. 119: 126). Time is short, and the creditor is impatient. A herald cries out every day. But the reapers in the field are few, and they are on the edges of the vineyard. They do not look, nor do they know fully where they are going. Assemble, friends, at the meeting place, garbed in mail, with swords and lances in your hands. Look to your equipment: counsel, wisdom, understanding, knowledge, sight, power of hands and legs. Appoint a king over you who has the power of life and death and who can utter words of truth, words that the holy ones above will heed, and that they will rejoice to hear and know.

Rabbi Simeon sat down and wept. He said: Alas, if I reveal! Alas, if I do not reveal!

The companions who were there were silent. Rabbi Abba arose and said to him: If it pleases you, master, to reveal, you know it is written, The secret of the Lord is for those who fear Him" (Ps. 25:14), and these companions do fear the Lord, and they have already entered the assembly of the sanctuary. Some of them have entered, and some have also emerged [safely].

It is taught that the companions who were present with Rabbi Simeon were counted, and they were: his son, Rabbi Eleazar, Rabbi Abba, Rabbi Judah, Rabbi Jose bar Jacob, Rabbi Isaac, Rabbi Hezekiah bar Rav, Rabbi Hiyya, Rabbi Jose, and Rabbi Yesa. They stretched out their hands to Rabbi Simeon, and extended their fingers toward the heavens, and they went into the field among the trees and sat down.

Rabbi Simeon arose and prayed. He sat down among them and said: Put your hands in my lap.

They put out their hands, and he grasped them.

He began by quoting: *Cursed be the man that makes a graven or molten image . . . the work of the hands of the craftsman, and that sets it up in secret* (Deut. 27:15) And they all responded by saying, Amen.

Rabbi Simeon began by quoting: It is time to do something for the Lord. Why is it time to do something for the Lord? Because they have frustrated Your Torah. What does this phrase mean? It refers to the heavenly Torah, which is annulled. If this Name is not treated as it should be, and this alludes to the Ancient or Days.[2] It is written, *Happy are you, O Israel, who is like you?* (Deut. 33:29). And it is also written, *Who is like You, O Lord, among the mighty?* (Exod. 15:11) He called to his son, *Rabbi Eleazar,* and sat him down before him, and Rabbi Abba he seated on the other side. And he said: We comprise the whole. Thus far are the pillars set right.

They were silent. They heard a sound and their knees knocked together. What sound was it? The sound made by the entry of the assembly of heaven.

Rabbi Simeon was glad, and said: *O Lord, I have heard the sound of You, and I am afraid* (Hab. 3:2). At that time it was right to be afraid, but with us it depends on love, as it is written, *And you shall love the Lord, your God,* (Deut. 6:5) *because the Lord loved you,* (Deut. 7:8), *and I have loved you,* (Mal. 1:2) and so on.

Rabbi Simeon began by quoting: He that walks about as a talebearer reveals secrets. *But he that has a faithful spirit conceals a thing* (Prov. 1:13). This verse is difficult. It ought to have said, "The man that is a talebearer." What is the significance of "He that walks about"? It means that the man who is unsettled in his mind and insecure keeps whatever he hears moving about inside him, like bran in water, until he casts it out. Why is this? because he does not have a stable mind. But of the man of stable mind it is written "But he that has a faithful spirit conceals a thing." "A faithful spirit" means here "a secure spirit," *as in I will fasten him as a peg in a secure place* (Isa. 22:23) The thing depends on the spirit. It is written *Do not allow your mouth to cause your flesh to sin* (Eccles. 5:5), and the world endures only because of the mystery. And so, if in mundane matters there is a need for secrecy, how much more need for secrecy is there in the most mysterious affairs of the Ancient of Days, which have not been transmitted even to the angels in Heaven.

Rabbi Simeon said: I do not ask the heavens to listen, nor do I ask the earth to give ear, for we are the worlds' support. (Zohar III, 127b–128a, Idra Rabba)

The Exit from the Great Assembly

It is taught that before the companions left the assembly Rabbi Jose bar Rabbi Jacob, Rabbi Hezekiah, and Rabbi Yesa died, and the companions saw the holy angels carry them up in a litter. Rabbi Simeon said a word and the companions were pacified. He cried aloud and said: Perhaps, God forbid, it has been decreed that we should be punished, because matters have been revealed through us that had not previously been revealed since Moses stood on Mount Sinai, as it is written, *And he was there with the Lord forty days and forty nights . . .* (Exod. 34:28). Of what worth am I if they were punished because of this?

He heard a voice: Blessed are you, Rabbi Simeon, blessed is your portion, and blessed are these companions who stand with you, for things have been revealed to you that have not been revealed to any power above. Look, it is written, *with his firstborn he shall lay its foundation, and with his youngest he shall set up its gates* (Josh. 6:26). With how much greater delight did their souls cleave to the uppermost realms when they were taken from the world. Blessed is their portion, for they have ascended in complete perfection.

It is taught that during the process of revelation the upper and the lower regions trembled, and the sound traveled through two hundred and fifty worlds, for venerable matters were being revealed in the world below, and while the souls of these men were being perfumed with these words, their souls departed with a kiss, and attached themselves to the litter,[3] and the angels of heaven carried them away to the regions above. And why just these? Because these were they who had entered, but had not emerged [safely] on the previous occasion, whereas all the others had both entered and emerged.

Rabbi Simeon said: How blessed is the portion of these three, and blessed is our portion in the world to come on account of this.

A voice was heard a second time, which said: *But you that cleave to the Lord, your God, are alive every one of you this day* (Deut. 4:4).

They arose and departed. Every place they looked at exuded perfume. Rabbi Simeon said: This means that the world is blessed because of us.

All their faces shone, and people could not look at them.

It is taught that ten entered and seven emerged. Rabbi Simeon was happy and Rabbi Abba was sad. Rabbi Simeon was sitting one day with Rabbi Abba. Rabbi Simeon said something and they saw those three. The angels of heaven were taking them and showing them the hidden storerooms on high, because of the honor due to them. And they brought them to the mountains of pure balsam. Rabbi Abba was consoled.

It is taught that from that day forward the companions did not leave Rabbi Simeon's house, and that when Rabbi Simeon was revealing secrets, only they were present with him. And Rabbi Simeon used to say of them: *We seven are the eyes of the Lord, as it is written, "these seven, the eyes of the Lord* (Zech. 4:10) Of us is this said.

Rabbi Abba said: We are six lamps that derive their light from the seventh. You are the seventh over all, for the six cannot survive without the seventh. Everything depends on the seventh.

Rabbi Judah called him "Sabbath," because the [other] six [days] receive blessing from it, for it is written *Sabbath to the Lord"* (Exod. 20:10), and it is also written *Holy to the Lord* (Exod. 16:23). Just as the Sabbath is holy to the Lord, so Rabbi Simeon, the Sabbath, is holy to the Lord. (Zohar III, 144a–144b)

The Illness of Rabbi Simeon Ben Yohai

Our rabbis taught that when Rabbi Simeon ben Yohai became ill he was visited by Rabbi Pinhas, Rabbi Hiyya, and Rabbi Abbahu.

They said to him: Can a man who is the pillar of the world be near to death?

He said: It is not the heavenly court that is concerned with my case. I know that I am beyond the jurisdiction of any angel or judge in heaven, for I am not like other men. But the Holy One, blessed be He, not His court, judges my case. This is similar to the plea that David made to Him, *"Judge me, O God, and plead my cause"* (Ps. 43:1). And Solomon also said likewise, "That He may execute justice for His servant" (1 Kings 8:59)—He Himself, and no one else. And we have learned that when a man is on his deathbed the heavenly court examines his case. Some of them are inclined to acquit him, and they point out his merits. Others are inclined to convict him, and they point out his guilt, and the defendant does not emerge from the case as he would wish. But whoever is judged by the supreme King, who has dominion over all, is fortunate, and in a trial of this kind man must inevitably be successful. Why is this? We have learned that the attributes of the supreme King are always inclined toward acquittal, and He is entirely merciful, and He has the power to forgive iniquities and transgressions, as it is written, For with You there is forgiveness (Ps. 130:4)—and not with anyone else. Therefore I asked Him to judge my case, so that I might enter the world to come through the thirteen doors, which Only the patriarchs have passed through, with no one to prevent me; and, furthermore, so that I might not have to seek permission [from the doorkeepers].

Rabbi Simeon said something, and his visitors realized that he was no longer present. They were astounded, and none of them could utter a single word because of the deep fear that had fallen upon them. While they were sitting there, perfumes from many spices wafted over them, and they began to regain their courage, and at last they saw Rabbi Simeon talking, but they did not see anyone else except him.

After a while Rabbi Simeon said to them: Did you see anything?

No, said Rabbi Pinhas, but we were all astounded that we could not see you for a long time in your sickroom. And when we did see you, perfumes from the spices of the Garden of Eden wafted over us, and we heard your voice speaking, but we do not know with whom you were talking.

And you heard no other words, except mine?

No, they replied.

You are not sufficiently worthy to see the countenance of the Ancient of Days. Let me tell you something, he continued. I am surprised that Rabbi Pinhas did not see anything, for I saw him just now, in that world, below my son, Rabbi Eleazar. And they have now sent for me from above, and shown me the place of the righteous in the world to come. And the only place that satisfied me was one near Ahija, the Shilonite, and so I chose my place, and went there, together with three hundred righteous souls. Above them was Adam, who sat by me and spoke with me, and asked that his sin should not be revealed to the whole world, apart from what the Torah says of it, and that it should remain concealed with the tree of the Garden of Eden. But I told him that the companions had already revealed it. And he said: Whatever the companions have revealed among themselves is good and proper, but not to the rest of mankind.

What is the reason for this? The Holy One, blessed be He, is concerned for His own honor, and does not wish to publicize [Adam's] sin, except in respect of the tree from which he ate. But the Holy One, blessed be He, revealed it to me, by the Holy Spirit, and to the companions, so that they might discuss it among themselves, but not to the younger companions or to those who are still to come into the world, this is something that is not known to everyone, and they err thereby; not because of the sin that he committed, but because of the honor of the supreme name, which people do not treat with sufficient care, and it is written, *this is My name for ever* (Exod. 3:15),[4] and they will begin to ask unnecessary questions. This is referred to in *lest they break through to the Lord, to gaze, and many of them fall* (Exod. 19:21), which we interpret as follows: the companion that teaches the sacred name to all will fall and be more tightly trapped by that sin than they, as it is written "and many (rav) of them fall," that is, the Rav will fall, and be trapped by that sin.

Rabbi Eleazar, his son, approached him, and said: Father, what was my position there?

He replied: Blessed is your portion, my son. A long time will elapse, and you will not be buried next to me. But in that world I have selected a place for me and a place for you.

Blessed are the righteous, who in the future will praise the Master of the universe, like the angels who minister to Him, as it is written, Surely the righteous shall give thanks to Your name; the upright shall dwell in Your presence (Ps. 140:14). (Zohar Hadash, Bereshit 29b–d, Midrash ha-Ne'elam)

Revelation of Mysteries Before His Departure

It is taught that on the very day that Rabbi Simeon was to depart from the world and he was busy arranging his affairs, the companions gathered in Rabbi Simeon's house. Rabbi Eleazar, his son, Rabbi Abba, and the other companions were there with him, and the house was full. Rabbi Simeon raised his eyes and saw that the house had become full.

Rabbi Simeon wept and said: On a previous occasion when I was ill, Rabbi Pinhas ben Yair was with me, and the companions waited for me until I had selected my place. And when I returned, fire surrounded me increasingly, so that no man could enter without permission. But now I see that it has ceased, and the house is full.

While they were seated there, Rabbi Simeon opened his eyes, and saw what he saw, and fire enveloped the house. They all left, except Rabbi Eleazar, his son, and Rabbi Abba. The other companions stayed outside.

Rabbi Simeon said to Rabbi Eleazar, his son: Go and see if Rabbi Isaac is there, because I have given a pledge to him. Tell him to arrange his affairs and sit by me. Blessed is his portion.

Rabbi Simeon arose and smiled, and was happy. He said: Where are the companions?

Rabbi Eleazar arose, and brought them in, and they sat down before him.

Rabbi Simeon raised his hands, and prayed, and was happy, and said: Let those companions who were at the assembly present themselves here.

They all left, except Rabbi Eleazar, his son, Rabbi Abba, Rabbi Judah, Rabbi Jose, and Rabbi Hiyya. In the meantime Rabbi Isaac had entered. Rabbi Simeon said to him: How pleasant is your portion! How much joy is to be added to your life today!

Rabbi Abba sat behind his back, and Rabbi Eleazar sat in front of him.

Rabbi Simeon said: Now is a propitious hour, and I am seeking to enter the world to come without shame. There are sacred matters that have not been revealed up till now and that I wish to reveal in the presence of the Shekhinah, so that it should not be said that I departed from the world with my work incomplete. Until now they have been concealed in my heart, so that I might enter the world to come with them. And so I give you your duties: Rabbi Abba will write them down, Rabbi Eleazar, my son, will explain them, and the other companions will meditate silently upon them.

Rabbi Abba rose from behind his back, and Rabbi Eleazar, his son, sat in front of him.

He said to him: Arise, my son, for, behold, another sits in that place.

Rabbi Eleazar rose. Rabbi Simeon wrapped himself in his cloak and sat down.

He began by quoting: *The dead do not praise the Lord, nor do any that descend to silence* (Dumah) (Ps. 115:17). "The dead do not praise the Lord." This is certainly true of those who are called "dead," for the Holy One, blessed be He, is called "living," and He dwells among those who are called "living," and not with those who are called "dead." And at the end of the verse it is written, "nor do any who descend to Dumah." And all those who descend to Dumah will remain in Gehinnom (hell), unlike those who are called "living," in whose glory the Holy One, blessed be He, takes pleasure.

Rabbi Simeon said: How different is this moment from the assembly, for at the assembly the Holy One, blessed be He, was present with His chariots, but now, see, the Holy One, blessed be He, has come here with the righteous from the Garden of Eden. And this did not happen at the assembly. The Holy One, blessed be He, is more concerned with their reputation than with His own, as it is written of Jeroboam. He used to offer incense to and worship idols, but the Holy One, blessed be He, was patient with him, until he raised his hand against Iddo the prophet, and then his hand withered, as it is written, *and his hand dried up* (1 Kings 13:4)—not because he worshiped idols, but because he raised his hand against Iddo the prophet. And now the Holy One, blessed be He, is concerned with our reputation, and they have all come with Him.

He said: Look, Rav Hamnuna Sava[5] is here, surrounded by seventy righteous men, marked with crowns, each one of them reflecting light from the shining countenance of the Holy, Ancient One, the most mysterious of mysteries; and he has come to listen with joy to the words that I utter.

While he was seated, he said: Look, Rabbi Pinhas ben Yair is here. Prepare a place for him.

The companions who were there trembled. They rose and moved further away into the house and sat down, but Rabbi Eleazar and Rabbi Abba remained with Rabbi Simeon.

Rabbi Simeon said: When we were in the assembly, all the companions used to speak [Torah], and I joined in with them. But now I speak on my own and they all listen to my words, the upper and the lower worlds. Blessed is my portion on this day! (Zohar III, 287b–288a, Idra Zuta)

THE WONDROUS CHILD

J ewish esoterical literature includes several figures of young children who envisioned great secrets and became legendary in the history of Jewish mysticism. One of the earliest is a brief, tragic sentence included in the tales concerning the secrets of Ezekiel's chariot. It states that there was a child (*yenuka* in Aramaic), who dealt with the *hashmal*, the enigmatic term used by Ezekiel in his description of the *merkavah*. Fire emerged from the *hashmal* and burned him.[1] A late-medieval example is the legend of the youth Nahman Ketofa, who lived in the Galilee and pronounced several rhymed prophecies that were interpreted as describing future historical and apocalyptic-messianic events.[2] The narratives of the *Zohar* include several wondrous figures who reveal great secrets, most of them invented by the author of the work; the best known among them is Rav Hamnuna Sava, an old man who presented the members of Rabbi Simeon bar Yohai's circle with supernal visions and secrets.[3] The figure of the *yenuka*, the young child who is the hero of the following text, is identified as the son of that old man.

The *yenuka* of the *Zohar* is endowed with supernatural powers: He knows whether the sages have prayed properly or not; he knows whether they have washed their hands properly or not. He recognizes the moral and intellectual merits of people by a "smell," probably referring to a kind of aura engulfing them. The sages were deeply impressed and recognized in him angelic qualities. Yet his powers are employed concerning minute, mundane matters. He is not portrayed as a miracle-worker. This characteristic is prominent also in the contents of his visions and revelations. The wondrous child explains the reasons for common, everyday rituals and customs, based on the exegesis of verses, and despite the "lowly" nature of the subjects, the sages are immensely impressed by his discourse.

In order to understand this fact, one should take into account one of the main concerns of Jewish thinkers in the Middle Ages: the need to present spiritual meanings to the Jewish commandments, precepts, and customs. A different example of this meaningful drive is found in Rabbi Bahya Ibn Paquda's *Hovot ha-Levavot*.[4] Many sections of the *Zohar* are dedicated to the interpretation of the meaning of the commandments. The author, like other kabbalists, believed in the important spiritual role that these commandments have in the context of the dynamic inner life within the Godhead, in the realm of the divine manifestations, the ten *sefirot*. Actions that seem to be routine and mundane matters are revealed to carry immense spiritual significance, when one knows their relationship to the processes going on in the divine realms. These visions of the impact of actions in the celestial world, in the struggle between good and evil, between the right/sacred side and the left/evil side, give spiritual significance to every ritual performed by people on earth. According to the *Zohar* there is a parallelic relationship between the realms of the divine and the human, and there is a constant flow of spiritual power from each side to the other.

The Child

Rabbi Isaac and Rabbi Judah were on a journey, and they came to a place called Kfar Sikhnin. They lodged with a woman who had a young son, and he used to spend the whole day at school. On this particular day he left school, went home, and saw these scholars.

His mother said to him: Come near to these famous men, and you will obtain blessings from them.

He approached them, but before he got too near he turned away again.

I do not want to get near them, he said to his mother, because they have not said the Shema[5] today, and I have been taught that whoever does not say the Shema at its proper time should be shunned the whole day long. They heard and were astonished, and they raised their hands and blessed him.

They said: It is true; we have been preoccupied today with a bridegroom and his bride. They did not have the necessary prerequisites, and had to delay their marriage, and there was no one else to assist them. So we occupied ourselves with their affairs, and did not say the Shema at the proper time, for whoever is occupied with fulfilling one commandment is exempted from fulfilling another. But how did you know this, my child?

He replied: I knew it from the smell of your clothes as I came toward you.

They were filled with astonishment. They sat down, washed their hands, and began to eat. Rabbi Judah's hands were dirty, and he pronounced the blessing before washing.

The child said to them: If you are disciples of Rav Shemaiah, the Pious, you should not have pronounced the blessing with dirty hands. Whoever pronounces the blessing with dirty hands deserves to die.

The child began his discourse by quoting: *When they go into the tent of meeting, they shall wash with water, that they die not* (Exod. 30:20). We learn from this verse that whoever does not take care of this, and appears before the King with dirty hands, is punishable by death. For what reason? Because a man's hands dwell in the topmost part of the world. There is one finger on a man's hand that is the finger that Moses raised.[6] It is written, *And you shall make bars of acacia-wood: five for the boards of the one side of the tabernacle, and five bars for the boards of the other side of the tabernacle,* and then it is written, *and the middle bar among the boards shall pass from end to end* (Exod. 26:26–28). Now you might think that this middle bar is a separate one, and not included in the five. But it is not so. The middle bar is one of the five—two on one side, two on the other, and one in the middle. This is the central bar, the pillar of Jacob, the mystery of Moses. Parallel to this are the five fingers of the human hand. The middle bar in the center is larger and more important than the others, and the others depend on it. These five bars are called the five centuries, through which the Tree of Life passes.[7] And the holy covenant of circumcision is effected through the five fingers of the hand. This is a secret matter that I have spoken. It is for this reason that all the priestly benedictions depend upon the fingers, and Moses spread out his hands for this purpose. Since so much depends on them, it is only right that they should be clean when one uses them to bless the Holy One, blessed be He, for through them and through their representative [on high] the holy name is blessed. Therefore, since you are so wise, why have you not paid special attention to this, and followed the dictum of Rav Shemaiah, the Pious, who said: Dirt and filth are offered to the other side[8] for the other side is nourished by dirt and filth; and so water used in washing the hands at the end is hovah?[9]

They were astonished, and unable to speak.

Then Rabbi Judah said: What is your father's name, my child?

The child was silent for a moment, and then went to his mother and kissed her.

Mother, he said, these scholars have asked me about my father. Shall I tell them?

Have you tested them, my child? said his mother.

I have tested them, he said, and I have found them lacking.

His mother whispered something to him, and he returned to them.

He said to them: You asked about my father. He has departed from the world, and whenever holy, pious men embark upon a journey he drives the mules behind them. If you are exalted, saintly men, how is it that you have not discovered him driving the mules behind you? I summed you up at the very beginning, and now I know that I was right, for my father has only to see the mule [of a holy and pious man], and he straightway drives it along behind, in order to bear the yoke of the Torah. Now, since you are not worthy enough for my father to be your mule-driver, I shall not tell you who he is.

Rabbi Judah said to Rabbi Isaac: This child does not seem to me to be human.

They ate, and the child spoke words of Torah, and gave new interpretations of Torah.

They said: Come, let us bless [God].

The child said: You have well spoken, because the holy name is not blessed through this benediction unless one first expresses one's intention to say it.[10] He began by quoting: *I shall bless the Lord at all times* (Ps. 34:2). What need was there for David to say "I shall bless the Lord"?

David saw that it was necessary to express his intention. And he said "I shall bless," for when a man is seated at table the *Shekhinah* is present, and the other side is also present. As soon as he expresses his intention to bless the Holy One, blessed be He, the *Shekhinah* is able to prepare itself to face the realm above in order to receive blessings, and *the other side* is humiliated. And if a man does not express his intention to bless the Holy One, blessed be He, *the other side* rejoices, and shakes with mirth, for it gains a share in that blessing. You might ask why, in that case, we do not have to express an intention with the other blessings? The answer is, because there the object of the benediction itself represents the intention. Let us learn how this applies. If one says a blessing over a piece of fruit, the fruit itself represents the intention, and one says the blessing over it, and *the other side* has no share in it. Before this, when the fruit is still in the power of *the other side*, one does not say a blessing over it, for it is written *it shall not be eaten* (Lev. 19:23), to prevent us from saying a blessing over the fruit, and to prevent the other side from being blessed. But when it emerges from its power it may be eaten, and a blessing is pronounced over it, and it represents in itself an expression of the intention to say a blessing. Similarly, with all the good things of the world over which blessings are said—they all represent the intention to bless, and *the other side* has no share in this blessing. You might say, In that case the cup of wine in the grace after meals also represents this intention. Why say explicitly: Come, let us bless [God]? This is because the cup of wine has already fulfilled that function when it was drunk [during the meal] and when the blessing, "He who creates the fruit of the vine," was said over it. When we come to the grace after meals we need an additional expression of intention, for the cup is now needed for the Holy One, blessed be He, and not for food. Theefore we have to express our intention verbally. You might say that "Let us bless Him of whose bounty we have eaten" is the expression of the intention, and "Blessed be He of whose bounty we have eaten" is the actual benediction. That is correct. But "Let us bless . . . " is a second expression of intention. The first expression is for the cup of blessing on its own, but when this cup is raised it is associated with the second expression, in the phrase "Let us bless . . ." in relation to the upper world, whence come every food and every benediction. That is why it is expressed in the third person, for the upper world is hidden, and there the intention to pronounce a benediction can only be expressed on this level, with the cup of benediction.

Rabbi Judah said: How fortunate we are, for we have never in our lifetime heard words such as these, until this moment. As I said, this [child] is not human. He said to him: My child, angel of God, and His beloved, you interpreted the passage *And you shall make bars of acacia-wood; five for the boards of the one side of the tabernacle . . . and five bars . . . and five bars . . . and five bars for the back part toward the west*. Now there are many bars mentioned here, but a man has only two hands.

He said: This illustrates the saying: You can tell a man from his mouth. But since you have not understood, I shall tell you.

He began by quoting: *The wise man, his eyes are in his head* (Eccles. 2:14). Now, where would a man's eyes be if not in his head? In his body, or in his arm? Is this the way in which the wise man is distinguished from the rest of humanity? This verse must be understood in the following way. We have learned that one should not walk four cubits bareheaded. Why? because the *Shekhinah* rests upon the head, and both the eyes and the words of the wise man are "in his head," that is, they are directed toward Him who rests upon his head. And when his eyes are there, he knows that the light that burns upon his head needs oil, for man's body is the wick and the light burns above it. King Solomon exclaimed: *Let your head never lack oil* (Eccles. 9:8), for the light on the head needs oil, and that is good deeds. And so it is written, *The wise man, his eyes are in his head*—and not elsewhere.

Now you are surely wise men, and the *Shekhinah* rests upon your head, and yet you could not understand the passage, And you shall make bars . . . *for the boards of the one side of the tabernacle, and five bars for the boards of the other side of the tabernacle*. The verse stipulates "one" and "other." It does not mention a third or a fourth. So "one" and "other" represent the two sides, and it therefore calculates only with these two.

They came and kissed him.

Rabbi Judah wept and said: Blessed is your portion, Rabbi Simeon, and blessed is the generation in which, through your merit, even the little children of their master's house are tall and mighty rocks.

His mother came and said to them: Masters, only look upon my son, I pray you, with a good eye.

Blessed is your portion, they said to her, worthy woman, the most precious of all women, for the Holy One, blessed be He, has chosen your portion, and raised your banner above all the other women in the world.

The child said: I do not fear the evil eye, because I am the son of a great and noble fish and fish do not fear the evil eye, for it is written *And let them swarm as a multitude in the midst of the earth* (Gen. 48:16). What does "as a multitude" mean? It means: in order to have mastery over the [evil] eye. We have learned: "The fish of the sea are covered by the waters and the evil eye has no [power over them][11] "As a multitude in the midst of the earth" means: among mankind that are upon the earth.

They said: My child, angel of God, there is no evil eye in us, and we do not come from the side of the evil eye. But may the Holy One, blessed be He, shelter you with His wings.

He began by quoting: *"The angel who has redeemed me from all evil, may he bless [the lads; and let my name be named in them, and the name of my fathers, Abraham and Isaac; and let them swarm as a multitude in the midst of the earth]"* (Gen. 48:16). This verse was said by Jacob through the holy spirit. Since he said it through the holy spirit, then it must contain a secret of wisdom. "The angel"—he called the Shekhinah "angel," but he also called her by other names. Why is she called "angel" here? She is called "angel" when she is a messenger from above, and receives glorious light from the supernal mirror, for then father and mother bless her, and say to her, "Go, my daughter, and keep your house. Look after your house. This is what you shall do to your house: go and feed them. Go, for the world below is waiting for you. The members of your household expect food from you. You have all that is necessary to provide for them." Now you might say that there are several places where she is called "angel," without her coming to feed the worlds; and, furthermore, that she does not feed the worlds under this name, but under the name *Adonai*. This is true, but when she is sent from the father and mother she is called "angel," and when she dwells in her place, upon the two cherubim,[12] her name is Adonat.

When the *Shekhinah* first appeared to Moses she was called "angel." She did not appear thus to Jacob, but in an earthly form, as it is written, *Rachel came [with the sheep of her father; for she tended them]* (Gen.

29:9). This was the image of another Rachel, as it is written, *Thus says the Lord: A voice is heard in Ramah . . . Rachel weeping for her children* (Jer. 31:15). "Rachel came"—pure and simple; "with the sheep"—with her accompanying "levels"; "of her father"—really; and all of them were counted and entrusted to her care; "for she tended them"—she guided them and was put in charge of them. However, in the case of Moses it is written, *And the angel of the Lord appeared to him in a flame of fire* (Exod. 3:2). Now you might say that Abraham was even more highly regarded, for with him "angel" is not written, but simply "*And the Lord appeared to him by the terebinths of Mamre . . .*" (Gen. 18:1). There, with Abraham, it was *Adonai* that appeared to him, for at that time Abraham had accepted the covenant [of circumcision], and He was revealed to him as master and ruler, something that had previously been concealed from him. And it was right for this to be so, for at that time he became associated with this particular level, and no farther, and so, through the name *Adon*, He became his master. But with Moses there was no differentiation in time, for it is written "Moses Moses" without disjunctive punctuation, while "Abraham, Abraham" (Gen. 22:11) is written with disjunctive punctuation. Abraham was at one time imperfect, and later became perfect, so there is a difference between the later Abraham and the earlier Abraham. But with Moses, as soon as he was born, a shining mirror was with him, as it is written, *And she saw him, that he was good* (Exod. 2:2), and it is also written, *And God saw the light that it was good* (Gen. 1:4)—So Moses was immediately associated with his level. That is why it says "Moses Moses" without disjunctive punctuation. Therefore, in Moses' case, she belittled heself, and it is written "the angel of the Lord." Jacob called her "angel" when he was about to depart from the world. Why? Because at that moment he took possession of her in order to rule [over her]: Moses in his lifetime, Jacob after he departed from the world; Moses in body, Jacob in spirit. Blessed was the portion of Moses!

"Who has redeemed me from all evil"—[Jacob] never approached *the evil side*, and evil could exercise no power over him. "May he bless the lads"—Jacob was setting his house in order, like a man who goes to a new house, and sets it in order and provides ornaments for it. "May he bless the lads"—these are they who are designated, appointed over the world, so that blessings may flow from them, the two cherubim.

"And let my name be named in them"—he now sets his house in order, and ascends to his level, because the conjunction occurred with Jacob; the body became attached to the necessary place, and the two arms with it. Once the lads had been blessed properly, then, immediately, "let them swarm as a multitude in the midst of the earth." Fish customarily spawn in water, and if they come out of the water on to any land they die right away. But these are not like that. They come from the great sea, and when they disperse in order to procreate they do so "in the midst of the earth"—something that happens with no other fish in the world. What is written before this? *And he blessed Joseph, and said* (Gen. 48:15). But we do not find Joseph's blessings here. He blesses him later, as it is written, *Joseph is a fruitful vine* (Gen. 49:22). But since he blesses these lads he also blesses Joseph, for they cannot receive blessing except through Joseph. And because he is hidden, and it is not right for him to be revealed, it is written in the third person, "and let my name be named in them, and the name of my fathers"— they are blessed through the patriarchs, and from no other source. "In the midst of the land"—this is the covering that conceals what is necessary.

They came and kissed him, as they had at the beginning. They said: Come, let us bless [God].

Let me say the blessing, he said, for all that you have heard so far has emanated from me, and I shall fulfill in myself the verse, *He that has a good eye shall be blessed, [for he gives of his bread to the poor]* (Prov. 22:9). Read rather "he shall bless." Why? Because "he gives of his bread to the poor." You have partaken of the bread and sustenance of my teaching.

Rabbi Abba said: My son, the beloved of the Holy One, blessed be He, surely we have learned: The host says the blessing before the meal, and the guest says the blessing after the meal.

I am not the host, he said to them, and you are not my guests. I have discovered a verse that I shall implement, for surely I am the one "who has a good eye." I have spoken Torah quite voluntarily up till now, and you have partaken of my bread and sustenance.

He took the cup for the blessing, and began to say grace, but his hands trembled, and he could not hold the cup. When he came to "for the land and for the food" he said, *I will lift up the cup of salvation, and call upon the name of the Lord* (Ps. 16:13), and then the cup steadied itself in his right hand, and he continued the grace. At the end he said: May it be God's will that one of these present may be accorded life from the Tree of Life, upon which all life depends. And may the Holy One, blessed be He, vouch for him, and may he also find a surety below, so that he might be joined through his pledge with the Holy King.

When he had concluded grace he closed his eyes for a moment, and then he opened them. He said: Friends, may peace light upon you from the good Master, to whom all peace belongs.

They were amazed, and wept, and blessed him. They stayed there the night, and in the morning they arose and went. When they came to Rabbi Simeon ben Yohai they told him what had happened.

Rabbi Simeon was astonished, and said: He is the son of a mighty rock, and most worthy to be at a stage higher even than man can understand; he is the son of Rav Hamnuna Sava.

Rabbi Eleazar became agitated, and said: I must go and see this burning lamp.

He will not achieve fame for himself in this world, said Rabbi Simeon, for there is something of the celestial in him, and it is a mystery. A continuing light shines upon him from his father, and this mystery is not current among the companions.

One day the companions were sitting together and were waging war [arguing over matters of Torah]. There were present Rabbi Eleazar, Rabbi Abba, Rabbi Hiyya, Rabbi Jose, and other companions. They said: We find it written in Scripture *Be not at enmity with Moab, neither contend with them in battle* (Deut. 2:9). This is because Ruth and Naamah were later to be descended from them. But should not this have applied even more forcibly to the Midianites? Moses' wife, Zipporah, was from Midian, and Jethro, and his children, all of whom were truly righteous, came from Midian, and, furthermore, they reared Moses in Midian. And yet, the Holy One, blessed be He, said, *Take vengeance for the children of Israel on the Midianites* (Num. 31:2)—It looks as if there is some bias here, because the Midianites have more reason to be saved than the Moabites.

Rabbi Simeon said: A man who is going to pick figs in the future is not the same as a man who has picked them in the past.

Rabbi Eleazar said to him: Even though he has already picked them, [the tree] still deserves to be praised.

The man who has not yet picked his figs, he replied, looks after the fig tree all the time, so that it should not suffer any blemish, for the sake of the figs that he will gather later on. But once he has picked his figs he leaves the fig tree, and does not look after it any more. So Moab, which was going to produce figs in the future, was protected by the Holy One, blessed be He, as it is written, "Be not at enmity with Moab." But of Midian, whose figs had already been produced and gathered, it is written, *Harass the Midianites* (Num. 25:17), because this fig tree was not going to bear any more fruit, and could be burned.

He began by quoting: *And Moab said to the elders of Midian* (Num. 22:4). It was the Moabites who made the first move, and because of the figs that Moab was to bring into the world, they were saved from punishment.

Rabbi Eleazar wanted to visit his father-in-law, Rabbi Jose, the son of Rabbi Simeon ben Lekunya. Rabbi Abba and Rabbi Jose went with him. They set off, and discussed Torah throughout the journey.

Rabbi Abba said: It is written, "And the Lord said to me: Be not at enmity with Moab, neither contend with them in battle." And it is also written, "When you approach the Ammonites [do not harass them, or contend with them]." Is there any difference between these two? They seem to be treated equally. And yet we have learned that when Israel approached the Moabites they were visibly equipped for battle, as if they wished to wage war against them. But in the case of the Ammonites they were all enveloped in their cloaks and no weapons of war could be seen at all. And yet the verses quoted show that they were to be treated equally!

Rabbi Eleazar said: So they are, but we have learned that one daughter was barefaced and said "Moab," as it is written: *And she called his name Moab* (Gen. 19:36). Consequently, Israel confronted them in as barefaced a manner as she, when she said "Moab," [meaning] *from my father did this son come* (Gen. 19:38). But the younger, who said, "Ben Ammi," disguised her conduct. And so Israel disguised their conduct in relation [to the Ammonites]. They wrapped themselves in their cloaks and presented themselves to them as real brothers. These matters have already been reconciled.

As they were going along Rabbi Eleazar remembered the child. They made a detour of about ten miles and came to the place. They were received in the house, and when they went in they found the child sitting down while a meal was being laid for him. As soon as he saw them, he approached them.

He said: Let the pious and holy ones enter. Let the pillars of the world enter. They are praised by both the upper and the lower worlds. Even the fish of the great sea come on to dry land to meet them.

Rabbi Eleazar went and kissed him on the head, and then he kissed him on the mouth. Rabbi Eleazar said: The first kiss is for the fish that leave the waters and walk on dry land. The second kiss is for the eggs of the fish, which produce fine fruit in the world.

The child said: I can tell from the smell of your garments that Ammon and Moab have been contending with you. How did you escape from them? You had no weapons. For if you had, you would have walked in safety, without fear.

Rabbi Eleazar, Rabbi Abba, and the companions were filled with amazement.

Rabbi Abba said: How blessed is this journey, how blessed is our portion, that we have been enabled to see this!

They prepared the meal, as they had done earlier.

He said: Wise and holy men, do you like your sweetmeats battle-free, or do you prefer the bread of war and a meal with weapons? Would you like to bless the King with all the weapons of war, for the table cannot be exalted without war?

Rabbi Eleazar said: Beloved, adored, and holy child, we would prefer that. We have used all these weapons, and we know how to fight with sword, and bow, and lance, and sling-stones. But you are a child, and you have not yet seen how the mighty heroes of the world wage war.

The child laughed, and said: That is true. I have not seen it. But it is written, *Let not the man who puts on his armor boast like the man who is taking his off* (1 Kings 20:11).

They laid the table with bread and everything else that they needed.

Rabbi Eleazar said: There is so much joy in my heart because of this child. How many new interpretations of Torah will be spoken at this table. That is why I said before that I knew that there were clappers of the bells of the holy spirit within him.

The child said: Whoever wants bread, let him eat it with the edge of the sword.

Rabbi Eleazar rejoiced. The child turned and approached him. He said: Since you have boasted of your own prowess, you must begin the battle. I said earlier that the battle should begin after the meal, but now, whoever wants fine bread, let him bring his weapons with him.

Rabbi Eleazar said: You should show me some of your own weapons.

The child began by quoting: *It shall be that, when you eat of the bread of the land, you shall set apart a portion for a gift (tenufah) to the Lord* (Num. 15:19). This verse refers to the wave-offering of a sheaf of barley. What is this "wave-offering"? If it refers simply to the fact that the priest has to wave it aloft, what difference does it make to us whether he waves it [aloft] or holds it low? But it is in actual fact essential to raise it on high. And this is the force of the word *tenufah*. And even though we explain [that *tenufah* should be] one-fiftieth part, and so it is, yet this *tenufah* signifies "raising." One of wisdom's secrets is here. Alas, holy and pious ones, wielders of the lance, that you did not serve Rav Shemaiah the Pious, for if you had done so you would have known the meaning of *tenufah*, the meaning of "wheat," the meaning of "barley." The *tenufah* about which I have spoken, may be regarded as *tenu peh* and its secret significance is in *Give glory to the Lord, your God* (Jer. 13:16), for the celestial mouth is the glory that we should give to the Holy One, blessed be He. Therefore, we must raise it aloft to show that the "mouth" that we are giving belongs to Him, for the supreme King receives praise only when Israel prepares this glory, and gives glory to the King. So this *tenufah* is "give glory," and the verse with which I began really refers to the act of raising something.

(Zohar III, 186a–192a)

15 TO WRITE WITHOUT PEN AND INK

The relationship between mysticism and magic has always been a complex and intricate one. When the definitions of the two disciplines are presented, it seems that there is no point of contact between them. Magic views itself as a science, demands following linguistic instruction precisely, does not offer explanations of the methods by which it achieves its purposes, and, above all, is result-oriented, trying to achieve exact aims that are in most cases mundane or even material. The magician does not pray: he orders earthly and celestial entities to obey his demands. Most important is the fact that practicing magic represents complete faith in the communicative power of language. Mystics are different concerning all these characteristics. While magic is a quest of results and gains, mysticism is a quest of truth that is beyond the sensual and the intellectual, and therefore it is beyond language. Despite these vast differences, mystics occasionally combined magical practices with their efforts to ascend to celestial realms and used magic in their rituals when seeking hidden, supernal truth. The following text is an example of such combination: it expresses dedication to the revelation of divine secrets, which is achieved by magical practices.

Since the second half of the fifteenth century we find Jewish mystics increasingly relying on mediated divine revelation, in which a messenger from heaven, called *maggid* (literally: sayer), which is described as an archangel or a divine power (sometimes identified with the *Shekhinah*), who appears before the mystic and reveals to him secrets from the divine world. In many cases it is a voice without an image, while in others it is a clear apparition. Sometimes the voice emerges from within the mystic, who then is heard speaking in a different voice from his usual one. Another variation of this phenomenon is the belief that a celestial power is guiding the hand of the writing mystic ("automatic writing"), sometimes referred to in Hebrew as *shem ha-kotev* ("the writing holy name"). The number of such maggid revelations increased dramatically in the sixteenth century, and the most important and best-known such figure is the maggid who instructed Rabbi Joseph Karo, the great lawyer and mystic in sixteenth-century Safed in his life and work, which Karo recorded in his *Book of the Maggid*.[1] The believers in the messiah Shabbatai Zevi in the last third of the seventeenth century and the eighteenth often claimed to have such celestial revelations; it almost became a practice associated with the mystics of that movement. By the end of the eighteenth century we hear less and less of maggid appearances, and it became a relatively marginal phenomenon in later Jewish mysticism. The text presented here, however, refers to one of the early examples of the reliance on the maggid in the generation following the expulsion of the Jews from Spain in 1492. The mystic in the center of this phenomenon is Rabbi Joseph Taitazak, a revered leader of a group of Jewish mystics in Salonica in the beginning of the sixteenth century.

Taitazak's family was among the many Jewish refugees from Spain who settled in Greece and Turkey. Joseph Taitazak became a prominent halakhic teacher, famous and widely respected as a legal authority. He was fascinated by the kabbalah, and was influenced by the writings of Shlomo Molkho, the martyr.[2] Taitazak was the teacher of some of the prominent kabbalists who settled in Safed and established there the great center of kabbalistic learning later in the sixteenth century. A series of "revelations" (giluyim) given to Rabbi Joseph by his maggid has been published by Gershom Scholem,[3] a section from which is translated here.

It should be noted that the text includes detailed instructions, clearly magical in character, of receiving written secrets from heaven, but the content that is to be revealed can be described as mystical secrets. The miraculous nature of the revelation confirms the veracity of the messages included in it.

Writing Without Pen and Ink

With the assistance of heaven. This is what the maggid revealed to our teacher, the Rabbi Joseph Taitazak of blessed memory. I have copied it from the end of the [manuscript of the] book *Hesed le-Abraham*, [by] our teacher Rabbi Abraham Azulai of blessed memory, a manuscript which was written in Egypt in the year 1664, copied by Menahem ha-Cohen son of Jacob ha-Cohen, may he rest in peace.

You shall now hear the wonders of the living God about this subject, the secret of the celestial writing, without a hand, without a foot, without ink. You shall then know of your own knowledge that the spirit of God has been flourishing in you, when you understand the secret of the celestial ink and the celestial pen, because it is a wondrous secret. It is the same secret by which the Tables of the Covenant were written, with the finger of God.[4] You shall then know the secret of the celestial finger and the celestial hand, and understand the secret of the hand of Daniel.[5] When these subjects will be clarified and written in a book you shall realize that your knowledge of this wisdom originated and was caused by God and you shall understand the secret of celestial writing and celestial ink. The [celestial powers] write their messages in brief, in headlines, in order to exhaust the subject in a short note, because writing long passages is characteristic of lowly writing, while brief headlines represent the supreme stage. Many scholars in Israel have learned this wisdom in the past, so that their words will be believed by future generations.

Now, after I have informed you of this, I shall tell you who is the one who writes this wisdom and who is the celestial scribe. Gabriel is the one who writes, and Michael the angel is the scribe. These two angels have the power, derived from their station, to write, if you invoke them, and they write without ink, which is a wonder—how can they write and preserve the writing. The writing is in Assyrian letters[6] which is written with the adorning crowns (tagin) and rounded. The secret meaning of "hand" is that for the time being the writing is observed on the wall or in the air or on paper, if you request this, and it is made of linen sheets.

Now I shall go deeper into the subject of this wisdom in order to explain it well, so that you shall understand, because this wisdom is deeper than the sea. Many [scholars] in Israel have fathomed it, and so do Joseph and me,[7] we have learned it with great effort and toil. [a detailed section concerning the writing of the holy names of twelve and seventy-two letters.]

I have sworn in the name of the living God of Hosts, that immediately a [secret][8] angel will descend downward, in order to write, without a hand, without a foot, without a pen. This is what you should say, after reciting those holy names, "may there be the will of God," and every time you read the names say the following: I hereby invoke you by the explicit names which I have mentioned, that you should immediately show your power and your writing in the lower world, in this paper or this book or this wall or this air, right now, at this time, [show] it and subjugate it by the secret of the celestial ink, whatever it is that I wish, in abbreviated words and the letters and the vocalization marks above, and you should anounce it, the meaning of the words, what each word means. I am invoking you with all the power of the letters which I have mentioned that immediately, at this time, you should write and engrave and imprint in fire these letters in paper[9] and that the divine fire will not burn the paper, and that the writing will be visible to every eye, even that of gentiles and Jews and Muslims, so that all will know and recognize that this is a divine phenomenon, when they see that there is no ink in it.

I am invoking you, the princes of the celestial writing and the princes of the writing of divine writing[10] with the finger of God; I am invoking you with all the power of the sanctity which I have mentioned and which I intended, that you should immediately demonstrate your power and your writing down here, without delay and without any hindrance. I invoke you with the full power of "one God whose name is one"[11] and with the full power of the sanctity which is hidden in the secret of every point[12] and the full power of the secret of his fire and its color, and in the power and secret of the point, and in the power and secret of the hidden thought, and in the full power of the two halves of a ball[13] and the full power of "one God whose name is one" which is connected to the supreme point,[14] that immediately your power and your fire will come down and will immediately write this thing which I demand on this paper which I have placed in a certain place, a true thing, or on the wall if it is white. You shall then mention the wall or the air or the place you wish them to write and imprint the writing. You shall then use four kinds of ketoret[15] three times with a smoking paper, and in order to give it the needed strength the paper should be treated by smoke before that, and after it is smoked you should enter a room clean of any tumaah, and you should recite the names which I have instructed you, forward and in reverse.

After you have recited it seventy times with the invocation every time, immediately the secret of Gabriel and Michael will descend, their whole stature and their power, and they will write what you ask them to or what you will wish to know whether it is true or not. I am swearing in the name of God, blessed be He, that it will happen exactly as I am telling you. And then, when you envision this celestial writing you shall know that there is a God in Israel, you and everyone else who observes this, and they will believe that there is God in Israel, and the spirit of God will inhabit you.[16]

I shall now explain this in detail. The secret of this supernal writing is the secret of the descent of the power of God in his glory, and the people of the world call it "a written question."[17] The secret included in this writing should be believed by everyone, like the one who had written it originally, for it is real prophecy and will come true fully. This is the secret of the supernal writing. With this power you can achieve the ability to write whatever you wish, be it a great deal or just a little. You shall understand the secret of the *writing Name*,[18] guided by an angel, whenever you wish it, and everything written in this way you should believe to be true as if it were done by God himself . . . With this secret there is nothing which you cannot achieve, like actual prophecy itself, and this is one of the greatest wonders of the living God. A person who reaches this stage, after he has observed the process in his own eyes, will render praise and thanks to God, and will receive everything he wants in the celestial realms, and he will be like a member of the household [in heaven], he who has mastered the secret of the supernal writing . . . Do not hesitate to try it alone or in any way you wish, only the room should be clean and pure of any unclean thing, and this you should observe.

This practice should be done with full observance, without any neglect. The woman of the house should be clean of any impurity. It should begin by two days of complete fasting, and on the third day it should be performed. The person doing it should not drink any wine and he should eat on that day only after performing the practice. Before that he should eat three eggs, to give him the power for the Names. It should be performed in the morning and also after midnight. This is the right way to do it immediately, without delay. Try it, and you shall observe it yourself. But you should not use it only in sanctity and purity, and after he has separated himself from a woman for three days and night; the practice should be performed on the fourth day.

You should preserve this writing, not showing it to scholars and ordinary people, for if he reveals how it was written he will frighten anyone who sees it. This is the secret of the supernal writing, which should be revealed only to those who worship God and revere His name and to the righteous, only they deserve to know it, and not the evil-doers and the sinners of this evil generation, a sinful generation which is completely guilty.

FROM EXPERIENCE TO LEGEND

The story of the attempt to bring forth the redemption by magical and mystical means, the hero of which is Rabbi Joseph Della Reina, became one of the best-known Jewish messianic legends. We have several literary versions of the narrative, and it has been adopted in drama, fiction, and poetry. It is possible to follow in some detail how the story was embellished into a full-fledged folk legend, yet it seems that at its core is a real mystical experience, and that the hero was a historical figure, working in specific historical and ideological circumstances.

The history of Jewish mysticism includes several examples of directing mystical experience and knowledge into redemptive, messianic endeavor. One of the best-known is that of Rabbi Abraham Abulafia (see above) who saw himself as a prophet and believed in his redemptive mission to the pope. Others include Shlomo Molcho, Nathan of Gaza (see below), and Moshe Hayyim Luzzatto (see below). In such cases the sense of empowerment that is derived from the belief of the mystic's proximity to God and the intimate knowledge of his secrets is translated into a belief in the ability of the individual mystic to bring forth dramatic changes. Mystical knowledge is transformed into magical knowledge: The secrets are used to compel celestial powers to obey the mystic and enable him to achieve his worldly purpose. The theological assumption is that earthly events reflect spiritual and celestial situations. The government of evil in the universe is the result of its position in the spiritual realms. If it were dethroned above, it will lose its hold over the created world. Direct earthly activity is insufficient, as the real source of all occurances is found in the dynamic events in the divine sphere. The mystic, endowed with divine powers, may thus achieve a revolutionary change in both realms. The activities of the historical figure of the mystic-magician Joseph Della Reina and the narratives that developed around them represent a typical example of this process.

Rabbi Joseph Della Reina was a kabbalist in Spain, who lived in the second half of the fifteenth century, in a period of intense persecutions of Jews in that country just before the expulsion of the Jews from Spain in 1492. He wrote several kabbalistic treatises, from which we may conclude that he belonged to a school of kabbalists—most of them anonymous—who remolded the kabbalah in a redemptive-messianic direction, a direction which became dominant in the late sixteenth century and the seventeenth.[1] It is entirely possible that he attempted to use his magical and kabbalistic knowledge in order to enhance the redemption, directing his efforts at overcoming the powers of evil that govern the world.

The earliest text describing these efforts is found in an epistle, "A Letter Concerning the Secret of the Redemption," written by a later kabbalist, Rabbi Abraham be-Rabbi Eliezer ha-Levi, in Jerusalem in 1519.[2] Rabbi Eliezer was a kabbalist from Spain who immigrated to the Holy Land for messianic reasons, and his numerous works are completely dominated by messianic calculations and apocalyptic narratives. The main element in the story of Joseph Della Reina that interested Rabbi Abraham be-Rabbi Eliezer was the conclusion, in which it is stated that as a punishment for Rabbi Joseph's transgression the redemption was postponed by forty years. If this conclusion is authentic—and there is no reason do doubt it—at the time it was first narrated the story was one of sorrow and misfortune, because an opportunity to achieve immediate redemption has been missed. But when Rabbi Abraham was retelling the story, most of these forty years have already passed, so that it became a positive prophecy of hope, signifying the imminence of the vanquishing of evil and the appearance of the messiah.[3] Several reference to the story are found in the writings of the kabbalists in Safed in the second half of the sixteenth century, including one by Rabbi Isaak Luria, the great kabbalist, who identified Rabbi Joseph as incarnated in the body of a black dog—an incarnation usually regarded as the punishment for fornication, which is Della Reina's sin in the concluding part of the narrative.

The standard, full-fledged narrative of this event has been published by Shlomo Navarro, a scholar and kabbalist from Jerusalem, who claimed that he found the notes written by the one surviving disciple of Joseph Della Reina in an old manuscript in Hebron. This claim may be regarded as part of the fictional embellishment of the story, which was written, in all probability, by Navarro himself, around 1660. A few years later Navarro was involved with the outbreak of the Sabbatian messianic-heretical movement, and converted to Christianity. The story, however, spread in this version and became popular and well known; we even have a Sabbatian version of it.[4]

The basic assumption of the story is the belief that proper use of kabbalistic and magical knowledge can be employed to overcome and bind the powers of evil, Satan and his female consort, Lilith. Rabbi Joseph, who is reported of having achieved it, is portrayed as a great scholar, but not as a messiah. The message delivered by the story is that this can be done by knowledge, without the hero being designated for the task by God as his emissary. The power of magic to employ celestial powers and make them follow the instructions of the kabbalist is manifest throughout the story. In his way to the ultimate achievement, Rabbi Joseph compels three great archangels, or even divine powers, to serve him and endow him with secret information. The narrative does not denote any specific, individual characteristics which enabled Rabbi Joseph to achieve this; he had the knowledge, and he was persistent and determined, but otherwise he was a scholar, a kabbalist, a magician, like many others. The power is found more in the knowledge than in the individual person. We may assume that indeed the original core of this elaborate legend is the experience of one person; both he and his ideological environment held such an attempt to be possible.

The personal element becomes evident only after Rabbi Joseph's mistake and failure. The Faustian story of his involvement with the queen may have been based on his name—"Della Reina," representing the depth of his fall from the pinnacle of redemptive achievement to the bondage of erotic, satanic realm, which ultimately brought him to his death. This part is absent in the early version, found in Rabbi Abraham be-Rabbi Eliezer's epistle, but it need not be an invention of

Shlomo Navarro: If Isaac Luria, a hundred years before Navarro, saw him as a fornicator, it is possible that this erotic ending or something similar to it was known in Safed in the 1570s. In this version, the story of Joseph Della Reina became one of warning: Attempting to overcome evil may be a worthy endeavor and a theoretical possibility, but the danger of failure is very great, and the result can be extremely tragic. It is a fact that we do not find in later kabbalistic literature narratives describing a similar attempt by other scholars (with the exception of the followers of Shabbati Zevi who converted to Islam; see below).

The Story of Rabbi Joseph Della Reina

There is an awesome story of Joseph Della Reina who was a great man, versed in the skills of the practical Kabbalah, who dwelt in the city of Safed in the land of Galilee. One day he resolved to insist upon bringing the Redemption and remove the rule of wickedness from earth. Now he had five disciples who stayed with him day and night and did anything he requested. He said to them: "My sons, I am resolved to use the knowledge God has given me in order to remove the pollution and idolatry from the world and bring our Messiah, who will release us from our oppressors." All five of his disciples answered together: "Master and rabbi, we are prepared for anything you may command us." "If so," he said, "do this: Purify yourselves and change your garments and be prepared within three days, and do not approach any woman during that time. On the third day we shall go out into the field, and we shall not return home until the Children of Israel are settled every man on his own farm in the Holy Land!" When the disciples heard these words of their master, they immediately rose up and energetically purified themselves and changed their garments. They took provisions and food, clean bread which they themselves had made in purity and which no woman had touched. On the third day they came to him and found him all alone in hallowed purity in his house of study, with his head between his knees. When they came, he lifted up his head and said to them: "May it be God's will that the Shekinah should inspire the work of our hands, and the Holy and Blessed One approve of us and aid us with respect to His glorious Name." And they all answered: "Amen." After all this, Rabbi Joseph took sundry spices and placed a scribe's inkhorn in his belt, and told them: "Let us go forth!" So they left the city of Safed and went to Meron, to the grave of Rabbi Simeon ben Yohai, at whose grave they prostrated themselves. Shortly before dawn Rabbi Joseph dozed, and Rabbi Simeon ben Yohai together with his son Rabbi Eleazar appeared to him in a dream and said: "Why are you getting involved in such a difficult task which you will not be able to carry out?" He answered: "God Himself knows my intention and will aid me for the sake of His profaned Name." They in turn said: "May the Lord your God grant your wish!"

When morning came, Rabbi Joseph and his disciples proceeded to the city of Tiberias, passing through the open country till they reached a forest, and seeing neither man nor beast, but birds alone. There they engaged in the permutations of the holy Names, and the contemplation of formulas which they knew. Every morning they went to immerse themselves in the Lake of Tiberias, twenty-six successive immersions in accordance with the numerical value of the letters of Havayah [the tetragrammton], the Name of God the Ever Present. This they did for three consecutive days and nights, likewise fasting by day and by night.

Toward evening when it was time for the afternoon prayers Rabbi Joseph and his disciples rose up and recited the afternoon prayers in pleasant voices with great devotion and closed eyes. When they reached the words "Hearken to our voices," they added "Answer us." And wherever the text mentions the Holy Name of God as "The Lord," they pronounced the Great Name as it is written with the proper vowels and the necessary formulas. The rabbi entreated in a long prayer and great conjurations of all the heavenly angels and finally he pronounced the Name of Havayah, combined with the Name of Forty-two Letters, together with the words "Answer us." By the power of that great Name he adjured Elijah the Prophet to appear. And, lo and behold, Elijah came at speed and suddenly appeared to them and said: "Here I am, and what can I do for you and what is your request to entreat so much in your prayers?" Then they bowed down to the ground and said: "All peace to our lord, 'My father, my father, the chariots of Israel and the horsemen thereof' (2 Kings 2:12)." And the rabbi began: "Let not my lord take it amiss that I have entreated to bring you hither. Indeed, I am zealous for the honor of the Holy and Blessed One and His Shekinah. Therefore let me entreat you to show me the way whereby I can subdue the powers of Satan and strengthen holiness." To which Elijah the Prophet answered: "Know that your purpose is welcomed. If you can fulfill your thoughts in action, happy are you and good is your portion. Yet my counsel is: Let it be and cease, lest Samael and his band strike you down, for you will not be able to prevail against him."

But Rabbi Joseph said: "I pray you, my lord, do not discourage me! For I have taken oath that I shall not return home until I bring the holy Shekinah to light and raise her from the dust!"

When Elijah the Prophet heard these words, he said: "This is what you must do. You and your disciples, go out into the fields far from any inhabited place, for twenty-one days. Do not eat your fill, but only what you yourself know will keep you alive. Reduce the amount you eat every night, and accustom yourselves to smell spices in order that your corporeality may be pure and clear, so that you may be capable of bearing the sight of the heavenly angels whom you will bring down to speak with you. Likewise immerse yourselves each day twenty-one times, that being the numerical value of the letters of the Name Eheyeh (Exod. 3:13–14); and after the twenty-first day make an interval and fast for three days and nights. On the third day after the afternoon prayer mention the great Name of Forty-two Letters which you know, together with its permutations and intents; and also pronounce the great Name which is derived from the verse "Above Him stood the seraphim" (Isa. 6:2). When you do this, be wrapped in your prayer shawls and wear your tefillin and cover your faces, and by those holy Names summon the Angel Sandalphon and his host to appear before you. When they come, strengthen yourselves with the pleasant scent, for you will fear and tremble and grow exceedingly weak at the great commotion and the mighty fire. Request the said angel to strengthen you and give you the might wherewith to speak. He will tell you what you should do, for he guards the ways and paths to prevent Samael from entering the holy places, and he knows the spots where that one gathers his strength."

As soon as Elijah the Prophet went his way, Rabbi Joseph and his disciples gathered their strength and united their hearts. They added sanctity to their earlier sanctity, and they did all that Elijah had told them. When they had completed the term of days exactly as Elijah had commanded, they adjured the Angel Sandalphon to reveal himself to them at that very time. No sooner did they finish their conjuration than the heavens opened and Sandalphon the Angel suddenly came to them with all his host. And, behold, there was a fiery chariot with fiery horses and a great host, while flaming fire filled the whole countryside; there was a great commotion, but it did not continue. Rabbi Joseph trembled and shook exceedingly, and he and his disciples were left without any breath within them. They fell to the ground, and their hearts melted and a trembling possessed them. Still, they found the strength to smell the pure frankincense in their hands and came to themselves.

Then the Angel Sandalphon and his host came down to them and said: "Son of Adam, worm that you are, what gave your heart the audacity to set the upper and the lower worlds shaking? Have the self-respect to stay at home or my forces may strike you and burn you with their breath!" But Rabbi Joseph answered in a low and broken voice: "My lord, holy angel of God, what can your servant say in your presence? I am left without breath as though I were dead, so great is my fear and awe!"

As soon as the angel heard this, he touched him and said: "Stand up and say what you have to say, for I have strengthened you." Indeed, when the angel touched him, he rose up and gathered strength and prostrated himself, and then removed his shoes from his feet; but as for his disciples, they still had their faces to the ground and could not rise.

Then Rabbi Joseph spoke: "Welcome, peace be with you, angel of the Lord of Hosts and peace be with all your holy forces. I entreat you, give me the strength and courage to carry out my will! For it is not to honor myself or my father's house that I do this but for the sake of the Living God, the King who is King of Kings! I entreat you, holy one with all your holy forces, to agree to wage war against Amalek and his prince together with me, and instruct me as to what I must do to remove the rule of wickedness from the earth."

The angel answered Rabbi Joseph, saying: "Indeed, your words are good and proper, if only you might be heard, and God be with you! But you must know, son of Adam, that all you have done until now is nothing. If you were to know the high position which Samael with his forces has reached, you would not engage in this matter. For who can prevail against him except the Holy and Blessed One Himself until the time comes to fulfill His word. I have come to you now in respect to the great Name you pronounced; but what can I do for you? For I am unable to learn what is the extent of the strength of Samael and his host and on what his fall and his rise depend. None know this except the great Angel Akhtariel and his hosts and Metatron, Prince of the Presence, and his hosts. Yet who can stand before such mighty angels? For if you were frightened by me, how will you be able to even exist in their presence?"

But Rabbi Joseph answered: "I am youthful and puny and I myself know that I am not worthy of doing this thing. Yet I also know that God will not despise a broken and depressed heart. I have made up my mind to sacrifice myself for the sanctity of the Holy and Blessed One and His Shekinah! Therefore, holy Ministering Angel of the Lord, instruct me as to what I should do to bring down Akhtariel and Metatron, and what further privations I must add in sanctity and purity, and what is the Name by which I can conjure them."

The angel spoke again, saying: "Please hear my words and God be with you! Continue for forty days whatever immersions, fasts, and purification of thought that you have done until now. Let not your thoughts depart from the concepts even for a single moment by day or night. After forty days pronounce the holy Name of Power which consists of Seventy-two Letters (Exod. 14:19–21) with all intents and vocalizations and with its source which is known to you. Therewith you can conjure those two great and mighty angels, who shall instruct you as to the ways of Samael and how you can bring him down. May the Lord guard you from all evil and preserve your soul!" Then the angel of the Lord went heavenward in a tempest.

They rose up and went away from there through the wilderness to a certain mountain near Meron, where they found a cave in which they dwelt. For forty days they followed all their instructions in holiness and purity. They missed nothing until they could sense nothing corporeally of themselves; all those days they saw neither men nor beast. When they had completed the forty days, they went out into the wilderness to a place near the source of the River Kishon, for there they had been bathing all those forty days. They prepared themselves to pray the great afternoon prayer. They marked a circle on the ground and entered into it. Each one gave his hand to his friend, so that their hands were linked together in a circle. Then they cried unto the Lord after prostrating themselves and they pronounced the Expressed Name, and they conjured the Angel Akhtariel and his hosts together with the Angel

Metatron and his hosts. When they pronounced the great Name, the Earth heaved and shook and there were lightnings and thunders, and the heavens opened; the angels with all their hosts came down and sought to smite Rabbi Joseph and his disciples. But they kept their hands together and strengthened their concentrations on Names they knew in their minds though they did not pronounce them, because they did not have the strength to speak. They all fell to the ground but held their hands linked together and did not separate.

As soon as the said angels came down, they began to speak in a great fury, saying: "Who and where is the one who has had the audacity to use the Royal Scepter?"

When Rabbi Joseph saw this great vision, he felt as though he were dumb and slumbering with his face down, and he and his disciples were completely exhausted. But the Angel Metatron touched him and said: "Speak up, answer, you stinking drop, what is this great alarm which has brought us to you? And woe betide you because you have not been concerned for the honor of your Maker!" Then, when the angel touched him, Rabbi Joseph opened his mouth and said in a faint voice with closed eyes: "What can this abject and worthless slave say in the presence of pure and holy angels if you do not strengthen me?" Then the Angel Akhtariel also stretched out his hand and touched him, saying: "See, I support you, say your say!"

At this Rabbi Joseph answered: "God Almighty assuredly knows that I have not done any of this in revolt or deceit, but to honor the Holy and Blessed One and His Shekinah. Therefore, I entreat you, Ministering Angels, by the power of the great and holy Name, show respect to His Name and instruct me where the strength of Samael and his hosts is to be found, and what I must do to bring him down."

The angels answered together: "This is a difficult request. Had you only known how mighty and powerful he has become because of the transgressions of Israel! None can bring him down, for his nest is amid the stars where his seat is surrounded by three barriers. You cannot prevail against him and none can do so except the Holy and Blessed One Himself when it is time to fulfill His word."

Rabbi Joseph went on again, saying: "I have already risked my soul for the honor of the Holy and Blessed One and His Shekinah. After I have seen the holy Hosts and my soul has been delivered, I trust in the loving-kindness of God that He will aid me and I shall succeed, if your pure words will instruct me and tell me what to do. Whatever you may tell me I shall indeed fulfill."

Then the angels answered: "Joseph, hear the word of the Lord! He who spoke and the world came into being is aware that your intention is desirable; but the time is not yet come and the decree has already been made that 'You stir not up, nor awake love' (Songs of Songs 2:7). Yet nevertheless, in view of your wisdom and knowledge of hidden secrets which the Rock of the Universe has granted you, and by reason of them we are compelled to honor His great and holy Name to tell you and instruct you as to the way you should go."

And after this the Angel Akhtariel began: "You should know that on one side, facing me, Samael has two powerful barriers, one is an iron wall which rises from earth to heaven and the other is a great barrier of ocean." Similarly, the Angel Metatron answered that on his side and facing him Samael had a barrier consisting of a mighty snow mountain, whose summit reached the skies.

"Now," said they, "pay careful attention to all we tell you, for you have to bring down these three barriers and eliminate them. This is what you must do: When you leave this place, make your way to Mount Seir; and we shall arrive before you to Mount Seir on high.

"Whatever you do below in accordance with our instructions to you, that we shall do above. The likeness of your soul would be on high with us; whatever actions you perform below your soul will perform above.

"When you go to Mount Seir, continue to be as holy as you have been till now in all your deeds; for your souls have already risen to such a height that you yourselves have almost attained the degree of angels and have forgotten the ways of the corporeal world; continue in this fashion.

"Along the way you will encounter a great horde of black dogs, these being the companies of Samael whom he will send to confuse you in your intention. But have no fear and pronounce the expanded Name HVYH in such a fashion that its numerical value shall be fifty-two (that being the numerical value of the Hebrew word for dog which is Keleb). Concentrate on its correct vocalization and formula and they will flee away from you. Go on from there and climb the mountain where you will find a great mass of snow up to the skies. Then mention the Name which is derived from the verse 'Have you entered the treasuries of snow' (Job 38:22), and the mountain will be removed from its place. After that, pronounce the name derived from 'It snows in Zalmon' (Ps. 68:15), and the mountain will vanish entirely. Continue with these concentrations until you reach the other barrier of ocean, whose waves mount up to the skies. Pronounce over it the Names that are derived from the Psalm (29:1): 'Ascribe to the Lord, O you sons of the mighty,' and it will dry up and you will pass dryshod through its midst.

"Go forward after that and you will encounter a great wall of iron rising from the earth to the skies. Take knife in your hand and write upon it the Name which is derived from the verse 'The sword for the Lord and for Gideon' (Judg. 7:20) and cut with the knife into the iron, make an opening and enter through it. But be careful to hold the opening fast until you and your disciples have passed through so that it should not close; for after you have all gone through the opening will close again. After that, go forward until you reach Mount Seir.

"At that very time we shall fling Samael from his place, and he will already be entrusted into your hand. And then let the holy Name be prepared, written, and engraved by you on a plate of lead. Likewise prepare another plate on which you shall engrave the Name which is derived from the verse in Zechariah (5:8), 'And he said, This is Wickedness. And he cast her down into the midst of the measure and he cast the weight of lead over its mouth.' After this, you may go wherever you desire in Mount Seir; and there you will find the wicked Samael and Lilith his mate in the form of two black dogs, a male and a female. On the male set the plate with the holy Name and on the female set the other plate and put a rope around their necks at once to which the plates are attached; and they will follow you together with all their band. Then the Lord's desire will already have been achieved by you and you will bring Samael to Judgment upon Mount Seir, which you have already passed. There a great shofar will be blown and Messiah will appear and will purify the earth from the spirit of pollution. The Holy and Blessed One will slaughter that spirit in the presence of the righteous and there shall be a full Redemption. But be very cautious with the said intentions. Also take exceedingly great care, for when Samael and his mate are in your hands they will cry and appeal to you to give them something to eat or drink or any food to maintain their bodies. Pay no attention to them and do not give them anything. May the Lord be in your guide and guard your feet from snares!" And with that the two holy angels ascended to heaven in a tempest.

After the angels had ascended, Rabbi Joseph and his disciples rose and started toward Mount Seir. Bands of black dogs came toward them, but at once they uttered the Name which they had been commanded, and the dogs scattered and disappeared. After this, they encountered a great mountain of snow, and immediately they strengthened themselves with the aforementioned Names and combinations, and the mountain shifted from its place. And with the other aforesaid combination it vanished entirely. They went on two more days, and on the third day they saw before them a huge and spacious ocean. As soon as they mentioned the proper Names, they passed through it dryshod.

At noon they reached the iron wall. Rabbi Joseph took the knife on which he had written the prescribed Name, and he made an opening with it. They held the opening, but as they passed the last of the disciples was slow and the opening slipped away from Rabbi Joseph's hand and closed on the disciple's foot, so that it was caught. At once Rabbi Joseph took out the knife and cut the iron away round the disciple's foot, and he passed through. They climbed Mount Seir to its summit.

There they found a crater within which were several ruins, from where they heard dogs barking. They entered one of the ruins where they found two great black cowering dogs, a male and a female. When they approached, the dogs leaped at them to rend them. But Rabbi Joseph had the plates in his hand. Sensing at once that these dogs were Samael and Lilith, he stretched out his right hand and set one plate upon the neck of the male dog and with the left hand set the other on the neck of the female. His disciples had the ropes ready in their hands and tied them up with the plates upon them.

As soon as they realized what had befallen them, they put off the shapes of dogs and put on their own shapes like that of humankind, except that they had wings that were full of eyes, like flames. They entreated and begged Rabbi Joseph to give them food and water, but Rabbi Joseph refused as he had been commanded.

Then Rabbi Joseph and his disciples set out on their way, rejoicing and of good cheer with bright faces, while Samael and Lilith and all their hosts went weeping. Rabbi Joseph rejoiced and his mind was at ease, and he said: "Who could have believed our story? Upon this day the heavens will be joyful and the earth rejoice." Then Samael responded: "Indeed, we are all in your hands, for you to do whatever you desire, but let some little thing be given to us to maintain our spirits, otherwise how can we exist till we come there." But Rabbi Joseph answered: "I shall give you nothing!"

When they approached Mount Seir, Rabbi Joseph took a pinch of frankincense and smelled it. Samael said: "If you do not give me any food, let me at least sniff at a little of this frankincense of yours!"

Then Rabbi Joseph stretched out his hand and gave him a few grains of the frankincense he had; and Samael blew a spark of fire from his mouth and burned the incense while Rabbi Joseph was still holding it.

The vapor entered Samael's nostrils, and he snapped the bonds and ropes and flung the leaden plates from him, and he and his hosts began striking at the disciples. Two of them died at once upon hearing the mighty roar of Samael and his hosts, while two others were stricken and went out of their minds.

Rabbi Joseph remained alone with a single disciple, weary and exhausted and astonished. For he did not know that he had risked his soul when he gave the incense to the demon who turned it to vapor, and thus unwittingly was engaged in idolatry, thereby bringing all the holy forces in the leaden plates to naught.

At that very moment the whole mountain began to smoke amid gloom and darkness and a voice was heard, saying: "Woe unto you, Joseph and woe to your soul, because you did not observe what you were commanded but engaged in idolatry and offered incense to Samael, for now he will pursue you to drive you out of this world and the next!"

The single disciple remained together with Rabbi Joseph, weary and exhausted and weak, reaching the very gates of death. They stayed there under a tree and rested. Then they buried the two disciples. But demons had obsessed the other two who fled and finally came to the city of Safed, where they soon perished of the pains which the demons inflicted upon them.

After these events, Rabbi Joseph came to the city of Sidon where he settled and turned to evil ways. Since he saw that his intention had not succeeded, and particularly since he had heard the said voice, he gave up all hope of the World to Come, and made a covenant with the malicious Lilith and handed himself over to her so that she became his wife. He polluted himself in every way possible using the holy Names and other Names and conjurations that he knew in order to do evil. Every night he would conjure spirits and demons to fetch him whatever he might desire.

This was his practice for many a day until more than all other women he came to love the wife of the king of Greece; and he had her brought to him almost every night, and in the morning he would give orders to take her back.

One day the queen said to the king: "Every night in my dreams I find myself in a certain place where a certain man sleeps with me, but in the morning I find myself in my bed without knowing how it comes about."

When the king heard this, he summoned the magicians and set them on guard in the queen's house. That night the demons came by order of Rabbi Joseph, but the guardians noticed them at once and performed their works and conjured them in order to know what this was and how it came about. And the demons stated: "We are sent by Rabbi Joseph, who lives in Sidon." Immediately the king sent a certain minister with letters and a gift to the lord of Sidon, asking that Rabbi Joseph should be sent to him alive at once in order that vengeance might be executed on him. When Rabbi Joseph realized that his deeds were known and evil had finally fallen upon him, then even before the letter reached the lord of Sidon he went and threw himself into the sea and died.

As for me, the fifth disciple, I was left alone on a sickbed all my life, and there is no remedy for my ailment, nor do I have any reprieve from the demons. I have written this tale for a memorial.

WALKING WITH THE
SHEKHINAH

THE PALM TREE OF DEVORAH

T
omer *Devorah,* "The Palm Tree of Devorah," is a brief
treatise, written in the middle of the sixteenth century by
the great kabbalist Rabbi Moses Cordovero in Safed, in
the Upper Galilee in the Holy Land. It is one of the
most influential mystical works in the history of Jewish
mysticism. The treatise is dedicated to presenting the
reader with a coherent *via mystica,* the way to follow in
order to adhere to the divine realm, by a series of
detailed instructions based on the concept of *imitatio
dei,* which was at the time a new concept to be
employed in Jewish ethical works. This treatise represents the beginning of a vast mystical literary phenomenon—the emergence of kabbalistic ethical literature in
Safed, in which the kabbalah broke away from its segre-
gation in closed circles of esoterics and mystics, and
became the dominant theological worldview and main
source of religious direction to Judaism as a whole for
several centuries. Hasidic literature in the eighteenth
and nineteenth centuries followed the main norms of the
Safed ethical-mystical teachings, as well as other modern Jewish movements (most notably the *musar* movement of the anti-Hasidic *mitnagdim* in eastern Europe
in the nineteenth century).

Rabbi Moses Cordovero (1522–75) is one of the
greatest kabbalists of all times.[1] His family came from
Spain, as his name indicates, and there can be found in
his work references to the devastating experience of the
expulsion of the Jews from that country. He viewed himself as a loyal follower of the teachings of the *Zohar* and
the Spanish kabbalah, and regarded his writings as com-

mentaries on that classical, normative source of Jewish mystical speculation. His most extensive work is indeed a detailed commentary on the *Zohar*—the voluminous *Or Yakar* ("Precious Light"), which because of its vast dimensions remained in manuscript and was printed only in the last decades in a score of large volumes. His best-known work is the two-volume Pardes *Rimonim* ("An Orchard of Pomegranates"), which is a systematic presentation, in the form of a theosophical doctrine, of the teachings of the *Zohar*. It is a coherent, profound presentation of the kabbalah as a whole as Cordovero viewed it, including numerous new ideas and concepts formulated by Cordovero or derived from other kabbalistic works that he collected and studied. This work can be viewed as both the great systematic summary of Spanish kabbalah and the beginning of the new, modern kabbalah that took shape in Safed in the sixteenth century. Cordovero was in close touch with kabbalists in other countries, especially Italy, and his writings spread quickly and influenced generations of kabbalists throughout the Jewish world, in the East and in the West. His other works include commentaries on the prayers and monographs on many of the major subjects of the kabbalah.

Tomer Devorah differs from most of Cordovero's other works in its dimensions—a brief, succinct treatise—and in its immediate instructive, rather than discursive, character. In ten short chapters Cordovero presents detailed directions on how to mold a person's life to resemble, and be harmonized with, the structure of the divine world. The main concept, according to which the work is structured, is that a person should imitate in the various aspects of his life the characteristics of the ten divine emanations, the *sefirot*. By performing deeds and acquiring spiritual qualities that are in harmony with each of them, a person causes the divine flow of spiritual force from each divine power to vitalize his soul and create a link between himself and that particular *sefirah*. Thus, for instance, the performance of *teshuvah*—repentance—connects a person to the divine entity called by that name, which is the third *sefirah*, *binah*, which gives him the power to renew himself, to return spiritually to the infinite divine goodness and emerge from there purged of all sin and all the evil in him transformed into goodness.[2] The performance of charity connects a person to the fourth *sefirah*, *hesed*, and so on, concerning all aspects of the divine world. In this way Cordovero transformed the abstract, mystical speculations of previous kabbalists concerning the nature of each divine aspect into a way of life, dedicated to the imitation of the qualities of the divine powers in daily life. He thus gave the traditional Jewish norms of behavior—legal and ethical—a dynamic mystical significance, which can be drawn from the divine realm and engulf the human soul.

Tomer Devorah begins with two chapters dedicated to the imitation of the first and highest divine power, *keter* (Crown), and the chapters then continue in a descending order, to the last one, the *Shekhinah*, the tenth divine manifestation that represents the feminine aspect of the Godhead. It is evident in some of the chapters—though not in all of them—that the descending order of the divine powers represents also a descending order of types of human beings that the author is addressing. Thus, the adherence to the second *sefirah*, *hochmah* (wisdom), to which the third chapter is dedicated, is achieved by the teaching of the Torah and the leadership of the people, obviously directed to the intellectual elite of the community and not to everybody. The chapter describing the imitation of the last *sefirah*, the *Shekhinah*, presented here, seems to be directed to simple people, to everybody, and does not demand any particular status or religious achievement. The instructions presented in this chapter are the matters that everybody should do and that all can do. This is indeed a new concept in the history of the kabbalah: a clear statement, by one of the greatest kabbalistic authorities, that every individual can achieve communion with the *Shekhinah* by continuing to live the ordinary schedule of his daily life. The requirements presented by the author are surprisingly minimal, while the mystical achievement promised is very significant. The images used by Cordovero are radical indeed, suggesting a union with the *Shekhinah* in sexual terms, not to the dedicated mystic whose life is centered around the attempt to achieve proximity to God, but to the simple Jew who leaves his home and travels pursuing his livelihood. When dealing with the other divine powers in the previous chapters the author emphasized the element of imitation, which leads to contact and identification. When describing such a relationship with the *Shekhinah*, an erotic aspect is introduced, and the result of a successful religious endeavor is presented in sexual terms. Some such tendencies were present in earlier kabbalistic works, including the *Zohar* itself. Here, for the first time, it is presented in a short, clear, and exoteric way to every individual, hardly demanding any training in kabbalah or in any kind of unusual religious effort.

The work has been translated into English by Louis Jacobs (Hermon Press: New York, 1974). The editor added a brief commentary, adding some references to the sources employed by Cordovero, especially from the *Zohar*. This chapter is quoted from pp. 114–21.

Chapter IX

How should a man train himself to acquire the quality of Sovereignty (the *Shekhinah*)? First and foremost he should not be proud in his heart because of all that is his, but he should behave constantly like a beggar, standing before his Creator as a poor man begging and offering supplication. Even if he is wealthy he can train himself to behave in this way by considering that none of his possessions are attached to him and that he is forsaken requiring the mercies of Heaven at all times, for all he has is the bread he eats, and he should humble his heart and afflict himself. Especially at the time of prayer, for this is a wonderful aid. Of the opposite it is said: "and thou forget . . . . Then thy heart be lifted up, and thou forget (Deut. 8:14), for the forgetting belonging to the Outside Ones is found there. David behaved in this way to a great extent when he said: "For I am solitary and afflicted" (Ps. 25:16). For all the people of his household have themselves to consider. What are they all to him? What can even his wife and children do for him when he is judged before the Creator or when his soul departs? Can they accompany him beyond the grave? Of what use are they to him from the entrance of the grave and onwards? He should therefore humble himself and perfect himself according to the secret of this quality.

A second method is explained in the *Zohar* and it is very important. He should exile himself from place to place for the sake of Heaven and in this way he will become a chariot to the Exiled Shekhinah. He should imagine: "Behold I have gone into exile but, behold, my utensils go with me. What shall be with the honour of the Most High seeing that the Shekhinali is in exile without Her utensils which are lacking as a result of the Exile?" Because of this he should be satisfied with as little as possible, as it is written: "Prepare thee stuff for exile" (Ez. 12:3), and he should humble his heart in exile and bind himself to the

Torah and then the Shekhinah will be with him. And he should carry out expulsions,[3] by divorcing himself from his house of rest constantly, after the fashion of R. Simeon and his company who divorced themselves to study the Torah. And how much better if he bruises his feet wandering from place to place without horse and chariot. Concerning him it is said: *"His hope (sibhro) is with the Lord his God,"* (Ps. 146:5), which they explained from the expression *shebher* ("to break"), for he breaks his body in the service of the Most High.

A further most excellent quality of Sovereignty from the gate of divine service as a whole is to fear the Lord, the honoured and the awful. Now, behold, fear is very dangerous in the making of a flaw and to allow the Outside Ones to enter, for if he is afraid of sufferings or death or Hell, behold, this is the fear of the Outside Ones; for all these things are from the Outside Ones. However, the main fear is to fear the Lord, which is achieved by considering three things: The first is that the greatness of the Creator is above all existing things. Now, man is afraid of the lion, the bear, the robber, fire and falling masonry, yet these are but puny deputies. Why then should he not fear the Great King? And his fear should be constantly on his face because of His greatness. And he should say: "How dare despicable man sin before such a great Lord?" Behold, if it were a lion it would eat him, but merely because the Holy One, Blessed is He, is patient is this a reason for not fearing Him? Secondly, he should consider the constancy of Providence, that He looks at him and gazes upon him. Now, a slave is afraid in the presence of his master and man is always in the Creator's Presence Whose eyes are open to all his ways. He should be afraid and terrified to nullify his commands. Thirdly, He is the root of all souls, all of which are rooted in His Sephiroth. And since sin makes a flaw in His Palace how should he not be afraid to soil, with his evil deeds, the King's Palace? Fourthly, he should observe that the flaw in his deeds pushes away the Shekhinah from above. He should fear to cause this great evil of separating the love of the King from the Queen. This kind of fear is that which puts man on the right path for the perfection of this quality and by means of it he cleaves to it.

Furthermore, a man must be very careful to behave so that the Shekhinah cleaves always to him and never departs. Now, it is obvious that the Shekhinah cannot be with a bachelor for the Shekhinah is mainly from the female. Man stands between the two females, the physical female below who receives food, raiment and conjugal rights from him, and the Shekhinah who stands above him to bless him with these which he, in turn, gives to the wife of his covenant.[4] This is after the pattern of Beauty, which stands between the two Females: the Higher Mother, which pours out all that it requires, and the Lower Mother, which receives from it food, raiment and conjugal rights,[5] namely, lovingkindness, justice and pity, as is known. And the Shekhinah cannot come to him unless he resembles the Supernal Reality.

Now, a man separates himself from his wife at times for one of three reasons: (1) when she is in her period of separation, (2) when he studies the Torah and lives apart from her during the week-days, (3) when he journeys from home and keeps himself from sin. During these times the Shekhinah cleaves to him and is bound to him and does not leave him so that he be not forsaken and separate but always the perfect man, male and female.[6] Because, then, that the Shekhinah unites with him a man should take care that She does not depart from him while he is travelling. He should be industrious and profit by reciting the traveller's prayer and by holding fast to the Torah, for by virtue of this the Shekhinah, which guards the way, stands by him always when he takes care not to sin and to study the Torah. So, too, when his wife is in her period of separation the Shekhinah stays with him if he keeps the laws of separation properly. Afterwards, on the night of her purification or on the night of the Sabbath or on his homecoming from the journey each one of these is a time of dutiful cohabitation. The Shekhinah is constantly open above to receive holy souls so it is likewise fitting that he have congress with his wife and by virtue of this the Shekhinah will always be with him. So it is explained in the *Zohar* to the first section of Genesis.

Congress with his wife should only take place when the Shekhinah is in Her place, that is between the Two Arms. During a public disaster, however, when the Shekhinah is not between the Two Arms, it is forbidden, and so it is stated in the Tikkunim to Genesis.[7]

He who wants to be united with the King's Daughter, that She never depart from him, must first adorn himself with all the adornments and fine garments, and these are all the Tikkunim of the qualities mentioned. After he has so adorned himself he should intend to receive Her while studying the Torah and bearing the yoke of the precepts, according to the secret of the perpetual union. Immediately then She becomes married to him and never more departs from him. But this is conditional on his purity and sanctification and when he is then so pure and holy he can intend to fulfill for Her the duty of providing Her with food, raiment and conjugal rights which are the three things a man is obliged to do for his earthly wife.

The first is to provide Her from the Right with the flow that is Her food by virtue of his deeds. The second is to cover Her from Power so that the Outside Ones have no dominion over Her, namely, that there be no trace of the evil inclination in the carrying out of the precepts, not for the benefit of the body nor for the hope of illusionary honour, for instance; for then the evil inclination is present in that Precept and She flees from it, for it is shame. Therefore he should cover the shame and hide Her ever that it have no dominion over Her. How should he do this? By doing all his actions for the sake of Heaven and without any trace of the evil inclination. *Tephillin*[8] and *Tzitzith*[9] are also powerful in shielding Her that the Outside Ones have no dominion over Her and he should be accustomed to wear them. Thirdly, to make union with Beauty during the time of reading the *Shema* and by setting aside periods for the study of the Torah. And when he sets aside a period for any purpose he should intend that this is the time of the Shekhinah, the King's Daughter. And there is a hint of this in the Tikkunim.

18 THE MESSIANIC DREAMS OF RABBI HAYYIM VITAL

"The Book of Visions" (*Sefer ha-Hezyonot*) is a unique document in the history of Jewish mysticism. It is an intimate, candid personal diary, covering more than forty years, of one of the most prominent authors of kabbalistic works, Rabbi Hayyim Vital Klipers, the greatest disciple of Rabbi Isaak Luria Ashkenazi (the "Ari"), who revolutionized the kabbalistic worldview in Safed in the last quarter of the sixteenth century. Rabbi Hayyim Vital was among the young prominent kabbalists in Safed before the arrival of Rabbi Isaak Luria in that remote town in the Upper Galilee, and he started writing the diary before his meeting with Luria in 1570, and continued to do so after his teacher's untimely death in 1572. Vital himself lived till 1620, the last decades in Damascus.

Vital's prominent place in the history of the kabbalah rests on his voluminous works presenting the teachings of Luria, especially the *Etz Hayyim* ("Tree of Life") and the *Sefer ha-Shearim* ("The Book of Gates," a series of monographs on the main subjects of the kabbalah), which became the classic texts of the kabbalah after the *Zohar* and were regarded—and still are—as the "last word" of kabbalistic tradition. The *Sefer ha-Hezyonot*, however, was not known in its original form. A selection from it was published under the title *Shivhey ha-Rahu* ("In Praise of Rabbi Hayyim Vital," corresponding to the better-known *Shivhey ha-Ari*, "In Praise of Rabbi Isaak Luria"), and was regarded as hagiographical work. The complete work was published by A. Z. Eshkoly in Jerusalem 1954, by the orthodox publishing house Rav Kook Institute, which never republished it.

Eshkoly died before completing the project, and the book was published without an introduction and very few notes. It seems that Eshkoly believed that the one manuscript of the work that he had was the author's authograph.

From its beginning, when Vital was hardly out of his teens, to its last entries, which were written by the old, prominent, and highly respected scholar, the book has one aim, to which every single entry is dedicated: to prove that Rabbi Hayyim Vital, the author, is the Messiah son of David, and that his revelation as the redeemer and the king of Israel is imminent. The work is divided into four parts, each of which includes one aspect of the assembled proofs of Vital's destiny. The first is autobiographical, presenting events in his life that demonstrate his messianic mission. The second is a recounting of dreams he had, every one of them including in its core a mystical-messianic experience. The third describes incidents, dreams, and prophecies that other people had that prove his destiny. The fourth part, the most extensive and detailed, comprising half of the book, includes information given to Vital by Rabbi Isaak Luria, which recounts the history of Vital's soul from Adam to the present, as the history of the soul of the Messiah.

Luria and Vital developed the concept of reincarnation of the soul in a manner unparalleled in the history of Jewish thought. The idea was rejected by Jewish scholars until the late twelfth century, when it appeared in a prominent place in the first work of the kabbalah, *The Book Bahir*. From then on kabbalists made use of it, but it was not incorporated in the core of the kabbalah; it plays a part in numerous kabbalistic works, while many other kabbalists ignored or marginalized it. An anonymous kabbalistic treatise written in the sixteenth century, *Galya Raza* ("The Revelation of Secrets") is one of the few examples of this concept being central in a Jewish worldview. Rabbi Hayyim Vital, however, wrote two detailed and extensive monographs on the subject (*Sefer ha-Gilgulim* and *Shaar ha-Gilgulim*), following the teachings of Luria, and made the subject central for Lurianic kabbalah. After this peak, the interest in this concept declined among kabbalists and its use in modern writings, including modern Hasidic teachers, is sporadic and inconsistent.

Reincarnation, or the metempsychosis, was integrated in the Lurianic teachings concerning the nature of the human soul. Following traditional psychological concepts, Vital discerned in the soul five parts, which correspond to the five main aspects of the divine world: *nefesh, ruah, neshama, haya, yehida.* The last two—representing the most elevated and hidden divine realms, appear only in the souls of few, selected pneumatics in every generation. Each of these parts can be incarnated in a body independently of the other parts of the original whole. Thus the souls that were emanated from God in the beginning of the world are scattered and spread in each generation. They will be reassembled and united only in the time of the redemption.

The original soul of the Messiah first appeared in the body of Cain, the first murderer, Adam's first son. Supreme evil and supreme good are thus united in it. The separate parts of this illustrious soul appeared in the bodies of prominent people throughout history (one meaningful assemblage of these parts was represented by Rabbi Akibah, the second-century sage). They have been collected now in Rabbi Hayyim Vital, and Luria revealed to him the details of their transition from body to body throughout history. According to the fourth part of *Sefer ha-Hezyonot,* Luria had no doubt that Vital's soul is the prefect messianic restructuring of the original soul, and that it will be he who will redeem Israel and the whole world.

It is interesting to note that besides keeping this diary, Vital never acted as a messiah and never published his pretensions. He did not use the great truths that he received from Luria to establish a position of leadership outside the closed circle of Luria's disciples.[1] He even prevented his own writings from being copied and published, and legend has it that his manuscripts were stolen from his house when he was ill and copied without his permission. He behaved throughout his life as the unambitious, humble disciple of Luria, dedicating himself to the formulation in writing of his teacher's doctrines, never seeking anything for himself, and keeping the revolutionary ideas secret and hidden.

This attitude can be understood on the background of the Lurianic theory of messianism. The Messiah, according to Luria, is the result of the process of redemption rather than its cause. The spiritual process that enhances the redemption is performed by every Jew in every ethical and ritualistic deed of his; everybody contributes to this process in every moment of his life, and the Messiah will appear when the process has reached its end, all the elements of evil have been vanquished, and all the elements of divine goodness restored to their original rightful place. Then, and only then, the Messiah will be known and assume the government of the people. The Messiah does not bring the redemption; he is its crown. Thus, Vital did not have to do anything to fulfill his messianic role. He had to contribute to the spiritual struggle like every other person, until the culmination of the process; then his unique mission will be recognized.

1. Year 1570

Friday night, 13th of the month of Av. I dreamt that it was the festival of New Year or that of Shavuot. I was sitting with my father and my mother and my relatives, eating at the table. Suddenly [I observed] in a window which is not open to the outside[2] which was in the southern wall, in the window there was an egg of a snake, and one side of the egg began to crack. I took it and threw it to the earth and it broke completely. Two big snakes emerged from it, a male and a female, and they were clinging to each other and enmeshed in each other like in a sexual intercourse between male and female. I took a stone, which was white like snow, and threw it at the head of one of the snakes, and it severed its head; yet the head remained enmeshed with the second snake. Then the severed head jumped and ran out of that house. I went out to look for it. I then saw a tent, made of very white cloth. I went inside the tent to look whether the head of the snake entered it, but did not find it. I said to myself: I am not worried about it, for there is no doubt that it will not live after evening comes, and when the sun goes down it will die completely.

Then I raised my eyes, and saw written on the cloth above, these words, some of it in Aramaic and the end in the holy language (Hebrew), and this is what it said: "Anyone who overcomes and breaks the power of evil[3] and anyone who pursues the sinners in order to remove from them the dirt [of sin and evil] and to bind the powers of evil I shall put his chair above that of my servant Metatron."[4]

It seemed to me then [in the dream] that the text is actually a verse from Solomon's book of Proverbs. I said then: If so, if such a great reward is promised to the person who will overcome the power of evil, I shall go and kill the second snake as well, after having killed the first one. Then I woke up. It was in the early morning.[5]

2. Year 1607

12th of the month of Kislev. The night of Tuesday, whose planet is Mars and whose angel is Samael, and it was on the week of the torah portion of Vayishlach, in which the battle between Jacob and Samael is found,[6] as well as the matter of the chieftains of Esau.[7] As our Rabbis of blessed memory said: The chieftain of Magdiel—this is Rome. The portion from the prophets at that week is the vision of Ovadia.[8]

I saw in my dream a big and very high mountain, which is the rock of halamish. It was hewed and cut squarely from each of its four sides, like for walls of one square fortification. I ascended on the eastern wall, from the south-eastern side, and asked: Which city is this? And I was told: This is Ninveh. Then they were telling me: This is the evil Rome.

The writer, Hayyim, says: Remember that this [statement] can be found in the manuscript of the Book of Zerubavel.[9]

I then observed that from the inside, on the eastern wall, there was a lance stuck in the wall, a very long one, and it was protruding towards the houses of the city, and it was situated in the middle of the height of the wall. And there was a sword, up-side-down, its edge down, stuck in the lance. And its handle was high above at the top of the wall, for the length of the sword was that of half the height of the wall. And I was told: This sword is stuck in this lance since the day the world was created until now, and no person has ever touched it. I looked at it and saw that it was a strong one—nothing like it—which can cut all sorts of iron as if it was dry weed. It had four edges on its four sides. At the top of the sword, at its tip, there was like the mouth of a snake, and they said that anyone who is touched by this sword is doomed.

I thought in my heart: It is such a long time—from the creation of the world till now—maybe rust has crept on the sword. I looked at it, and saw that it was completely new. I took it in my hand. The emperor of Rome was then told: That sword, that no man has ever touched, is now in the hand of a Jew. The king then ordered to look for me and to kill me. When I was still up there on the wall, I threw the sword from my hand into the city and its tip was inserted in the ground in one of the city's courts. I then ran away and hid in a cave there in Rome in which poor people dwelt, and I hid there until the time of the noon prayer on Saturday. Then I came out, and the emperor's servants found me and brought me to him.

He then ordered: remove everyone from here, and he and I remained alone. I said to him: Why are you looking for me, to kill me? All of you go the wrong way in your religion, like blind people, for the only true torah is the torah of Moses and there is nothing that is true beside it. He said to me: Now, because I know all this, I have sent to find you, because I knew that there is no one who is as wise and knowledgeable as you are in the true wisdom. I wish that you will instruct me in the secrets of the torah and some of the names of God, blessed be He, your God, because I have already realized the truth. Therefore do not be afraid that I have sent people to pursue you, because I truly love you.

I then related to him some of this wisdom, and woke up.

3. Year 1566

Sabbath eve, 8 Tevet. I said the kiddush and sat to the table to eat, and my eyes were shedding tears, moaning and saddened because on the tenth day of the month of Heshvan I married my wife Hanna, and I fell victim to sorcery and became impotent. I said to God, blessed be His name: I brought her back by a dream-question, how did I get into such a great misfortune? Especially as this causes the sin of night emission in vain when I check myself with her. I also cried because of the neglect of the study of the torah during these two years, as it is written in my notes concerning the matters of my soul, section two. Because of these worries I did not eat at all, and I lied in my bed on my face, crying, until I fell aspleep exhausted by weeping. And I dreamed a wonderful dream:

I saw myself sitting in the home of the Rabbi Shem Tov ha-Levi of blessed memory, praying the afternoon prayer which is called "a time of good will" on the Sabbath. After the prayer I saw standing in front of me an old man, who looked like the Rabbi Hayyim ha-Levi of blessed memory who was my neighbor. He called me by name and said to me: You, Rabbi Hayyim, would you like to come out with me now to the field to accompany the queen, the Sabbath, as it goes out, in the same way that you are used to welcome her when she enters; and I shall show you some great things. I said to him: Here I am, let us go. We went to the wall of the old tower in Safed, on the west, across from the inn, in the place that there was an opening in the wall.

I saw there a tall mountain, its top in the sky. He said to me: Ascend with me to the mountain and be there, and I shall tell you the words I was sent to deliver to you. Instantly I saw him standing at the top of mountain, while I was sitting at the bottom, because I could not ascend at all, for it was straight like a wall and not sloping like other mountains. I said to him: I an astonished, for I am a young man and could not ascend at all, while you are old and you ascended instantly. He said to me: You, Hayyim, don't you know that every day I ascend and descend this mountain a thousand times to perform the missions I am given by God, why are you surprised by what I do? I noticed in the beginning he called me "Rabbi Hayyim" and now just "Hayyim" without "Rabbi," and also when I heard his terrifying words, I realized that he was Elijah of blessed memory, from the tribe of Levi, undoubtedly. My eyes then became full of tears and I was terrified.

I beseached him, weeping, and said: Please care for my soul and bring me up with you. He said to me: Do not be afraid, for this is the purpose of my mission to you. He held my arm, and elevated me instantly to the top of the mountain with him. I then saw a ladder reaching the earth at the top of the mountain and its head reaching the heaven. There were only three stages in the ladder, and between each stage it was like the height of a man. He said to me: I was given permission to assist you reach this point but no farther, from here on you have to decide what you should do. He went and disappeared from my eyes, while I was crying, in great trouble.

Then there was an imposing woman, beautiful like the sun, standing at the top of the ladder. I thought in my heart that it was my mother. She said: What are you doing here, Hayyim, crying? I heard your crying and came to assist you. She extended her right hand and brought me up to the top of the ladder. I saw there a large, round window, and great flame of fire coming out of it, to and fro, like lightening,[10] with great force, burning everything that was there. I realized in my heart that this was the fire of the revolving sword,[11] in the gate of paradise. I cried bitterly to that woman and told her: Mother, mother, help me so that the burning sword will not consume me. She said: Nobody can help you escape this fire but you yourself. I shall give you advice what to do. Put your hand on your head and you shall find there wool, white like snow, take it and put it in the burning window and it will close, and you can quickly pass.

It seems to me that the wool on my head was the result of the turning of my black hair—black is judgment—to white, by the power of my merits, as attested by the verse: *and the hair of whose head was like the pure wool* (Dan. 7:9). I did [what she said], and passed quickly, and immediately the heat again emerged from there as it was in the beginning. Then the woman vanished from before me.

Elijah then appeared again, like the first time, and took hold of my right hand and said to me: Come with me to the place that I was sent originally to bring you there. He brought me to a courtyard, huge without measure. In it there were rivers, in which living waters were flowing to water that garden. On the banks of the rivers, on both sides, there were trees bearing fruit, looking very enticing, full and fresh immeasurably. Most of them were apple-trees, spreading wonderful smell like the best perfumes. The trees were very tall, and the tips of the branches which emerged from the trunk of the trees were turned down until they were close to the ground, and created the likeness of a hut (*sukkah*). There were in that garden numerous birds, in the image of white geese, walking in the garden, its length and width, reciting portions of the mishnah, the tractat of Shabbat, for this was the evening of the Shabbat, as I said above, in the beginning of the dream. As they were walking they would read one section or one chapter, then raise their necks and eat apples from the tree itself (= directly), and then would drink water from the rivers. This they do constantly. I immediately understood that they were the souls of the righteous, the authors of the mishnah, but I did not understand why they were in the form of geese and birds and not in the form of people.

I was led then further into the garden, until I saw in the garden a structure like a tower, large and tall, as if it were situated on a high hill, but there was no other house below it. It was above the ground in the height of a man's height, and its entrance was on the west side, and a ladder of three stages of stone leading from the ground to the entrance to the tower. Elijah then disappeared from my eyes, and I ascended the ladder alone and entered the door of the tower. I saw there God, blessed be He, sitting on the chair near the southern wall, in the middle, in the image of a very ancient,[12] His beard white as snow, beautiful beyond anything, and the righteous sitting there on the ground before him on new carpets and sheets, learning torah from Him. I knew in my soul that these are the righteous ones who are called *bney aliya*[13] and they have the image of people, they always envision the face of the shekhinah and always study the torah from His mouth directly. Theirs is a different station from that of the masters of the mishnah, for they are in the form of birds and geese, about whom it is said: He who sees a goose in his dream should expect wisdom.[14] They stand in the court and in the garden and do not accept the face of the shekhinah constantly, as do the *bney aliya*, and do not study the torah directly from Him.

When I entered [the tower] and saw His face I was shaken and began to tremble, I fell to the ground on my face between His feet and lost all my strength. He extended His hand and took hold of my right hand and said to me: Hayyim, my son, stand up, why do you fall on your face? You should not be frightened. I said to Him: My Lord, I lost all my strength, and . . . because of your numinous grandeur, and I have no power to stand up. He said to me: I am giving you now strength and courage, stand up and sit down on my right side, here, in this vacant place, in which nobody is sitting, as near to me as possible. I told him: How can I sit on your right side in this place, which has been prepared for Rabbi Joseph Karo to sit in? He answered: This is what I intended originally, but later I gave him another place and I gave you this place and has already prepared it for you. I said to him: This place belongs to [the prophet] Samuel of Ramah of blessed memory. He said to me: It is true, this is his place, but when the Temple was destroyed he took it upon himself not to sit in this place until the Temple is built in the future (= the redemption). Since then he went to Jerusalem, to the ruins of the Temple, and he stands there and mourns constantly, until the End of Days when it will be built. This is why his place remained vacant, and I hereby give it to you to sit in. I then set on His right, immediately beside Him, on the carpets on the floor, like the other righteous ones who were there.

He said to me: Do you like this place? I answered Him: Who can tell the greatness and honor of this elevated place? . . . [15] I repeated and said to Him: My Lord, may my soul be precious to you, leave me in this place and do not let me return to the lower world. It is well-known to you that I intend to obey your will and I am afraid that the evil inclination[16] will cause me to sin and I shall loose this holy place. He said to me: You are still young, you have time to study the torah and perform the commandments, and you must go back and bring your soul to perfection, and when your days [of life] come to an end you shall come to this place. And if you are afraid to go down because of the danger of sinning, swear to me by your right hand that you shall never neglect the study of the torah because of anything else whatsoever, and I shall also swear to you that if you do so I shall not change your place or give this place to somebody else under no circumstances, and this will be your place, on my right, for ever. I then raised my hand and swore to perform all that was mentioned, and He also swore to me to carry out all that He had said. He said to me: Go in peace, and remember and never forget all these things. I then descended from there, from that elevated tower, alone, and found myself standing in this lowly world in the dream itself, and did not see any more what I have seen when I ascended in the beginning.

19 A PROPHETIC VISION BY NATHAN OF GAZA

During the twenty-five centuries that have passed since the "end of prophecy," a process that declared Malachi to be the "last prophet," Jewish religious culture included numerous visionaries and mystics, redeemers of various kinds, people who envisioned the future and spiritualists of every possible character. Yet between Malachi and the present there was only one person who was widely recognized as a prophet: Nathan ben Elisha Ashkenazi of Gaza (1644–80), the prophet of Shabbatai Zevi (1626–76), who in 1665–66 confirmed and popularized the messianic message of the Messiah from Smyrna. There were a few people who claimed to be prophets, and the term was used from time to time to praise religious leaders. Nathan of Gaza, however, is the only visionary and mystic who was accepted as a prophet by a vast Jewish messianic movement, and his message shaped Jewish history in the late seventeenth century and during the eighteenth. The following text, one of the most influential texts published by Nathan, is the only one in the collection presented in this volume that had immediate historical impact and influenced the events of that period.

When Shabbatai Zevi began to present his claim as a messiah in public in the middle of the seventeenth century, he was not taken seriously: There was nothing unusual in the phenomenon of a kabbalist claiming to have a personal redemptive mission. This happened frequently among Jewish spiritualists, and such cases increased considerably in number since the expulsion of the Jews from Spain in 1492 and the intensification of messianic expectations that followed that upheaval. Neither Shabbatai Zevi nor any of the others who presented such a claim in that period succeeded in creating a substantial following, and starting a sizable messianic movement. The Sabbatian movement began in 1665, when Nathan of Gaza, just twenty-two years old, joined Shabbatai Zevi and confirmed him as the Messiah who was going to redeem the people of Israel in the next few months.[1] It is possible to say that Jewish society was immune to messianic claims by mystics, but it had no immunity concerning a claim of prophetic power. One of the reasons was the belief, expressed in the talmudic tradition, that there is no possibility of prophecy outside the Land of Israel.[2] Nathan presented the one and only such claim when residing in a place that was regarded at that time to be a part of the ancient homeland. The fact that Shabbatai Zevi had been going from town to town declaring his messianic vision made no impact; the fact that a prophet has arisen in Gaza and declared that the messianic era has arrived excited Jewish communities wherever they were. The movement engulfed, in a few months, Jews in the Netherlands and Poland, Italy and Egypt, with very few feeble opposing voices. As Gershom Scholem summarized the phenomenon: "The great messianic awakening began on the seventeenth of Sivan [June 1665]. A prophet as well as a king had arisen in Israel, but the people accepted their king only because the prophet had confirmed his kingship."[3]

The following text is not a direct experience or prophecy; it is a pseudepigraphic document, written by Nathan but attributed to a sage who lived four hundred years before him. It is one of a series of Sabbatian pseudepigraphic literature, some of them written by Nathan, many by other believers. It is an apocalypse, which includes the detailed identification of the future redeemer as Shabbatai Zevi. It is attributed to a Rabbi Abraham, who is described as an ascetic visionary who lived in Germany in the beginning of the thirteenth century. The details of the vision bear the influence of previous messianic literature, including the narrative of Joseph Della Reina (ch. 16), and the apocalyptic visions of the martyr Shlomo Molcho (executed in 1533). Even though Nathan was accepted as a prophet, he preferred to present his vision and his message in a pseudepigraphic structure, to which he added his own confirmation. As Scholem has noted, the traditional historical characteristics of Jewish apocalyptic literature have been transformed in this and similar visions into kabbalistic ones, emphasizing the struggle against monstrous celestial evil powers rather than earthly ones.

And I, Abraham, after having been shut up for forty years grieving over the power of the great dragon that lieth in the midst of his rivers, [wondering] how long it shall be to the end of these wonders [cf. Dan. 12:6], when behold the voice of my beloved knocketh [saying], "behold a son will be born to Mordecai Sevi in the year 5386 [1626] and he will be called Sabbatai Sevi. He will subdue the great dragon, and take away the strength of the piercing serpent and the strength of the crooked serpent, and he will be the true messiah. He will go forth to the war without hands [that is, without weapons], [until the time of the end]. His kingdom will be forevermore and there is no redeemer for Israel besides him. Stand upon thy feet and hear the power of this man, although he be poor and lean. He is my beloved, the apple of my eye and my very heart . . .⁴ and he shall sit on my throne, for the hand [is] the throne of the Lord' [Exod. 17:6].

And I was still wondering at this vision, and behold a man stood before me, his appearance was like that of polished brass from the appearance of his loins even downward, and he had the brightness of fire round about. And from the appearance of his loins even upward like bdelliun and like the body of heaven in its clearness. He called with might: "Loose the knots [of the demonic powers] and make war [against them], and prepare a refuge for there is no provision." And a deep sleep fell on me, and lo, a horror of great darkness in all the land of Egypt. And there came a ferret and a chameleon and brought forth a great light, "the light of the hiding of his power." And behold there was a man, his size was one square cubit, his beard a cubit long and his *membrum virile* a cubit and a span. He held a hammer in his hand and tore up a great mountain of ten times sixscore thousand. And the man went up the mountain, and there was a pit that went down to the bottom of the mountain and he fell in. And he [the man resembling polished brass] said unto me: "Do not grieve [over the fall of the messiah], for thou shalt see the power of this man." But I could no longer restrain my grief, and I fell into a deep sleep and saw no more vision for a month until the awesome man came again and said unto me: "My son, how great is thy strength, since I reveal unto you things that are unknown even unto the angels. And now write the vision and conceal it in an earthen vessel, that it may continue many days. Know that the man of which I have spoken shall strive hard to know the faith of heaven, and Habakkuk prophesied concerning him, 'the just shall live by his faith,' because for a long season Israel will serve 'without the true God,' but he shall restore the crown to its pristine glory. His contemporaries shall rise against him with reproaches and blasphemies—they are the 'mixed multitude' [cf. Exod. 12:38], the sons of Lilith, the 'caul above the liver,' the leaders and rabbis of the generation. He will do wondrous and awesome things, and he will give himself up to martyrdom to perform the will of his Creator.

"Let him be well remembered, the man called Isaac, by whom he will be taught the ways of serving God. From the age of five to six he will make himself like unto an ox bearing the yoke and an ass bearing a burden to serve the Lord. When he is six the Shekhinah, which has revealed herself to us, will appear to him in a dream as a flame, and cause a burn on his private parts. Then dreams shall sorely trouble him, but he shall not tell anybody. And the sons of whoredom will accost him so as to cause him to stumble, and they will smite him but he will not hearken unto them. They are the sons of Na'amah, the scourges of the children of men, who will always pursue him so as to lead him astray."

20 NATHAN OF GAZA FACING THE MONSTERS OF EVIL

THE MYTH OF THE DOENMEH

Thousands of Jews followed Shabbatai Zevi and converted to Islam. It seems that the Messiah himself encouraged this, but there were many among his adherents who refused to take this radical and paradoxical act: leaving one's own religion as a result of devotion to that religion's messiah. Among them was Nathan of Gaza, who remained very close to the converted Shabbatai Zevi, but did not convert. The followers of Shabbatai Zevi established in Turkey a separate Muslim sect, known as the Doenmeh. It underwent several schisms and upheavals, but succeeded in preserving its separate identity to this day. In the present it is threatened by the universal processes of assimilation and westernization, but it has not been persecuted by the Turkish Muslim authorities or populace. It is a remarkable chapter in the history of Judaism—a Jewish sect surviving for more than three centuries within the framework of a rival religion, and remaining loyal to at least some of its traditions. It is most surprising that this intriguing phenomenon did not attract more scholarly attention; we have few studies of some of the works of these Jewish-Muslim-Shabbatians, and almost no historical studies of its development.

Gershom Scholem dedicated to this chapter in the history of Jewish mysticism several studies, and published some of the literary texts that survived, and gave some glimpses of the peculiar religious world of these converts.[1] His point of view was focused, however, in the quest for authentic information about the history of the Sabbatian movement itself. The same texts can be read

217

also as intense spiritual expressions of a desperate, paradoxical devotion to a converted Messiah who died many decades ago, and to his prophet, Nathan of Gaza (died in 1780), who represented for these believers a supreme achievement of proximity to God and the direct experience of the turmoils of the messianic process.

The section of the text translated here is an apocryphal, pseudepigraphic spiritual biography of Nathan of Gaza. It is a part of a collection of documents that reflect the spiritual upheavals among the believers in Shabbatai Zevi who converted to Islam between 1666 and 1683.[2] It is presented as a series of visions and experiences of the prophet. This and similar texts served to create a fictional-mystical history of the events that led to the present situation, in which thousands of crypto-Jews, living within the Muslim society in Turkey, are waiting for the messianic redemption.

The author of this myth combined in his narrative several elements that transform actual history into an individual vision that derives its materials from the Jewish mystical and messianic traditions. Nathan of Gaza is presented here in an image strikingly similar to that of Rabbi Joseph Della Reina in the messianic story presented above in this volume [ch. 16]. Nathan—with whom the author identifies himself—is the leader of a small group of devotees who undertake to fight the core of evil using his unique spiritual power, and achieving a victory—though a temporary one—in subjugating it. Evil is portrayed as a male and female entity, described as a terrifying monster. The hero follows the orders of his master, the Messiah (Shabbatai Zevi), who dies after the failure of this enterprise. Another traditional source is the ancient Jewish apocalypse, The Book of Zerubavel, which described the wars of the messianic era.[3] The evil emperor in that work is called Armilus (i.e., Romulus, the founder of Rome), a name that has been transformed here into the Hebraized form of Armeel.[4] The story of Della Reina attracted the narrator because it is the narrative of a failure and the delay of the redemption; the myth he created explains the failure of Nathan of Gaza and Shabbatai Zevi to bring forth the messianic victory (another part of this text includes the list of commandments that adherents should follow in the current, unredeemed era). As a mystical text, this series of visions represents the internalization of historical experience, transforming it into a spiritual experience that may sustain the believers in their prolonged wait for the fulfillment of their dream.

It happened on the night of the festival of Shavuot, while I and my friends were studying in my home in Gaza, after midnight I heard the voice talking to me from behind the *parochet*: Stand up and go out to the external yard, and there I shall speak to you. My heart was excited and I went out to the yard and I saw there a man wearing a cloth *efod* and he looked like an angel of God, very frightening. He said to me: You know that there is a war being conducted against our king, by the princes[5] of Esau and Ishmael, and the prince of Ishmael has become very strong. You should be strong and brave, do not be afraid, because it is God who is fighting for you. I came from the battleground to inform you and the friends and to assist you. You should inform the whole people that he who does not go to the war following the king and the Matron,[6] shall be executed, and he shall not live to see the flag of the camp of Judah in the end of days. I was terrified when I heard his words and fell on my face and could not speak until the light of the morning. The friends then came to me, and I told them what happened; they marvelled very much about that vision and did not know how to respond. We were engulfed by that grief that day and the sources of wisdom were locked before me, and I did not cry.

That man then spoke to me and said: This is what I have been telling you, this is the subject of the prophecy which has alluded you, for it is forbidden to come to the gate of the king's palace wearing sack. Now shed from your body the clothes of sorrow, and I shall tell you what is hidden. As he was speaking to me my heart was turned and I became like a different person, and I became happy, and we sat down until evening. When the time of the evening (minchah) prayer came, the man said to me: Sanctify yourself and listen to what I am telling you. I heard his voice speaking to me: In the vision which was revealed to you you were informed concerning the coming years.[7] When the sun goes down it will be revealed to him and to those close to him. When those kings you have envisioned will be overcome, he shall be revealed to his people and those who are close to him and support him. This war was caused by the sins of people who opened their mouths to speak against his majesty, our master, and at that time some sparks were captured by the armies of Azael, the prince of Ishmael, and absorbed by him.[8] Because of this, people of good faith started the war to save them and assemble them back, because they are originally people of high station, as you know. Now observe the visions and you shall know the true nature of the events, the numbers of those joining the battle and what will be the sequence of the events and how it shall end in the appropriate time, everything explained clearly in writing, and this will bring you satisfaction. You should read all that you have envisioned to the knowledgeable people who are the close supporters and do not prevent them fron enjoying the good which they deserve. Then the man flew away, and I have not seen him. I was sitting, dumbfounded for an hour and then I turned my mind to understanding all the visions and dreams which I have seen since the spirit was revealed to me, and I wrote everything down, truely, and informed the friends. I sent a copy of this book to Rabbi Shmuel Primo, asing him to inform the friends, and I gave him the book *The Secret of the Messiah* and the book *Nearness of the Messiah*, and there I explained everything in the right way.

All the believers congregated and came to me on the first day of the month of Kislev. I was then apprehended, by the order of the king, in the land of the Chaldeans.[9] They sent for me, and I instructed them to wait for me in the land of Patros (= Salonica), until the day in which I am destined to be revealed to them. Then came the day and I went to the land of Patros, in the house of Rabbi Isaac Hanan, may God protect him, and there were all the believers celebrating together, and I sat with them. On that day there was great joy, and there I saw the visions which I described and interpreted in my book, the book of Raziel.[10]

When we were sitting and discussing this, there was a strong earthquake, and it seemed that the the house was falling upon us. We were dispirited, and all the faithful fell on their faces and asked me: "why did this happen?" I responded: Do not be scared, this misfortune happened because of me, because I came to you before I have accomplished what I had to do in the land of the Chaldeans, and I left that enterprise unfinished. The messengers which I sent to our majesty the king were late, and I said that meanwhile, until they come to you, I shall go and welcome the believers and not leave them alone, and now the messengers have come, and this is the earthquake. Now I am going to execute the order of our master the king.

A wind then carried me and brought me to the land of the Chaldeans, and there were the messengers with a letter from our master the king. The letter said: Peace be on you. I have seen all that you have sent me about the tribes of Zebulun and Naphtali who have ridiculed your words. Do not be discouraged, because that is their custom to ridicule since the time of my forefathers, and recently they are coming back. Be careful not to punish them, because there are some great people among them, people who are knowledgeable in secrets, and the sons of the king are being raised among them. Now go out and assemble all the congregation and tell them everything. Go with them out to the fields, and there is a large cave, and in the opening of the cave there stands the great demonic power Armael, the Prince of Edom.[11] You should arrest him and tie him with these chains brought by the messengers, and he should be bound under your supervision until I inform you what you should do. I hereby appoint you to carry out this endeavor, do not be afraid of him, because he is yielding to the Prince of Ishmael, and it is better to be captured by you then by the Prince of Ishmael. You shall then go with the faithful to Rome, and outside the city you shall find a big abomination, and you shall find there a large stone in the form of a female, as you know.[12] You should then do the yihhudim[13] which I have conveyed to you, and be very careful from her, because there are strong powers supporting her, but they should not frighten you. The power of feminine evil is greater than the power of masculine evil, as you know. You should know that she has seven heads from which she derives her power, and when these heads fall down she will be devastated and frightened and she will yield to you of her own accord, and all her supporting forces will be slain before you. At that time the prophecy of the verse will come true: "Out of Ya'akov shall come a ruler and shall destroy him that remains of the city" (Num. 24:19).[14] When both the male and the female will be captured by you, you shall come to me, head uncovered, and I shall instruct you what to do. Go and do it and be successful, because this is a time of good will in heaven. When I heard that I hastened and called the faithful and they came to me, and we assembled all the people in the land of the Chaldeans and I performed everything that I was ordered to do by his majesty the king.

I and the faithful got up and went to the cave and I found there the demon, and he rose against me with all his supporting powers. I then executed one of the *yihuddim*, and they all capitulated, and I caught their princes, and I bound him in the chains in which the name of the great God was engraved. I then knew that the road was open for me. I then got up with the faithful to complete the enterprise, to go to evil Rome and face the abomination. I sat there in front [of the statue, the female devil] and performed the *yihuddim*, and every time I bowed down [in prayer] one of her heads fell down, and after six such acts six heads fell down. When she perceived this, she was enraged and she and her forces attacked me with great power; they frightened me during the *yihuddim* and they fled, hiding from me. They [the demons] carried me and my friends and they carried us to Gaza, to my home, and there we fell on our faces, crying all day and mourning our failure, which caused tthe redemption to be delayed at that time.

While we were crying, there came to me a messenger from our master, his clothes torn, crying and shouting, and in his hand there was a letter from His Majesty, our master. [In the letter the Messiah instructs Nathan and his adherents to refrain from further action because the powers of evil have become too strong. In the continuation of the text the death of Shabbati Zevi is described. The text ends without a definite promise of imminent victory.]

MESSIANISM AND SANCTITY

abbi Moses Hayyim Luzzatto of Padua (1707–47) was a unique figure in modern Judaism. His scores of treatises had—and still have—a remarkable impact in many aspects of Jewish culture, despite his untimely death and the fact that his writings in kabbalah were condemned by a court in Venice. He was accused of Sabbatianism and of dealing in magic, and was forced to leave Italy. He resided in Amsterdam for several years and then emigrated to the Holy Land, where he died a short time later.

Our knowledge concerning the life and works of Luzzatto is extensive; it is probable that we know about him more than about any personality represented in this volume. We have many volumes of his works; those that were published in his lifetime and those that were hidden and published later or are still in manuscripts.[1] We have numerous treatises written by his disciples, including a vast messianic commentary on the Bible written by his closest friend, Rabbi Moshe David Valle. Valle added to the manuscript of his commentary a mystical diary, in which he noted briefly spiritual events in his own life, including dreams and visions.[2] We have many hundreds of letters by Luzzatto and by others concerning him, establishing in great detail the major events in his life. It is evident from this material that Luzzatto behaved and impressed all those surrounding him as an ordinary Jewish-Italian intellectual, maybe a little bohemian, but not as an intense mystic and a dedicated messianic pretender. Yet it is clear that hardly out of his teenage years he had around him a secret group of adherents, who described themselves as a society dedicated to study and ethics, but among whom Luzzatto divided messianic functions—Valle was the Messiah son of David, Yekutiel Gordon of Vilna, a student of medicine in Padua, was the reincarnation of the biblical Samson and the commander of the armies of the Messiah, while Luzzatto himself was Moses, the redeemer in the past and the one destined to redeem again as the head of the messianic structure. It is probable that the role of the failed Messiah, the Messiah son of Joseph, was given to Shabbatai Zevi.[3]

In addition, Luzzatto had a personal, intimate avenue to the divine world: he had a *maggid* that was revealed to him, who spoke to him frequently and presented to him the greatest secrets of the divine world. Luzzatto described in detail the first appearance of this celestial messenger to him, and his attempts to get in touch, through him, with powers higher in the divine realm. Luzzatto's kabbalistic works, especially his "new Zohar," the *Zohar* of the time of the redemption, was dictated to him by this celestial messenger. We have descriptions, recorded by his disciples, in which it is claimed that Luzzatto was alone in his room, yet they distinctly heard another voice speaking there. Even his opponents did not doubt the existence of this maggid. Luzzatto described in detail in his diary the circumstances in which the maggid was first revealed to him, and the subsequent stages of their increasingly intimate relationship. Many of these mystical documents have reached us in autographs, in Luzzatto's and his disciples' own handwritings.

Luzzatto's activities evoked fierce opposition. The secret meetings of his friends, the writing of kabbalistic works dictated from heaven, and other activities aroused the suspicion that this was one more messianic-Sabbatian group, similar to numerous such associations in Italy in the late seventeenth century and the first half of the eighteenth. Luzzatto was formally accused of adherence to Shabbatai Zevi. He refuted this accusation by writing a book against Sabbatianism, which failed to completely satisfy his opponents.[4]

Luzzatto is the author of a brief text that I regard as the most unusual mystical document in Jewish literature, and as an outstanding one in mystical literature as a whole. Unfortunately, the text is untranslatable, because it is written in a condensed, rabbinic-kabbalistic style, which cannot be rendered into another language without every sentence being accompanied by a page of explanations. A brief description of it, however, should be included here.[5]

Luzzatto wrote this text himself on the day of his marriage ceremony, in August 1731, and it constitutes a commentary on his own marriage legal instrument, the *ketubah*. The *ketubah* is a traditional Jewish legal document, written in Aramaic, in which the rights of the bride are listed both within the framework of marriage and in case of a divorce. The bridegroom and witnesses sign this document during the marriage ceremony. While the text is fixed and unchanged, a few details are added in each case—the date, the place in which it is signed, the names of the bride and bridegroom. Luzzatto wrote his exegesis both on the fixed text and the particular details of his own marriage ceremony.

It is clear from the commentary that the ceremony is being held on three levels, simultaneously: It is that of Moshe Hayyim Luzzatto of Padua and his bride, Zipora; it is the wedding of Moses, the redeemer of Israel, the once and future leader, and his bride, Zipora daughter of Jethro; and it is the union of the male and female principles in the divine world, the *Shekhinah* and her husband *Tiferet*, expressing the achievement of perfection in the divine world after aeons of struggling against the powers of evil. Luzzatto was older when he was married than was the custom in his time and place; it is evident that he was waiting for the right "Zipora." This three-level event expressed, according to Luzzatto, the actual acievement of the final stage of the redemption, and the culmination of messianic hopes. It does not represent something that is about to happen or should happen; it is the event itself, the final, ultimate spiritual achievement, which is performed with the sexual union between the three levels of bride-bridegroom couples, which are indeed one and the same. Luzzatto does not represent or symbolize Moses or the masculine element in the Godhead; he is identical with them, completely unseparable. Some additional texts from Luzzatto and his circle of adherents support this conclusion: After that marriage ceremony, messianic times have begun. The world is already redeemed, even though the redemption is not apparent yet in every corner of existence. From now on, they live in the messianic era.

It is difficult to find in the history of religious and mystical expression a parallel to such an intense mystical experience, in which the erotic event is conceived as completely identical with the messianic-redemptive one, and the human and divine are united is such a complete fashion. There is no diminution of the actual earthly ceremony and the sexual expression of the marriage; they are conducted in the ordinary, traditional, and carnal way. Yet at the same time they constitute an enormous spiritual and divine upheaval in history and in the divine realm. It is not one meaning hidden within the other or one act symbolizing another: Everything is what it always has been, and the power of the Messiah brings them, together and united, into a different level of existence. The "erotic" is not a metaphor, it is itself, and at the same time it is the culmination of the spiritual redeeming power.

The court in Venice ruled that Luzzatto must cease writing kabbalistic works, and that his previous works in this field should be banned. Eventually Luzzatto could not continue to reside in Italy, and moved to Amsterdam. Here he wrote a series of ethical-philosophical works, in which he refrained from using kabbalistic terminology. These treatises—"The Way of God" (*Derekh ha-Shem*) and "The Knowledge of [supernal] Intelligences" (*Da'at Tevunot*), became very popular and influential. But his most important work in this period was "The Path of the Righteous" (*Mesilat Yesharim*), a brief treatise that became the masterpiece of Jewish spirituality, printed and reprinted scores of times, and knowing it by heart became a distinguishing mark of circles of pietists. The work describes the path of the aspiring spiritualist from the depth of sin toward the ultimate achievement of adherence to the holy spirit, purging his soul from evil and bridging it to the gate of unity with the divine. The last step, according to Luzzatto, cannot be achieved by human efforts alone; divine grace must be extended to the mystic to elevate him to this last stage. The following is a translation of the concluding paragraphs of *Messilat Yesharim*:

The matter of sanctity has two aspects, that is, its beginning is worship and its culmination is reward; its beginning is in efforts and its end is a present. This means that the beginning of sanctity is when a person sanctifies himself, and its end is when he is sanctified. This is the meaning of what the sages said: When a person sanctifies himself a little, they sanctify him a lot; he sanctifies himself below, and they sanctify him from above.[6]

A person should dedicate his efforts towards achieving a complete separation and severance of himself from the material realm. He should cling (*le-hitdabek*) always, every moment, to his God. Because of this the prophets were also called "angels," as it is said concerning Aharon: *For the priest's lips should keep knowledge and they should seek Torah at his mouth for he is a messenger[7] of the Lord of hosts* (Mal. 2:7), and it is said: *But they mocked the messengers[8] of God* (2 Chron. 36:16).

Even when a person is dealing with the material things necessary for his body, his soul should not move away from its supernal adhering (*devekutah*), as it is said: *My soul clings to thee, thy right hand upholds me* (Ps. 63:9).

However, as it is impossible for a person to place himself in this state by his own endeavors alone, because the task is beyond his abilities—he is, after all, flesh and blood—this is why I said that the achievement of sanctity is a gift from above. What a man should do is to dedicate all his efforts to the acquisition of knowledge of truth, and sustained striving towards enlightenment in the sanctity of the deed. If he does this, the end will be that the Holy One, Blessed Be He, will direct him in this path in which he wishes to go and will inspire him with His sanctity and sanctify him. Then he will be successful in achieving this endeavor, being in a state of communion (*devekuth*) with Him, Blessed Be He, continuously. What nature prevents him from achieving will become possible with the assistance of Him, Blessed Be He, and with His help, as it is said: *No good thing will he withhold from those who walk uprightly* (Ps. 84:12). This is why the sages said in the statement which I quoted above, that when a person sanctifies himself a little, which is what a person can acquire by his own efforts, they sanctify him a lot from above, which is the assistance he gets from the Holy Name, will He be blessed. And, as I have stated, the person who is sanctified by the sanctity of his creator, even his mundane, material deeds are transformed into matters which are truly sacred. A hint of this process is found in eating from the sacrifice of *kodashim* (= sacred, dedicated), which is a positive commandment, and the sages said about that: The priests eat, the owners (those who present the sacrifice) are being forgiven.

You can now understand the difference between he who is pure and he who is sacred. The pure person treats his material deeds as things which are necessary, and he does not intend them to be anything but that which is absolutely necessary. By this these deeds become separated from the realm of evil, which is the material realm, and remain pure, but they do not achieve the status of sanctity, because in this context they are regarded as things which if existence were possible without them — it would be better. It is different concerning the holy person who is always in communion with his God and his soul is integrated with the spiritual truths in love and fear of his Creator. This person is regarded as someone who walks before God in the realm of eternal life[9] while he is still in this world. Such a person is regarded like the holy tabernacle, like the temple, like the holy altar,[10] as the sages said concerning the verse: *And God went up from him* (Gen. 35:13), the patriarchs are the holy chariot.[11] They also said that the righteous ones are the chariot, because the shekhinah resides on them as it did reside in the Temple. Therefore, any food that they eat now is like a sacrifice presented to the holy fires, because there is no doubt that these things (= which are sacrificed) undergo a most meaningful transformation and elevation when they are presented upon the altar and given to the shekhinah. They achieved such a great elevation that their whole kind in the world was blessed by this, as the sages stated in the Midrash. In the same way, food consumed by the holy person constitutes the elevation to that food and to that drink as if it were actually presented on the sacred altar. This is the meaning if the statement of the sages that a present given to a scholar is like the presentation of first fruits.[12] They also said that filling their throats with wine is like presenting sacrifices. This is not because scholars are so eager for eating and drinking, heaven forbid, or wish their throats to be filled like an obsessive eater, but the meaning of this is as I have explained: Scholars, who behave like holy people in all their ways and deeds, they are actually like the altar and the temple because the shekhinah resides over them exactly as it used to reside in the temple. Therefore, anything which is offered to them is like that which is offered on the altar, and filling their throats is like filling the holy cups. In the same way, any mundane thing they make use of after they have been in communion with His holiness, blessed be He, will be elevated and uplifted because these things had the great benefit of being used by a righteous person. Our sages had mentioned the matter of the stones of the place (Beth-El) which Jacob put under his head,[13] that Rabbi Isaac said that each one of them demanded that the righteous person will rest his head on it.[14]

In conclusion, the essence of the matter of holiness is that a person becomes so deeply connected (*davek*) to his God that whatever he does, he is never separated and never moves away from Him, the Blessed One; so much so that the material things which he uses for any of his common needs will be elevated, rather than that he will descend from his communion and supernal status because he is using material things. This can happen only when his mind is completely fixed, always, in the contemplation of the greatness, numinosity and holiness of God, the Blessed One, until it is as if he has joined the supreme angels while he is still on this world.

I have already said that a man cannot achieve this position by his own efforts. All he can do is to wish it and aspire to it, after he has achieved all the good characteristics we have described in this book up to this point, from the [minimal stage] of carefulness, up to the fear of sin.[15] With these he can come to the stage of holiness[16] and succeed. For if he is lacking something from the previous, lower characteristics, he will be like an intruder or a handicapped person, about whom it is said: *And a stranger shall not come near to you* (Num. 18:4).

After a person has perfected himself in all these preliminary preparations, if he clings strongly, with the force of love and power of fear in the wisdom of His greatness, Blessed be He, and His immense grandeur; if he separates himself gradually from the realm of material things, and if he directs in his heart all his actions and all his movements towards the mystery of true communion; until a spirit coming from above will inspire him and the Creator, Blessed be He, will make His name dwell over him, as he does for all his holy ones,—than he will become really like an angel of God, and then all his deeds, even the most lowly ones and material ones, will be like rituals and sacrifices.

You realize now that the way to achieve this stature is by increasing abstinence, as well as by being absorbed in contemplation in the secrets of divine providence and the mysteries of the creation, together with the knowledge of His supernal greatness, Blessed be He, and His praises. This leads to his adhering to Him in intense communion (*devekuth*). He will know how direct his thoughts [towards God] even when he is walking in his mundane ways in the same way that a priest directs his intentions when he is slaughtering the sacrifice, receives its blood or sprays it, until he derives by this ritual from God blessing, life and peace. If he cannot achieve this, he can never reach this position and will remain mundane and material like all other ordinary people.

The possibility of achieving this status is enhanced by concentration on solitude and abstinence, so that in the absence of worldly obstacles a man's soul can gather more strength to cling (le-hitdabek) to the Creator. The things which disrupt the achievement of this status are: the absence of true knowledge, the indulging in social contacts with other people, for then the material character of a person finds its counterparts and is awakened and strengthened and the soul remains entrapped in it and will not break out of its imprisonment. But when he is separated from other people and remains alone, he can prepare himself to the acceptance of the inspiration of His holiness. The direction to which he wishes to go is the one to which he will be directed from above, and with the divine assistance exerted to him his soul will gather strength and overcome his corporeality, and will adhere (tidbak) in His holiness, Blessed be He, and will culminate in him.

From this position he will ascend to a higher one, which is the holy spirit,[17] for his spirituality will achieve a status which is above that designed for humanity. His communion can reach such an elevated place that the key to resurrection will be handed to him, as it did to Elijah and Elisha. This is the expression of his achieving such intense communion with Him, Blessed be He, that because His apellation is "the source of life," He who gives life to any living thing, [he also receives this power]. As our sages of blessed memory have said: Three keys were not entrusted to messengers and these are: the key of rains, the key of living and the key of resurrection.[18] The union with Him in complete communion can derive from Him, Blessed be He, even the flow of life itself, which is the characteristic which is most essential to Him in particular more than anything else, as I have explained. This is the meaning of the barayta's ending, that holiness leads to the holy spirit, and the holy spirit leads to resurrection.[19]

22 THE MYSTICAL PRAYER OF RABBI ISRAEL BA'AL SHEM TOV

ysticism, in most cases, is an esoteric phenomenon, cherished by individuals or small, closed circles. Modern Hasidism is one of the most important examples of mystical attitudes coming to the forefront of an exoteric, popular religious movement. In the historical context of this major modern Jewish pietistic-revivalistic phenomenon—and in the teachings of its founder, the Besht— the long process of the transformation of mysticism from a marginal, hidden aspect of Jewish religious culture into an essential, normative component of Jewish worship has reached its culmination.

Rabbi Israel Ben Eliezer, who was called the Ba'al Shem Tov ("Master of the Good Holy Name," known by the acronym Besht), was born in 1700 and died in Meszibusz in 1760. Two generations of his disciples created the vast Hasidic movement, which by the middle of the nineteenth century engulfed about half of the Jewish people. It is today, despite the horrors of persecutions, pogroms, and the Holocaust, followed by about half the Jewish Ashkenazi (= of European descent) ultraorthodox communities. The other half is identified by its opposition to this movement, its adherents called simply "mitnagdim," that is, "opponents." It might be therefore said that this movement identifies the European Jewish traditional communities that are divided between those who accept its norms and those who reject them. This schism, which was formed in the last quarter of the eighteenth century, is still a dominant fact shaping Jewish religious life.

The information we have of his life indicates that most of his early activity was that of a wandering preacher, healer, and magician. He traveled from town to town, exorcizing demons from people and houses, writing amulets, giving blessings, and preaching a message of divine presence throughout reality, touching every person in every moment of his life. It seems that a central element of his teachings was the belief in the ability of a prominent person to affect the spiritual status of other people. Prayers do not always go directly to heaven; they have to be pushed along by the mystical power of a unique individual. In the forties and fifties of the eighteenth century several disciples gathered around him, and he was in close contact with other preachers of that age. He probably settled in the town of Mezhibuzh in the last years of his life, where he was known as a kabbalist and a healer.

The Besht did not write any books; his teachings were included in the sermons he preached and in oral discussions with his disciples. Several treatises were attributed to him after his death, but they were actually composed by his disciples. We have only one document that seems to be an authentic letter written by the Besht: an epistle he wrote to his brother-in-law, Gershon of Kutov, who immigrated to Jerusalem. The letter was probably never delivered to its destination, and a copy of it was published by the first writer of the Hasidic movement, Rabbi Jacob Joseph of Polonoi, appended to his book *Ben Porat Yosef*, published in Koretz, 1781.[1] This epistle describes a mystical experience — an "elevation of the soul" (*aliyat neshama*), during which the Besht's soul wondered in the divine realms, observing, learning, and trying to intervene on behalf of endangered Jewish communities. The Besht also tells about a meeting he had on this occasion with the Messiah, and his enigmatic response to the Besht's inquiry concerning the date of the redemption.[2] It also includes a most important section dealing with the mystical significance of language (see below).

It seems that the mystical practice of "elevation of the soul" was carried out in the context of prayer, and possibly even during the public ritual in the synagogue. The two narratives translated below can be viewed as a parallel to the events described in the epistle, as told by disciples who witnessed them, and their accounts were included in the collection of traditions and miraculous stories about the Besht, the *Shivhey ha-Besht* ("In Praise of the Besht"), which was published in Kopust in 1815.[3] The first is an account of an "elevation of the soul" which the Besht performed in the last year of his life, 1760, and the second, in which Rabbi Gershon of Kutov participated, occured several years earlier.[4]

As an account of a mystical experience, the first narrative is unusual in that it includes first an eyewitness account of the Besht's ecstatic behavior during the process, which is followed by the Besht's narrative concerning what happened to his soul during the time in which he seemed to have passed out in the synagogue. The concluding part of this tale includes references to the historical consequences of the Besht's endeavors in the divine world.

Another story which I heard from him [Rabbi Gedalyah of Linitz]. Once, on the eve of Yom Kippur, the Besht envisioned a great threat in heaven directed against the people of Israel, that the Oral Torah (= the Talmud, which is also identified by kabbalists with the Shekhinah) will be removed from them. The Besht grieved very much all that day, the eve of Yom Kippur. In the evening, when the whole town came to him to receive a blessing, he gave it to one person or two, and then said that he could not continue to bless them because of his deep sorrow. He then went to the synagogue, and admonished the people, and then he fell down in front of the holy ark, cried and said: Vay, for they want to take the Torah away from us, how can we survive among the nations even half a day. And his anger was directed against the Rabbis, for, he said, it was their fault, for they invent lies and false positions.[5] And he said that all the sages of the Talmud will be brought to trial.[6] Then he went to the *bet midrash*, and said more admonishing words, and they prayed the *kol nidrey*, and after *kol nidrey* he said that the threat is growing stronger. He told all the leaders of the prayers to make haste, because it was the custom that he himself would lead the concluding prayer of the day, the *ne'ilah*, and he wanted to do it long before sunset. Before the *ne'ilah* he started to say words of admonishment and cried, and he put his head way back on the praying-table and moaned and shouted. Then he began to pray the silent eighteen benedictions, and then started the loud repetition of the prayer. It was his custom always on the High Holidays not to look at the prayer-book, but the Rabbi, Rav Yekil of Mezhibuzh, would read from the prayer-book the hymn, standing before him, and the Besht used to repeat the words after him. When he reached the words: "open a gate for us," or the words "open the gates of heaven," when Rav Yekil said it and repeated it, he heard that the Besht was not repeating after him, so he stopped and remained silent. The Best than began to move in a terrifying way, he bent himself backwards until his head was close to his knees. The people in the synagogue were afraid that he might fall down. They wanted to help him and hold him up, but they were afraid. They notified Rabbi Ze'ev Kutzes, of blessed memory, and he came and looked at his face and motioned to them not to touch him. His eyes were protruding, and his voice sounded like that of an ox being slaughtered. He remained in this state for about two hours. Suddenly, he woke up, straightened himself at his stand and prayed very quickly and finished the prayer.

Later that evening, after the holiday of Yom Kippur was concluded,[7] everybody came to see him, for that was the custom always. They asked him what happened to that threat, and he told them:

When I was standing for the ne'ilah prayer, I could pray [without difficulty], and I ascended from one world to the other without meeting any obstacles, during all the silent eighteen benedictions. But when the loud repetition started, I still went on, and I reached one palace, and I had to enter only one final gate before I would stand before the Holy Name Blessed be He.[8] In that palace I found prayers of fifty years which could not ascend [to their destination]. Now, because on this Yom Kippur the prayers were said with great intention, all the prayers ascended, and each prayer was sparkling like the brilliant dawn. I asked those prayers: Why did you not ascend before? They said that they were ordered to wait for Your Highness to lead us. I told them: Come with me. The gate was open. And he [the Besht] told the people of his town that the gate was as large as the whole hall. When we started to walk with all the prayers an angel came and closed the door and put a lock on the gate, and he told them that the lock was as large as all of the town of Mezhibuzh. I started to move the lock around, trying to open it, and could not. So I ran to my teacher [the one known from the book, Toledot Ya'akov Yosef][9] and beseeched him and said: The people of Israel are in such great trouble, and now they do not let me enter, for at another time I would not try to force myself to get in. My Rabbi then said: I shall go with you, and if it will be possible to open it, I shall do it. He came and turned the lock and he also could not open it. Then he told me: What can I do for you? I began to complain to my Rabbi: How can you leave me in such a time of trouble? He answered: I do not know what I can do to help you. But you and I can go to the Palace of the Messiah, maybe salvation will come from there. I went, with great tumult, to the Palace of the Messiah. When our righteous Messiah saw me from afar, he told me: Do not shout, and he gave me two letters,[10] and I came to the gate, and thank God I succeeded to open the lock and opened he gate, and I led all the prayers. Because of the great happiness that the elevation of the prayers caused the mouth of the accuser was closed and I even did not have to argue against him. The threat was then cancelled, and all that remained was the impression of that threat.

From that impression[11] I [the narrator, Rabbi Gedalya of Linitz] remembered that there was a great tumult in the world. Some people sent their books to the province of Vallachia. The accuser was from the sect of Shabbatai Zevi, may his name be *araized*. And one Bishop from the town of Kaminitz burned two volumes from the Talmud. And the Rabbi of our community said that [the Bishop?] took from a renter in his village a copy of the Talmud by force, and put it in the fire, and because of our sins it was burned totally. But, praised be God, immediately when the Bishop stood in front of the fire he was hurt, and he was taken to the town of Kaminitz but they did not bring him there alive for that evil person died on the way. Later there was a debate before the Bishop of the holy community of Lvov, but the fear of the Torah fell on him and he did not convict. And that evil sect all converted [to Christianity], for he [the Bishop] abused them and degraded them for he shaved one *peah* (sideburn) and half their beards, so that it will be obvious that they are neither Jews nor Christians, and because of the great shame they all converted.

Once the pious Rabbi, our teacher and Rabbi Menachem Nachum of Tchernobil was visiting our town, and told this story before the people. I came in the middle of the telling of the story, and heard from him some things which were different [from the story told above], and also something new. [Menachem Mendel told] that the Messiah told the Besht [after giving him "the two letters"]: I do not know if you will succeed in opening the gate, but if you do open it, there will be salvation to the people of Israel. He also said that that gate was the gate of the palace of *kan zippor*,[12] into which no one ever entered but the Messiah himself, as it is stated in the holy Zohar. And he said that he heard the voice of God which told him: What shall I do with you, for I am compelled to fulfil your wish. [. . .] And concerning those who converted, I heard from the Rabbi of our community that the Besht said that the Shekhinah is wailing and saying: As long as a limb is connected [to the body] there is hope that its wounds will heal somehow, but when a limb is cut off there is no remedy forever. Every one of the people of Israel is a limb of the Shekhinah.

II

I heard this from Rabbi Falk. When Rabbi Gershon of Kutov travelled from the Land of Israel abroad for the betrothal of his son, he said that as I have, thank God, crossed the sea, I should go and visit my brother-in-law the Besht, of blessed memory. He reached him on the eve of the holy Sabbath. The Besht stood up to pray the afternoon prayer, and he used to extend his prayer until the stars came out in the evening. Rabbi Gershon also prayed according to the prayer-book of Rabbi Isaac Luria, of blessed memory.[13] After the prayer he read Torah-portions, in Hebrew and in the Aramaic translation. Later he asked for pillows to be brought to him, and lied down to rest [while the Besht was still praying].

On Sabbath eve, during dinner, Rabbi Gershon asked his brother-in-law the Besht: Why did you extend your prayer so long? I also prayed with intentions, and read the portion with its Aramaic translation, and had to lie down to rest, while you still continued to stand and shake and make the strange movements of yours. For he [Rabbi Gershon] wanted to extract some information from him. But the Besht kept his silence and did not give any answer. Rabbi Gershon repeated his question a second time, and then the Besht responded: When I reach the phrase: "Ressurection" (and Rabbi Falk was not sure whether it was the phrase "You [God] resurrect the dead" or the one "He who resurrects the dead in his mercy"), I made certain intentions and unifications (*yihuddim*), and then souls of the dead, in thousands and tens of thousands came to me, and I had to talk to each of them, to find out why each was rejected from the position which he should have occupied, and I do a *tikkun* for him, and I pray for him and elevate him, and I do that to each of them in the order of their importance. And they are so many, that if I wished to elevate all of them I should have been standing in the prayer [the eighteen benedictions] for three years. But when I hear the celestial anouncement, that "the holy is sanctified" and it is impossible to elevate any more souls, I step back from the [prayer of the] eighteen benedictions.[14]

Rabbi Gershon then said laughingly: Why don't they come to me? The Besht answered: If you[15] stay with me until next Sabbath I shall hand you the intentions, written on paper, and they will come to you too. He did so, and next Sabbath eve, when the Besht finished saying the *kaddish* before the prayer, Rabbi Gershon also stood up to pray. The Besht did not start his prayer yet, because he knew that Rabbi Gershon will not be able to stand it and will be terrified. So he stood and toyed with his watch and sniffed tobacco, waiting till Rabbi Gershon will pass the place of the intention in his prayer. When Rabbi Gershon made that intention, he saw that the dead people came to him like a great flock of goats, he fell down, fainting. The Besht then made him wake up and told him to go to his home. That night, at the dinner-table, during the meal, the Besht asked him: Why did you faint? Rabbi Gershon told him: When I made that intention the dead came to me in hordes. The Besht then said to his people: Beat him up, so that he does not try to poke fun at the Besht again.

I also heard from the pious Rabbi, our teacher and Rabbi Gedalya of blessed memory, that the Besht once prayed the afternoon prayer in a certain village in a room called spichler[16] and there were many barrels full of wheat there. During his prayer the barrels began to dance around forcefully, because of the shaking. As it is said: *Because the Lord descended upon it in fire . . . and the whole mountain quaked greatly* (Exod. 19:18).[17] And thank God I have perceived a soul from the level of Moses, of blessed memory.

A VISION AND A DREAM

abbi Nahman of Bratslav (1772–1810) is probably the most famous Jewish mystic. His narratives, dreams, and unique biography have captivated the hearts of modern readers and scholars, from Martin Buber to Arthur Green. He died 190 years ago, leaving behind him no family, and only a small group of adherents. These followers succeeded in surviving generation after generation, though with great difficulties. The European phrase, "poor like a church mouse" has its equivalent in Yiddish as "poor like a Bratslav hasid." They were rejected and ridiculed by other Hasidim as "dead Hasidim"—believers in a dead Zaddik. In the last few decades they are undergoing a new transformation: As they do not have any organization or clear-cut norms, they attract people who wish to get closer to Jewish life, who seek a spiritual existence, and who do not take kindly to authority and structure. It is becoming now a loose network of anarchic groups, among whom there are many artists, poets, architects, and "bohemians" in general—but also drug addicts, criminals, and fanatics. The one constant characteristic that did not change in more than two hundred years is their marginality in Jewish and Hasidic society, together with very high visibility and openness.

Rabbi Nahman's activity as a leader of a group of Hasidim occurred at the time when the hereditary element was becoming paramount among the newly established Hasidic communities. From this point of view, no one could surpass Rabbi Nahman, who was the direct descendant of the founder of the movement, Rabbi

Israel Besht, on both his father's and his mother's sides. According to the norms that were taking shape, he had every right to expect to be the supreme leader of Hasidism as a whole. Instead, he never had more than a handful of adherents; he felt persecuted, deserted, and in constant danger of being destitute. His health was frail, and in his last years he suffered from tuberculosis, of which he eventually died. His little son died when he was a few years old. Even though his writings and sermons demanded that a person shall worship God with great joy, he himself tended to melancholy and solitude. He demanded simple adherence to God, yet his own teachings are marked by paradox, dialectic, and sophistication.

In the center of the interest in Rabbi Nahman were his narratives, presented in the external form of folktales. Many readers, starting with Buber, tended to interpret them as exempla, tales that teach proper ethical and theological behavior and beliefs. Despite the popularity of this attitude, it seems to be a dead end: The stories are much more complicated and obscure than any didactic moral that may be learned from them. The notion that Rabbi Nahman elected to use "simple, popular" literary format in order to teach simple people crumbles in front of the obscure and incoherent nature of the stories. Rabbi Nahman's direct disciples read these narratives as expressions of the author's life and destiny, and so do contemporary scholars, like Joseph Weiss and Mendel Piekarz; this seems to be the only way by which they may be understood—actually, like any meaningful work of fiction that expresses the inner world of the author, and all the characters in them represent an aspect of the writer's world. When the stories are compared to Rabbi Nahman's didactic prose in his sermons, it becomes evident that the stories penetrate into those aspects of his life and thought that could not be expressed in the rhetoric of preaching. As Piekarz pointed out, Rabbi Nahman started to narrate these stories after his son's death in 1805, and this is closely connected with an intensification of the centrality of his messianic destiny in his spiritual life.

Rabbi Nahman was the one who introduced into Hasidic discourse the term "the true Zaddik" (*zaddik ha-emet*), which indicates that there are Zaddikim who are not "true." This term always appears in the singular, and, as his disciples insisted, it always refers to Rabbi Nahman himself. The transition from many Zaddikim to one true Zaddik is the transition to the identification of the Zaddik as the one redeemer of the whole people, a final, ultimate redeemer—a messiah in the full sense of the term. The stories, so we may conclude, express in a folktale garb the spiritual biography of the Messiah and his endeavors to bring forth the redemption and overcome all obstacles—and at the same time they are the secret autobiography of Rabbi Nahman, in the same way that a work of fiction is often a spiritual autobiography of the author.

"The Story of the Seven Beggars" is the last—the thirteenth—in Rabbi Nahman's collection, and it is distinctive by its being an unfinished one, like the first, "The Story of the Lost Princess."[1] Its outlines are well known: The first segment of the story narrates the spiritual fall of a king's son, "who fell from faith"; then the story moves, without any apparent connection, to an upheaval in a certain country that caused many people to flee from their homes. Among them were two children, a boy and a girl, who wandered as beggars in the forests and towns. During their wandering they met, in seven separate episodes, seven beggars, each of whom was also a cripple—a blind one, a deaf one, a stammerer, etc., who feed them and assist them. When they grew up, the other beggars decided that they should marry each other, and prepared a wedding feast in a hole in the ground, covered by weeds and garbage. During this celebration, the bride and groom crave for the presence of the seven crippled beggars. Each of them appears, in the order of their original meeting, and narrates a story in which he himself is the main hero, who possesses supernatural abilities that correspond to his particular disadvantage: The blind one sees better than anyone else, etc. Each beggar then gives his unique powers as a wedding gift to the children, thus allowing them to become masters of all the supernatural abilities of the whole group of beggars. The story ends with the narrative of the sixth beggar, so that the part which Rabbi Nahman never told included at least three segments: the story of the seventh beggar, who was legless (and, according to tradition, a wonderful dancer); the conclusion of the story of the wedding of the children and their ultimate fate; and the conclusion of the story of the prince "who fell away from faith" and the narrative as whole.

This structure can be explained as reflecting Rabbi Nahman's concept of the present moment in cosmic history, in the movement between creation and redemption according to the Lurianic messianic myth, which Rabbi Nahman internalized and absorbed as his own biography, the story of the fate of the soul of the Messiah.[2] The time of the final revelation of the Messiah and the implementation of the redemption on earth has not arrived yet, so the first story, as well as the last, could not be concluded. Traditional Bratslav commentators identified the last, seventh beggar with king David, who danced in front of the holy ark when it was moved from Shiloh to the Temple Mount in Jerusalem, where the temple was to be built by Solomon—a clear indication of the completion of the messianic process. The catastrophes with which both the first and the last narratives begin can be understood as representing the myth of the *tzimtzum* and *shevirah*, the primordeal catastrophes within the Godhead in the Lurianic mystical-messianic myth.[3] It seems that the bride and groom, in the hole in the ground coverred by garbage, are in the process of accumulating the powers of the divine manifestations, the *sefirot*, which they receive as wedding gifts from the beggars who represent these divine entities, and preparing themselves to their imminent role in the messianic event, of which the marriage ceremony, this *hieros gamos*, is a high point. From this ceremony the process of tikkun, the mending and correction of the mythical catastrophes, can reach its ultimate conclusion. Unfortunately, this is also the point in which Rabbi Nahman forsakes the mundane world, and the completion of the messianic process is delayed until his return, according to the belief of his followers.[4]

The tale of the third beggar is placed in the middle of the story, and it is suggested that it serves as the turning-point in the narrative between the segments dedicated to the myth of the creation and the primordeal catastrophes and the segments leading towards the correction and the redemption. It is neither "past" nor "future," but rather the description of the extended present, the situation in a universe which is at balance, though a tenuous and temporary one:

There is an entire tale about this. The True Man of Kindness[5] is indeed a very great man. And I (the stutterer) travel around and collect all true deeds of kindness and bring them to the True Man of Kindness. For the very becoming of time—time itself is created—is through deeds of true kindness. So I travel and gather together all those true deeds of kindness and bring them to the True Man of Kindness. And from this time becomes.

Now there is a mountain. On the mountain stands a rock. From the rock flows a spring. And everything has a heart. The world taken as a whole has a heart. And the world's heart is of full stature[6] with a face, hands, and feet. Now the toenail of that heart is more heart-like than anyone else's heart. The mountain with the rock and spring are at one end of the world, and the world's heart stands at the other end. The world's heart stands opposite the spring and yearns and always longs to reach the spring. The yearning and longing of the heart for the spring is extraordinary. It cries out to reach the spring. The spring also yearns and longs for the heart.

The heart suffers from two types of langour: one because the sun pursues it and burns it (because it so longs to reach the spring); and the other because of its yearning and longing, for it always yearns and longs fervently for the spring. It always stands facing the spring and cries out: "Help!" and longs mightily for the spring. But when the heart needs to find some rest, to catch its breath, a large bird flies over, and spreads its wings over it, and shields it from the sun. Then the heart can rest a while. And even then, during the rest, it still looks toward the spring and longs for it.

Why doesn't the heart go toward the spring if it so longs for it? Because, as soon as it wants to approach the hill, it can no longer see the peak and cannot look at the spring. (When one stands opposite a mountain, one sees the top of the slope of the mountain where the spring is situated, but as soon as one approaches the mountain, the top of the slope disappears—at least visually—and one cannot see the spring.) And if the heart will no longer look upon the spring, its soul will perish, for it draws all its vitality from the spring. And if the heart would expire, God forbid, the whole world would be annihilated, because the heart has within it the life of everything. And how could the world exist without its heart? And that is why the heart cannot go to the spring but remains facing it and yearns and cries out.

And the spring has no time; it does not exist in time (The spring has no worldly time, no day or moment, for it is entirely above time.) The only time the spring has is that one day which the heart grants it as a gift. The moment the day is finished, the spring, too, will be without time and it will disappear. And without the spring, the heart, too, will perish, God forbid. Thus, close to the end of the day, they start to take leave one from the other and begin singing riddles and poems and songs, one to the other, with much love and longing. This True Man of Kindness is in charge of this: As the day is about to come to its end, before it finishes and ceases, the True Man of Kindness comes and gives a gift of a day to the heart. And the heart gives the day to the spring. And again the spring has time.

And when day returns from wherever it comes, it arrives with riddles and fine poetry in which all wisdom lies. There is a distinction between the days. There is Sunday and Monday; there are also days of New Moon and Holidays. The poems which the day brings depend upon what kind of day it is. And the time that the True Man of Kindness has, all derives from me (the stutterer) because I travel around, collecting all the true deeds of kindness from which time derives.

Consequently, the stutterer is wiser even than the wise one who boasted that he is as clever as whichever day you wish. Because all of time, even the days, come about only through him (the stutterer) for he collects the true deeds of kindness from which time derives and brings them to the True Man of Kindness. He in turn gives a day to the heart. The heart gives it to the spring, through which the whole world can exist. Consequently the actual becoming of time, with the riddles and poems and all the wisdom found in them, is all made possible through the stutterer.

I have an affidavit from the True Man of Kindness that I can recite riddles and poems, in which all wisdom can be found, because time and riddles come into being only through him. And now, I give you my wedding gift outright that you should be like me.[7]

Upon hearing this, they had a joyous celebration.

It is remarkable that the basic terminology and processes described in this section of the narrative are rather simple, well-known, even mundane, Zoharic ones, expressing the mainstream, pre-Lurianic concept of divine providence. Upon this foundation Rabbi Nahman constructed in this parable the modifications resulting from his Hasidic and his personal worldview.

The spring is the third divine power in the kabbalistic system, binah, which is consistently described as the spring and the source of all existence, first and foremost that of the divine realms. The first two sefirot are conceived as potential rather than actual existence—divine will (*keter*) and divine wisdom (*hokhmah*). Real existence begins with the third sefirah, which is the springboard of all that is. Like a spring, it is half-hidden within the realm of divine potentiality, and only its outer aspects flow forth into existence like spring's waters. The "water" is the divine flow (*shefa*) which sustains all existence; if it is stopped, the world ceases to exist; if it is diminished, misfortunes and suffering come to the world.[8]

The heart is another rather common term, relating to the sixth sefirah, tiferet, which is conceived as the center of the "construction *sefirot*," the ones that support and direct all the affairs of the higher and lower realms of existence. The dependence of the "heart" on sustunance received from the third sefirah, the "spring," is a basic kabbalistic concept that is illustrated graphically by Rabbi Nahman in orthodox terms.

The dynamic aspect of this picture is supplied in this narrative by another basic kabbalistic concept, that of the impact of human deeds on the stature of the divine powers. In order to exist the universe has to be sustained by divine flow, coming from the hidden, supreme, and innermost realms of the divine powers. At the same time, this flow cannot come into being without being triggered by an upward flow of power, resulting from human rituals, ethical behavior, and piety. The ancient belief that the world is sustained by the righteous, that the zaddik is the foundation of the world (Prov. 10:25), has been extended in the kabbalah into a detailed relationship between righteousness and existence.[9] In Rabbi Nahman's parable, this concept is described as the one giving the spring "time." The spring tends, according to the narrative, to disengage from existence and recede into the realm of eternity, which is timelessness, in which reality cannot exist. In other words, without the "time" given to the spring, "one day at a time," God recedes into precreation eternity, in which the world does not exist. The flow from existence toward the spring is therefore necessary to hold God loyal to his own creative endeavor for one more day.

It is not difficult to extend this interpretation to include the other elements of the picture presented by Rabbi Nahman—the sun threatening the heart (probably the fifth sefirah, din, the harsh law and the source of evil), and the great bird—probably the fourth sefirah, hesed. Yet the text should not be regarded as a textbook allegory, to be mechanically interpreted detail for detail. Even the most mundane kabbalistic concepts have undergone some transformation in Rabbi Nahman's personal world, and presented according to his own, individual vision.

The process of providing one more day each day to the universe's existence as presented in this vision is different in a meaningful way from the dominant character of Rabbi Nahman's narratives. In most cases, his stories include elements of a catastrophe that [is being in the process of mending,] leading toward an expected final salvation. This is the basic structure of the story of the beggars as a whole, and of several of the stories of the individual beggars. This structure, as noted above, reflects the basic myth of Lurianic kabbalah—the road from the tzimtzum and shevirah to the final tikkun and redemption. In the story of the third beggar this element is absent: It is a description of a continuous, basically static situation, repeated unchanged every day. The processes described here do not contain any intrinsic crisis that demands radical change. It can continue indefinitely. This is a Zoharic myth, reflecting the mainly nonmessianic aspects of the early kabbalah, rather than the revolutionary, intensely messianic Lurianic myth, which serves as the foundation of Rabbi Nahman's worldview and his concept of his own place in the world.

Understanding this unusual characteristic of the third beggar's story seems to be closely connected with the nature of the hero of the narrative, the stutterer himself. He portrays himself as the wandering collector of deeds of charity and righteousness, who gives these treasures to the "True Man of Kindness," who, in his turn, uses this spiritual power to give another day of existence to the universe. It seems that we have here one character, divided into a celestial and earthly entities, who together fulfill this crucial role. They embody the process of delivering the life force, derived of human observance of divine commands, to the supreme powers that sustain the world. The supernal part, the "True Man of Kindness" or "Man of Kindness and Truth," seems to be combination of the characteristics of two sefirot, the fourth, *hesed* (usually rendered in English as "loving kindness"), and the sixth, tiferet, which is described in standard kabbalistic terminology by the terms *emet* (Truth) and *rahamim* (love, mercy, caring). It seems that Rabbi Nahman created in this character a dynamic figure that supplies "the spring" with all the good qualities of the these two *sefirot* combined. They are represented in the lower realms by the "stutterer," who actually fulfils the most important role of collecting the deeds of kindness which sustain the existence of the universe.

This is not a routine kabbalistic concept. It seems to be based more on the Hasidic doctrine of the role of the Zaddik than on traditional kabbalistic teachings. The most meaningful innovative idea that Hasidism introduced into Jewish thought is that of the intermediary power who stands in the middle, between humanity and God.[10] In the process of development of this central concept, which dominated Hasidism from the early nineteenth century to the present, Rabbi Nahman has a unique role. On the one hand, he contributed more than most other Hasidic thinkers to its development, and on the other, he is responsible, in thought and deed, to the emergence of an exception to the rule: the concept of the one-and-only Zaddik, the true Zaddik, who is the redeemer of the whole world, identified with the Messiah himself.

Rabbi Nahman's loyal disciple, Rabbi Nathan of Nemirov, included in his biography of his master, *Hayey Moharan* ("The Life of Our Master, Rabbi Nahman"), a chapter in which he preserved Rabbi Nahman's account of several dreams he had. This is an important source for the understanding of the mystic's inner life. It seems that in these narratives the author's doubts and fears are expressed in a way rarely found in mystical literature:

The month of Kislev 570 (December 1809). Here, in Bratslav. A dream. I was sitting in my home [that is, in the little house in which he dwelt][11] and no one entered to my room. I found this strange, so I went out to the next room and there was nobody there either. I went out, to the large house and to the beit ha-midrash, and there was nobody there. I then decided to go outside, and I went and saw people standing in circles and whispering to each other; one was joking about me and another was laughing at me and another was criticizing me. Even my own people were against me, some of them were criticizing me and others where whispering about me as did the others. I then called one of my people to me and asked him: What is this? He answered: How could you commit such a great sin? I did not have any idea about what they were gossipping about me. I then asked that person to go and assemble some of our people, and he went and I never saw him again.

I considered what to do, and decided to remove myself to another country. I arrived there but it was the same: there also people were standing and talking about that, because they also knew what happened. I thought and decided to settle in a forest, and five of my people joined me there, we went together to the forest and we sat there. When we needed anything, food and such, we used to send one of those people who bought for us what we needed. I used to ask him whether the turmoil has subsided, and he answered: no, the excitement is still very strong.

While we were sitting there, an old man came and called me and said that he has something about which he wanted to talk to me. I walked away with him, and he started to talk to me and said: How could someone like you do such a thing? Are you not ashamed, remembering your fathers? Considering your grandfather Rabbi Nahman?[12] And your grandfather the Besht of blessed memory? And how is it that you are not ashamed considering the Torah, given by Moses, and the sacred patriarchs, Abraham, Isaac and Jacob, etc.? What do you think, do you believe that you can sit here forever? Your money will be spent, and you are a weak person,[13] what can you do? Do you really think that you can sail to another country? Just think: If they, in that country, will not know who you are, you will not be able to survive there because they will not support you with money; and if they knew who you were, you also will not be able to survive there, because they will know about this affair. I responded to him: Because this is so, that I am driven away like this, I shall earn the next world.[14] He answered me: The next world? You think that you will achieve that? Even in hell there will not be a place for you, a corner in which you can bury yourself, because you have committed something like that, such a great defamation of the name of God. I answered: Go away, I thought that you came to console me and to talk [nicely] to me, but instead you cause me even more suffering, go away. The old man then left me.

While I was sitting there I considered that since I was staying there such a long time it was possible to forget all knowledge completely. So I ordered that person, whom we used to send to the town to acquire our necessities, that he should look for some book and bring it to us. He went to the town but did not bring a book, explaining that, obviously, it was forbidden to reveal who needed that book, and secretly it was not possible to acquire a book. This caused me great suffering, because I was wandering from place to place and I did not have any book with me; this way one can forget completely all that he ever studied. Later, the old man who was revealed to me earlier returned and came to me, carrying a book under his arms. I asked him: What are you carrying? He answered: A book. I said: Give me the book. He gave it to me. I took it, and I did not know even how to put it, and I opened the book and did not know anything about it at all, and it seemed to me as if it were written in another language and another script, because I did not understand anything in it at all. This caused me great pain, and I was also afraid of those people who were with me, that they also may depart from me if they know this. The old man then called me again and wanted to talk to me, and I walked with him. He again started to admonish me as he did the previous time: How could you do this, are you not ashamed, even in hell there will be a place for you to hide, as he said before. I said to him: If a person from the celestial world would say this to me, I would believe him. He responded: I am from there, and showed me something from there. This brought to my mind the well-known story about the Besht, when the Besht also thought then that he does not have a place in the next world, and he said: I love God blessed be He without the next world.[15] I then threw my head backwards in great bitterness. When I threw my head that way, the people that the old man said that I should be ashamed before them all came and assembled around me, that is, my grandfathers and the patriarchs, etc., and they recited to me the verse: *the fruit of the land shall be excellent and comely*.[16] And they said to me: To the contrary, we would like to be proud of you. They then brought to me all my men, and also my sons [for my sons left me before, when the affair began]. They talk to me in this way, so different from before. The way I threw my head back was such that even a person who transgressed all the commandments of the Torah eight hundred times, if he did throw his head back this way with such bitterness there is no doubt that he would have been forgiven. The rest of the good things I do not want to tell you, but it was certainly very good.

MYSTICAL POETRY AND MYSTICAL LANGUAGE

H ayyim Nahman Bialik (1873–1934), probably the most prominent poet in modern Hebrew literature, would have been horrified to find himself included in this anthology. He belonged to the Jewish enlightenment tradition, a devoted Zionist who was often described as a "national poet." Though he had a thorough traditional Jewish education, he lived as a secular, modern European intellectual. He did not express any particular interest in the kabbalah or any other aspect of Jewish esoterical tradition, though like every person of the same background he was familiar with its terminology and ideas. After settling in Tel Aviv he dedicated himself to a vast project of collection and publication of Jewish traditional literature, but he did not emphasize the esoteric-mystical works; he asked Gershom Scholem (in 1926) to deal with that. His lectures, essays, and letters do not indicate that he had any interest in mysticism, whether Jewish or Christian; it is possible that the term is not mentioned anywhere in his works.

It is my suggestion that Bialik's lyrical poetry includes elements that exemplify the problem of "mysticism sacred and profane"; can a person be a mystic without being, first and foremost, a devotee of a particular religion? Bialik's secular poetry seems to demonstrate that some of the main characteristics of mysticism, as described in the introduction, can be found in a context that is not a direct expression of a relationship between a mystic and his God. One of Bialik's early poems, entitled *Zohar*[1] (*"Brilliance"*), serves as an example. This extensive poem, written in 1909, begins with the following lines:

In the midst of my childhood I have been engulfed by loneliness,
And craved all my life for silence and the hidden,
From the body of the world I craved for its light,
Something which I could not fathom murmured like wine inside
    me.
I was looking for hiding-places. There I silently observed,
I was like a visionary looking into the eye of universe.
There my friends were revealed to me, I received their secrets,
And sealed their voices in my mute heart.
My friends, how numerous they were: any flying bird,
Any tree and its shadow, every bush in the forest,
The face of the meek moon shining into a window,
The darkness of a cellar, the creaking of a gate . . .
The sweet and awesome mixture of light with darkness
In the depth of a well,
Where the echo of my voice and my image are found,
The chiming of a clock, the tooth of a saw grinding within
    a log,
As if they are pronouncing the forbidden name of God . . .

It is striking how many of the terms and metaphors used by the poet are negative in nature: silence, mute, secret, hiding, sealing, etc. — serving as a testimony that his statement "something I could not fathom" is indeed something that he could not express in words. When positive terms are used, they are vague: "From the body of the world I craved to its light," indicating that he does not wish to be where he is, and craves to be somewhere else, probably a more spiritual place, which cannot be defined or described. The "friends" — the sounds and lights, shadows and images — seem to be connected somehow with the "its light," but nothing clearer can be gleaned from these phrases. If mystical language is one that denies itself, this is a good example of this phenomenon.

In the poem "Peeked and Died" (written in 1916) Bialik used a traditional Talmudic parable[2] and some terms taken from the ancient esoteric tradition in order to portray the poet struggling to express the truth behind language.[3] It is written in the manner of a ballad, and the hero, the mystic=poet, sacrifices his life in his quest for the impossible:[4]

Peeked and Died

He entered the secret treasuries of the *pardes*, his torch in his
    hand,
and the *pardes* had fifty gates
and there were obstacles in all its paths, deep depths
and mounting mountains,

and the brilliance of swords at the gates, and beyond the thresh-
    olds
snakes were lying in ambush —
He passed in peace among them all, passing over the snakes
and sneaking below the sword.

He hastened to enter the innermost, his torch in front of him.
Tarshishim[5] withdrew,
silently wondering: the brave one, will he endeavor to reach
the fiftieth gate?

He will endeavor! — He will come to the most hidden treasuries
where no trespasser has ever trodden.
He strove to reach borderless borders, the place where the oppo-
    sites
become one in their source.

He strove on, and found the most straight path —
the crooked one,
and turned to it, and came at one time to a place —
the absence of time, the absence of place.

He arrived where light ends, with darkness, to the ends of the void,
which no eye has ever observed,
Yet the last gate, the fiftieth — Oh, hiding God,
is still so far away!

The torch is dying out, dying out, the roads intersperse each
    other . . .
and the paths become more crooked —

and all of them are just corridors to corridors—where is the last
    gate?
And where is the palace itself?

His soul is tired of striving, his eyesight is failing
and his spirit loses its uprightness;
when he could no more walk on two feet, erect—
he crawled on his belly.

When his mouth was licking the earth, a last prayer on his lips
burning incessantly:
"If I only could reach the fiftieth gate, just for a moment, to peek
beyond the screen."

The prayer was answered; and before the dying torch
reached its end—
the fiftieth gate, the beauty of pure marble stones
appeared before him.

The hand was shaking, the eye stricken by the brilliance—should
    he knock?
He restrained himself for another moment,
and suddenly asserted himself and dared, stood up from crawling,
and knocked.

Then the torch went out, the doors of the gate were opened—
and he peeked inside,
and his body fell down, beside it the smoking coal
on the threshold of the belimah.

The terminology chosen by Bialik in this "mystical ballad" is taken, mainly, from four linguistic contexts. The first is biblical, especially images taken from the Genesis narrative of Paradise. The snake is present as a threat, and, later, the hero is crawling on his belly like the snake, after it was cursed and punished. The sword described in the beginning is, probably, the one protecting the Garden of Eden, and its edge of fire is clearly described.

The second linguistic stratum is the talmudic one, especially the narrative of the Four Sages who Entered the Pardes. Besides the pardes itself, the title is taken from that narrative — "peeked and died" is the talmudic description of the fate of one of the four sages — Ben Zoma in some versions, Ben Azai in others. Other rabbinic terms are those of *traklin* and *prozdor* — the preparation for the meeting with God and its achievement.

The number fifty itself is taken from rabbinic literature — the fifty gates of wisdom, which the medieval kabbalists interpreted as relating to the third *sefirah, binah.*

The third is the Hekhalot mystical literature descriptions of the ascension of the *yordey ha-merkavah* to the celestial realm and the throne of glory. The obstacles on their way are described in great detail, and price of failure is often cruel death.[6]

The fourth stratum is medieval philosophy and mysticism, from Maimonidean negative theology and classical kabbalah. The concept of the divine realm in which opposites become identical has been used by Bialik to indicate the realm in which semantic language loses its distinctive meanings and metalinguistic truth gleams at the end of the journey.

This same subject has been presented by Bialik in a most powerful and poetic essay, "Language Closing and Disclosing," which is presented here, in Yael Lotan's translation.[7] This is an intuitive, impressionistic presentation of Bialik's conception of language; it is not based on a study of any philosophical or linguistic monographs on the subject (though some traces of German nineteenth-century attitudes are discernible), but rather a forceful poetic-mystical assertion of the enormous power and inherent limitations of expressive language. The paradoxical nature of the relationship between language and truth, when linguistic expression is the only avenue by which truth can be glimpsed, while at the same time it hides and distorts it, is presented in this unique essay.

Language Closing and Disclosing

Men scatter words to the winds, deliberately or casually, masses of words in all their possible combinations, but only few know or consider what those words were like in their days of glory. Some words came into the world only after a long and difficult travail lasting several generations; others flared up like lightning and with a flash lit the whole world; through some passed untold souls, one after the other, each leaving behind it a certain shade and flavour; still others have served as vehicles for highly complex mechanisms of profound thought and exalted feeling in marvellous permutations. Some words are like great mountain ranges—others like a yawning abyss. A single small word may have encompassed the whole essence, the surviving soul of an entire philosophical system, the summary of a complete world-view. A word may have overcome nations and countries, unthroned kings and shaken the foundations of heaven and earth. And then the day came and these words fell from their heights into the marketplace, and today men toy with them in idle talk, as if they were no more than beads.

Is that such a strange thing? One does not question the ways of nature. This is how it has always been—some words rise to power, others come down in the world. Essentially, there is not a lightweight word in the language that was not born in a moment of stupendous spiritual revelation, a grand triumph of the soul. Thus, when the first man was struck by the sound of thunder—"The voice of the Lord is powerful, the voice of the Lord is full of majesty"—and fell on his face, amazed and shaken with awe, a wild sound breaking from his lips—imitatively, as it were—a bestial roar, a growl-like "r . . . rrr . . . r," a sound preserved in the word for thunder in many languages—did not that savage cry greatly relieve his thunder-struck soul? And did that cry, the echo of a profoundly-shaken being, reveal less of the force of creativity than the most telling phrase of the highest significance ever produced by a great visionary in a moment of spiritual elation? Did not that little syllable, the seed of a future word, contain within it the miraculous composition of *primeval* emotions, fiercely novel and wild—anxiety and fear, amazement, submission and admiration, the impulse of self-preservation and many others? And, if it did, was not the first man at that moment a great artist and visionary, intuitively creating a vocal expression—a very faithful one, at least for himself—for deep and complicated spiritual upheavals? And—as a certain wise man has said—how much profound philosophy and divine revelation was in the little word "I," when uttered by the first man? And yet we see that these words, and many like them, are absorbed in the language—and nothing happens. The soul is hardly touched by them. Their content has been consumed, their spiritual force has vanished—or been *stored away*—and only their shells, having become public property, remain in the language and are used automatically and carelessly, within the narrow boundaries of logic and social intercourse, as *outward* signals and abstract references for things felt and seen. We are now at a point where human language is divided in two, one part growing at the expense of the other—the inner language, that of the singular soul, whose principal aspect, as in music, is the "how"—in the sphere of poetry; and the external language of abstractions and generalizations, whose principal aspect, as in mathematics, is the "what"—in the sphere of logic. And, who knows?—perhaps it is better for man to inherit the empty shell of a word, so that he may fill it anew, or add to it of his own substance and illuminate it with his own light. Man seeks to have his own portion in this world, and were the spoken word to retain forever its original substance and luminescence, were it accompanied eternally by the self-same retinue of feelings and ideas which became associated with it in its days of glory, perhaps no "talking animal" would be able to disclose his own selfhood and spiritual light. For, after all, an empty vessel may be filled, but a full one may not—and if the empty word can enslave, how much more the full.

What is strange is the confidence and self-assurance with which men speak, as if they were conveying their expressed ideas and feelings across still waters over an iron bridge—little thinking how frail is that bridge of words, how deep and dark the abyss that gapes below, and how miraculous every step safely passed.

But it is plain that language, for all its intricacies, does not introduce us into the inner being of things but rather stands between us and them. Beyond the language, behind its screen, man's soul, bared of words, wonders without end. Mutely, an eternal "what" hanging upon the lips. And even the "what" is scarcely appropriate, for it carries the suggestion of hope for an answer. What, then, is there? "Surcease—a desistance from speech." And if, nevertheless, man made speech and thereby acquired confidence, it is only because of the terror of remaining even momentarily alone with that dark Chaos, with that "surcease," face-to-face, unmediated. "For there shall no man see me and live," says Chaos, and every word, every utterance, covers a fraction of the "surcease," becomes a shell concealing a dark drop of the everlasting impasse. *There is not a single word that can cancel a single question.* What then can it do? It can cover it up. It matters not what word, you may exchange it for another, so long as it suffices to cover and mediate. Those twin sisters, those parallel poles—wordless music and symbolic mathematics—prove that words are not of the essence, but a mere membrane over Chaos. But as objects become visible and their outlines are defined when they block the light, so a word receives its substance in the process of sealing a small crack through which the darkness of Chaos might otherwise seep. When a man sits alone and trembling in the midnight darkness, he talks to himself, says his prayers or whistles. *It is a sure remedy to divert the mind and dispel fears.* And this is the power of the spoken word, or of a whole system of words: not its explicit meaning, if such exist at all, but its capacity to distract the mind. Shutting one's eyes is, after all, the easiest and most convenient, if imaginary, escape from danger; and where opening the eyes is itself the danger, what better escape can there be?—"Moses did well to hide his face." Perhaps the earliest speech was not between one man and another, not a social tool, a means to an end, but the solitary expression of a man alone, an inner need, an end in itself—"My spirit wondereth within me, and I commune with mine own heart" . . . The first man did not rest till he heard himself speak. But that same speech, which in the beginning had raised his consciousness from the inchoate depths, now came to stand between him and "that which lies beyond," as if to say— From here on, Man, look only at what lies before thee. Never look back, never seek to glimpse the mystery; but even shouldst thou glimpse it, it will avail thee naught, for no man may gaze upon Chaos face-to-face and live. A dream once forgotten may be recalled no more. And thy desire shall be to Chaos and speech shall rule over thee.

And so, in fact, mind and speech only rule over what lies before us, and are narrowly circumscribed by time and place. But man walks in their shadow, and the closer he moves to the imaginary light before him, the greater grows the shadow behind, and so the enveloping darkness is not diminished. It may be possible to resolve everything which lies before us—resolve it poorly or well, no matter, so long as the mind of man is never for an instant left without a close covering of words, as tightly woven as the scales of a coat of mail. The illumination of mind and speech—the ember and the flame—is unquenchable. But what is the area bathed in that illusory light, compared with the limitless ocean of eternal darkness which still stretches, and will forever stretch, outside? And yet it is precisely the dreadful infinite darkness which always attracts the secret heart of man and arouses hidden longings to glimpse it, if only for an instant. All fear it, all are drawn to it. With our tongues we build superstructures of words and systems to hide it from sight— and at once the fingernails begin to scrabble and seek an opening, a tiny slit, through which to peer, if but for a second, at "that which lies beyond." Alas, man's labour is in vain! As soon as a crack appears, another barrier rises up, in the form of a new word or a new system, to screen the sight from our eyes.

And so it goes on forever—a word comes and a word goes, a system rises and a system falls, and the eternal impasse remains unaltered, undiminished. The issuance of promissory notes, or the recording of the debt, none of these constitutes payment; at best they serve temporarily to relieve the mind of its burden. And the same holds true of categorical speech, which is to say, the naming of names and the fixing of orders and qualifications for things observed and their combinations. No mere speech can give or imply an answer to the substantive question. Even the most explicit answer is only a rephrasing of the question; the question-mark is converted into a full-stop, which is a way of closing instead of disclosing. If we were to strip bare the final, innermost core of all words and systems, we would in the end, after the ultimate extraction of meaning, be left with the all-embracing, terrible "what," behind which looms an even more horrifying X, the "surcease." But man will always crumble the debt into small fragments, hoping vainly to ease the payment in that way. And when his hope is frustrated, he trades words and systems for others, which is to say, he issues new notes for old, putting off the time of reckoning, and, in the end, the debt is never paid.

When a word or a system falls from glory and makes room for another, it is not because of a diminution of its power to reveal, illuminate or cancel the impasse—wholly or in part—but rather the reverse: worn thin by constant use and handling, it no longer provides an adequate covering or serves to divert the mind. Glancing through the opening, man to his horror discovers dread Chaos looming beyond; quickly he stops up the crack with a new word, that is to say, he applies the old familiar cure, and is rescued from terror. And no wonder—the cure works for those who believe in it, just as belief itself is a diversion of the mind. An analogy may be taken from the protagonists themselves. So long as he is alive, striving, moving and acting, a man fills a space and everything appears clear; "all is well with me." The flow of life and all its contents are but a continued effort, a ceaseless endeavour to divert the mind. Every moment spent in the pursuit of one thing is also a moment spent in fleeing another—and that is all the profit therof. The profit of pursuit is the escape. At any moment, the pursuer finds present satisfaction not in what he has gained, but in what he has succeeded in escaping, and it is that which gives him temporary respite and security. "For to him that is joined to all the living there is hope." But then a man dies, and the space that he had filled is left void. Nothing diverts the mind—the screen is gone. The unknown rises before us in all its frightening dimension, and for a moment we sit on the ground before it, in darkness, mournful and still as stone. But only for a moment, for the force of life rushes in to seal the gap and provide us with a new remedy calculated to distract the mind and dispel the fear, and before the grave is quite covered, the void has been filled with a word. It may be a word of eulogy or of condolence, of philosophy or of belief in the after-life, and the like. The most dangerous moment— in speech as in life—is, therefore, the one between covering and covering, when Chaos glimmers. But such moments are rare in the routine of language as in the routine of life, and men generally skip over them, sensing nothing. The Lord preserveth the simple.

From all the foregoing comes the vast distinction between the language of speakers of prose and the language of speakers of poetry. The former, masters of the direct meaning, rely upon the common factor shared by words and phenomena, upon that which is firm and lasting in language, upon the accepted form—therefore they can make their verbal way in safety. Like one who crosses a frozen river by walking on its solid ice, they are free and able to ignore the swirling deep underneath their feet. Whereas the latter, masters of the hidden and secret meaning, are all their lives obsessed by the singularity of things, by that unique something, by that one point which binds into a coherent unit all phenomena and the language-forms that denote them, by the ephemeral moment which can never return, by the particular soul and immanent nature of things as grasped in a certain moment by the mind of the observer; therefore they must always flee from whatever is fixed and inanimate in the language, thus conflicting with their purpose, towards its living and mobile elements. Moreover, they are compelled at all times to introduce into it—by means of the keys in their possession— ceaseless movement, novel combinations and juxtapositions. The words vibrate under their hands, dimming and blazing, sinking and kindling, like the gems upon the *ephod*, emptying and filling, discarding one soul and taking on another. Thus the language is revitalized and trans-formed; a minute change can put a new gleam on an old word. The sec-ular becomes sacred and the sacred profane. Words which seemed immutable are momently removed from their settings and exchanged. And meanwhile, betwixt and between, the chasm glimmers. And that is the secret of the tremendous influence of the language of poetry. It tempts the sense of responsibility, the sweet terror of the test, so like the man who crosses the river in thaw, when the ice floes glide and roll. He dare not rest his foot on a floe for more than an instant, only just long enough to leap onto the next one and the next. And in between them twinkles the chasm, the foot slips, danger is near . . .

But, nevertheless, some cross safely from one bank to the other— for the Lord preserveth not only the simple.

Thus far about the language of words. But there are other, wordless languages—of music, weeping and laughter. And these too, belong to the "talking animal." They begin where words end, and their proper function is not to close but to open. They well up from the abyss, they are its tide. Therefore they overflow at times and sweep us away on the crest of their waves and none can withstand them; and sometimes they drive a man out of his mind or out of this world. But a spirit's creation lacking a single echo of those three, is not alive and should never have been born.

[*Translated by Yael Lotan*]

25 THE SWEET VOICE OF
THE LORD

FOUR CONTEMPORARY ISRAELI POETS

The last few decades may be viewed as a new golden age for Hebrew literature in Israel, both in prose and in poetry. Continuing the work of the great writers of the period before the establishment of the state, three generations of Israeli writers have demonstrated an unusual creative power, many of them achieving rare literary excellence and assembling a loyal and dedicated audience of readers. Hundreds of poets have published in the fifty years since the Israeli War of Independence, creating a vibrant and dynamic atmosphere in which poetry is still, despite adverse currents, prestigious and widely accepted. In this atmosphere it is not surprising to find many poets who tended to express either traditional Jewish mystical concepts, using kabbalistic terminology, or mystical experiences and aspirations in their own language. Some among them were (and are) scholars in the field of kabbalah. Isaiah Tishby, for instance, began his literary career as a poet in Hungarian, and in his last years—sixty years later—translated his poems to Hebrew. Other academics in this field used concepts and language of the kabbalah—Brachah Zack, Asi Farber-Ginat, Haviva Padaya, and others. Many other poets did the same, mainly influenced by the published work of Scholem and Tishby (as did some novelists—*Mahberot Itiel* by Aharon Meged, which is based on a scholarly study by Ephrayim Gottlieb, one of Scholem's best disciples). Artists also employed kabbalistic concepts and images, most notably Mordechai Ardon. Kabbalistic worldview and terminology has thus become an integral part of the literary language and convention.

Other poets developed their avenues of expressing mystical experience without use of traditional kabbalistic terminology, developing their own language and concepts. In such cases recognizing them as "mystical" is highly speculative and subjective, and selecting examples may be arbitrary. Yet it seems to me that ignoring this vibrant, creative realm when presenting the variety of Jewish mystical experience throughout history would be wrong. In every generation in the past some Jewish mystics followed the traditional terminology and modes of expression, while others presented their mysticism in new ways and forms. The present generation is not different, and should be recognized as a legitimate continuation, even when radical new ways of expression are presented. It should be noted that the poets of the last decades continue vigorously to make use of the inherent integration of mysticism and eroticism that is a characteristic of medieval and modern Jewish mysticism. Love and sex, God and woman are closely interwoven in these poems.

Yona Wollach

It is impossible to present here even a minute portion of the vast field, in which names like Hamutal bar Yosef and many others are prominent. There is little doubt, however, that the most original and forceful poet who included manifest mystical elements in her poetry was Yona Wollach (1944–85), one of the most outstanding Hebrew poets of the twentieth century. Wollach, who never left Israel and was not directly influenced by contemporary European and American literary trends, is regarded as the founder of Hebrew postmodern poetry, introducing revolutionary concepts in the use of language — alternating between the most literary levels and street vulgarity, presenting stark eroticism in an unusual way, bringing down taboos and ridiculing all conventions. Her short life, spent between mental hospitals and communities of drug addicts, is a saga of intense physical and mental torments, which are often expressed in religious and mystical terms that are fused with intense eroticism. Here are four examples:

When You Will Come to Sleep with Me Like God
When you will come to sleep with me like God,

Only in spirit,
Torture me as much as you can,
Be for me the eternally unreachable,
Find respite in my suffering,
I shall be in deep water,
Never shall I reach the shore,
Not even by a glance,
Or by a feeling,
Or in a deluge,
Water below and water above,
Never the heavens,
Open air,
The most tightly closed place in the world
An open place
Always a closed open place
Neither open nor closed,
That is, closed open
That is, neither closed nor open
So that I shall never imagine
That I was viewing everything from above,
To view from above the view,
Be only spiritual,
Pure pain isolated like a chord of pain
So that I shall never touch
So that I shall never know
So that I shall never really feel
At no time actually, really
Like all those others of yours
Always on the way

To the best of our knowledge, Yona Wollach never read systemati-
cally works by mystics or about mysticism, nor was she acquainted with
any mystic who had such extensive knowledge. Intuitively she expressed
some of the dominant motifs in mystical literature and language: Most
of the phrases are negative ones, and oxymorons abound. The erotic
element, which is presented rather bluntly in many of her poems, is
subdued here, and there is an emphasis on "only spiritual." Pain and
suffering are an unavoidable part of the experience, and the rest is an

endless, even hopeless, quest for a vision, or knowledge, which is destined always to remain unachievable: Always on the way, never to arrive.

I Shall Never Hear the Sweet Voice of the Lord

I shall never hear the sweet voice of the Lord
Never will his voice pass again below my window
Large drops will be falling in the wide vistas, signs.
The Lord does not come any more to my window
How can I envision again His sweet body,
To dive deep into His eyes I shall not descend any more to dig out
Glances will transverse in the universe like wind
How can I remember this beauty without crying
Days will pass in my life like tremors in the body
Near shards to remembered touch broken even more from weeping.
The air is charmed by the shape of his movement when He moves
Never will the sound of yearning again pass the threshold
At the time when a person will resurrect like the dead ones
     the memories, like essence
If only his sweet glance will stand by my bed and I shall cry.

A few subdued hints of kabbalistic terminology can be discerned here—the broken shards, the essence (a term which in Hebrew is comprised of the four letters of the tetragrammaton—HVYH, YHVH). This seems to be an expression of yearning to a past experience which will not be repeated.

Tefilin (Philacteries)

You shall come to me
Do not let me do anything
You shall do for me
You shall do everything for me
Everything which I shall just start to do
You shall do instead of me
I shall put on philacteries
I shall pray

You shall put also the philacteries for me
Encircle them on my hand
Play them with me
Move them gently over my body
rub me well with them,
excite me in every place
make me faint with emotions
Pass them over my clitoris
tie my hips with them
So that I shall climax quickly
Play them with me
Tie my hands and feet
Do things to me
Against my will
Turn me on my stomach
And put the philacteries in my mouth like reins,
Ride me, I am a mare
Pull my head back
Until I cry with pain
And you are satisfied,
Then I shall pass them over your body
With an intention which is not hidden in the face
Oh, how cruel will be my expression
I shall pass them slowly over your body
Slow, slow, slow
Around your neck I shall pass them
I shall encircle your neck several times by them, on one side
And on the other side I shall tie them to something stable
Especially something very heavy maybe which can turn
I shall pull and pull
Until your soul departs
Until I suffocate you
Completely by the philacteries
Which are stretched across between the stage
And the shocked audience.

It seems that here we find the opposite attitude compared to the previous two poems. Instead of memory and yearning to the sweet voice of God or the vision of the open-closed place, here the subject is religious ritual, which in Judaism is expressed by the philacteries that men, when praying, tie themselves with. The instrument that should be used as a means for approaching God is transformed into an instrument of torture in a sadomasochistic erotic game, which culminates in the orgasm reached by the woman and the suffocation of the male figure by the philacteries. The instrument of prayer is thus used to reach supreme pleasure as well as death.

When You Will Come to Sleep with Me Come Like My Father
When you will come to sleep with me
Come like my father
Come in the darkness

Speak in his voice
Which I shall not recognize
I shall crawl on four
And speak about what I do not have
And you will chastize me:
Take your leave of me
In the gate
Say goodby
A thousand times
With all the "missing you"
There are
Until God will say:
"Enough"
And I shall let go
And shall not sleep
Neither with God
Nor with my father
I shall wish to sleep with you
But you will not let it
Together with my father
You will be suddenly revealed
As the one responsible for
The inhibitions

My father will be an angel
Prince of hosts
And both of you will try to make of me
Something
I shall feel
like nothing
And shall do all
That you will tell me to do.
On the one hand you shall be God
And I shall wait for the afterwards
And you will not be the authority
And I just a poor one
Trying to be polite
I shall divide you into two
As well as myself
The part of the soul
The part of the body
You shall appear as two
And me too
Like two seals,
One wounded
limping a fin,
Or two women
One always limping
And you are one face
And one is hardly visible.

Benjamin Shvili

The collection of poems entitled *Songs of Yearning for Mecca* was published by Benjamin Shvili in 1992. This young poet is a devoted student
of religious and mystical texts, not only Hebrew ones but also Christian,
Moslem, Hindu, and Buddhist, and his poetry constantly refers to
images and concepts derived from all of them. His poetry, unlike that of
Wollach and others, represents a conscious immersion in mystical literature and a profound attempt to internalize and personalize them in
order to use them to express his own personal spirituality. It is apparent

that Shvili has found in the world mystical tradition a vehicle by which his own emotional reaction to the universal and the personal, the erotic and romantic, in his life can be expressed.

Creation[1]

I gave birth to air, and the air gave birth to wind, and from the
    wind
A wind was born and afterwards
Water and the water gave birth to air and from the air
Was born
Wind and afterwards water
And the water gave birth to air
and heat from the intercourse of the air in the wind and the wind
    in the water and from the heat
Was created fire which gave birth
To earth and the earth gave birth
To me
And I gave birth to love.

A Song of Desire for Krishna

Like water to the sea moon to the darkness and dusk to the star of
    my beloved Krishna
I am for you
My body is hungry for your body like the hunger of the body to
    the mirror
Your life has carved with a knife my life
When you are in fullness I am incomplete
Like a day without a sun and colour on the earth such is the day
    in which
You will forsake me
Your friends will say like a bird to the branch you are lucky.

With the Lines of Ibn El Arabi

A human being knows the God only
Because
It is the wish of God to know himself
Like

I knew the pounding of the heart of the
Burning vagina of my beloved
In order to
Fell the tremors of what is mine there
Was in love.

God Has Touched Me

The God has touched me with your fingers my beloved
Looked at me from your eye
Hummed at me from your throat
Wetted my face from your lips and your tongue
Clung to me from your womb

Agi Mishol

Agi Mishol is one of the most prominent Israeli poets today. Her early
poems were distinctive in their use of natural and agricultural images; she
is a veritable "nature poet," though her poetry included many other elements, including intense, profound eroticism. In the following brief
poems these are united in metaphors worthy of classical mystical poetry.

Meditation

1
The moon is in its fullness.
I am in my fullness.
Erecting like a Cobra from a basket to the tune of your flute
    within me.

2
Self-negated
and disrupted in the soft spot of the skull,
I am experiencing (hovva)
in my Yehovati[2]
and a lonely angel
without a stone
without a ladder
ascends and descends

until morning
in my body

3
Listening
to the metronome of life
of my breathing
and sun's butterflies
yellow
are quivering
within my veins
in the major scale of existence.

A Love Song

Why do you wander so far
in quest of the wondrous
When it is between my legs?

Come to me
deep
to my womb

Because dusk has descended
and the oranges were switched off.

My voice which is receding from me
Is listening to me

My gaze which is sent to the distance
Is observing me
What I am extending my hand to touch
Touches me and returns
To the God of which
I am made.

13
God is the sense of vision
which paves ways within the body

He is the blanket of love
covered in the skin

He is the sudden illumination
of all my cells.

Maya Bejerano

When Maya Bejerano started to publish her poetry she was regarded as
a "high-tech" poet, using extensively images and metaphors derived
from modern technology and science. Her poems expressed an absorp-
tion of contemporary terminology and worldview into an intense, internal spiritual life. In her later poems the scope of her language and sen-
sitivity has broadened, and the deep union she feels between the self,
the universe, and the divine realms is remarkable. It is a fitting conclusion for this anthology, because these three poems from her cycle of
poems, *The Hymns of Job*, represent, I believe, the loss of many distinctive terminological and metaphorical characteristics of religious
poetry, including spiritualistic and mystical ones, into the general
poetic expression of the end of the twentieth and the beginning of
twenty-first century.

My Garment Is Empty of Body
My garment is empty of body bereft of life
peeled off the flesh in which it was wrapped
in pale lightness eagerly inquisitive
in spite of the pain, brief as was mentioned,
this is another kind of alienation, we probably went sailing
after I've accepted this wondrous transformation simply
to meet up with the truest of the truest
the essence of life's principle nice to meet you
what exactly must I remove?
And how long will this meeting in black last
and without committing to remain outside the light—
overlaid like a tray of aches
a tray laden with grapes—
I cannot or don't want to.

Suddenly I Was Stabbed from Behind

Suddenly I was stabbed from behind,
and before me stood a black angel, a talking stone,
and he took me into his crackling wings
like an elevator shaft in an invisible tower
and I alighted with him, ascended with him, descended with
      him, I was consumed,
disgorged, discharged, and came back to myself with open eyes;
my dear ones hung over me, the more I smiled at them,
the more they blew my nose, wiped my tears that absolutely
      weren't
flowing from anywhere, but
in the main we successfully recognized one another, namely,
we took a picture together;
once again I was suddenly stabbed from behind, and an angel,
darker than the first of talking stone,
stood before me and took me into his crackling wings;
in a sweet-bitter flavor his knowledge was transmitted to me,
seeped into my ears, and I turned a dark tint,
smooth and glistening,
we alighted ascended descended as if in an elevator in an invisi-
      ble tower
his thick knowledge transmitted to me
received and absorbed and instantly squeezed
into a slimy fluid that dripped from the pores
of my black skin, as mentioned,
I was gleaming like a stone and all the other angels sang with me
in a discordant voice that infuriated me,
how can angels be so off-key,
they've been out of practice for thousands of years, emissaries of
      divine bidding

For years they've been fossilized
steeped in graves, in veins,
in coloring books, albums, carved in marble, steel
and cardboard, etched in glass
they tore themselves loose rose to sing with me

calling as one: come come
and I did I came I obeyed knowing
they'd take me to him
and they took me to him

Job: I Was Cast onto a New Life Cycle
Job: I was cast onto a new life cycle
an immaculate youth in the gentle light of morning
I awake naked as on the day of my birth
wish to begin my life afresh
only my great pensive eye contemplates the past
my pensive gloomy eye
it sees ahead
like the upside-down memory of an infant;
I've rejected all my former treasures
to return here
naked and young cast into a new life
after I've emerged from God's belly, the belly of pain
I roam the gulf of my soul
enter the recess of my person, the recess of my ocean,
up to the small reef that opens in the folds of my familiar brain,
I'm lit,
my consciousness before me like a set table.

"Hast thou entered into the springs of the sea?
or hast thou walked in the search of the depth?"
(Job 38:16)

NOTES

Introduction

1. Some recent examples include: Nelson Pike, *Mystic Union: An Essay in the Phenomenology of Mysticism*, Ithaca and London: Cornell University Press 1994; William McNamara, *Christian Mysticism*, New York: Continuum 1981.

2. A recent survey of definitions and attitudes toward the concept of mysticism is presented in an extensive chapter in: Bernard McGinn, *The Foundations of Mysticism*, New York: Crossroads 1994, pp. 266–342.

3. By the term "historical approach" I mean the acceptance of textual evidence as the dominant source of understanding and rejection of imposition of concepts and definitions derived from a theology, ideology, or philosophy of religion. See a detailed discussion in my essay: "In Quest of a Historical Definition of Mysticism: the Contingental Approach," in: *Pharos, Studies in Spirituality* 3 (1993), pp. 58–90 (now included in my *Jewish Mysticism*, vol. III, Northvale, N.J.: Aronson 1999, pp. 1–46).

4. In the case of Latin and Arabic sometimes such a barrier has been established, excluding people who are not proficient in these languages, yet the premise is that once one knows the language there is nothing that separates him from the divine message. In some cases the texts have been restricted, open only to the upper strata of the religious hierarchy; yet this practice also demonstrated that the

texts themselves are understandable, only that understanding should not be available to all.

5. This attitude is clearly manifest in the classical texts of Christian mysticism, from the Pseudo-Dionysius treatises to Meister Eckhart and Saint Teresa. One brief example will suffice here: "The Cloud of Unknowing," an influential English manual of mysticism (anonymous; the end of the fourteenth century) states:

A naked intention directed to God, and himself alone, is sufficient. If you want this intention summed up in a word, to retain it more easily, take a short word, preferably of one syllable, to do so. The shorter the word the better, being more like the working of the Spirit. A word like "God" or "love." Choose which you like, or perhaps some other, so long as it is of one syllable. And fix this word fast to your heart, so that it is always there come what may. It will be your shield and spear in peace and war alike. With this word you will hammer the cloud and darkness above you. With this word you will suppress all thought under the cloud of forgetting. So much so that if ever you are tempted to think what it is that you are seeking, this one word will be sufficient answer. And if you would go on to think learnedly about the significance and analysis of that same word, tell yourself that you will have it whole, and not in bits and pieces . . . . Just as meditations of those who seek to live the contemplative life come without warning, so, too, do their prayers. I am thinking of their private prayers, of course, not those laid down by Holy Church. For true contemplatives could not value such prayers more, and so they use them, in the form according to the rules laid down by the holy fathers before us. But their own personal prayers rise spontaneously to God, without bidding of premeditation, beforehand or during their prayer. If they are in words, as they seldom are, then they are very few words, the fewer the better. If it is a little word of one syllable, I think it is better than it is of two, and more in accordance with the work of the Spirit.

Thus, in a few sentences, a complete denial of language, thinking, learning, traditional prayer, and religious institutions is expressed. See: *The Cloud of Unknowing and Other Works*, translated into modern English with an introduction by Clinton Walters, Penguin Books, 1961, 1978, Chapter 7, pp. 68–69.

6. Analogically, it can be said that we may never know whether God exists or not or what is its nature, but we can study efficiently the impact of the belief in God on human civilization.

7. In modern Hebrew the word "kabbalah" is used for a receipt as well as "reception" in a hotel.

8. See the detailed analysis of this story and its implications concerning the authorship of the *Zohar* in G. Scholem, *Major Trends in Jewish Mysticism*, New York: Schocken 1954, pp. 190–93; I. Tishby, *The Wisdom of the Zohar*, vol. I, Oxford: Oxford University Press 1989, pp. 78–102.

9. Talmudic tradition states the paradox that when Moses ascended Mount Sinai God revealed to him all the secrets of the Torah, including "everything that a scholar will innovate in the future." Thus, all possible interpretations of scriptures, which seem to be brilliant, new discoveries, are actually ancient ones, always hidden within divine wisdom, and revealed to Moses in the great theophany. See the detailed discussion in my *On Sanctity*, Jerusalem: Magnes 1997, pp. 112–26 (in Hebrew).

10. A series of attempts to bridge this gap are presented in the volume: *Midrash and Literature*, ed. Geoffrey H. Hartman and Sanford Budick, New Haven and London: Yale University Press 1986.

11. One of the most important among these midrashic methodologies, which is very difficult to explain outside the range of Hebrew discourse, is *temurah*, letter-substitution, which enables the midrashic exegete to exchange every letter by every other one and thus create new words to substitute those in the scriptural text. This was used already in the Bible itself, when Jeremiah referred to Bavel as *Sheshakh* (Jer. 25:25), using the *temurah* system of ATBS. To do this, one has to list, vertically, all the letters of the alphabet from *Aleph* to *Tav*, and then, parallel to it, all the letters in an inverse order, from *Tav* to *Aleph*, and then substitute each for the other — T instead of A, S instead of B, etc. In this way Bvl becomes Ssk. This can be done in an infinite number of such arrangements: B replacing A, C replacing B, D replacing C in ABGD, or skipping to letters: C instead of A, D instead of B etc., and so on ad infinitum.

12. See below, pp. 44–48.

13. Rev. 13:18, and see Bernard McGinn, *Antichrist: Two Thousand Years of Human Fascination with Evil*, New York: HarperCollins 1996, pp. 52–53.

14. Seven of the most important manuscripts of this literature have been presented in a scholarly format side by side in Peter Schaefer's *Synopse zur Hekhalot Literatur*, Tübingen: J. C. B. Mohr (Paul Siebeck), 1981. Studies surveying the whole field are: P. Schaefer, *The Hidden and Manifest God*, Albany, N.Y.: SUNY Press 1992; J. Dan, *Ancient Jewish Mysticism*, Tel Aviv: MOD 1991; Rachel Elior, "Mysticism, Magic and Angelology—The Perception of Angels in Hekhalot Literature," *Jewish Studies Quarterly* 1 (1993/94), pp. 1–53.

15. Scholarly edition by N. Sed-Rejna, *Revue des etuted Juifs* 123 (1964), pp. 259–305; 124 (1965), pp. 23–123.

16. See below, pp. 21–22.

17. Concerning the history of Merkavah speculation, and its beginnings within the book of Ezekiel itself, see David Halperin's detailed monograph, *The Faces of the Chariot*, Tübingen: J. C. B. Mohr (Georg Siebeck) 1988, pp. 38–48 et passim.

18. Scholarly edition by I. Gruenwald, *Temirin*, vol. I, Jerusalem 1972, pp. 101–39.

19. Schaefer's *Synopse*, sections 81–280.

20. Schaefer's *Synopse* sections 335–426; and see the scholarly edition by Rachel Elior, Jerusalem Studies in Jewish Thought Supplement, 1981.

21. Schaefer's *Synopse*, sections 544–596; Published by G. Scholem as an appendix to his *Jewish Gnosticism, Merkavah Mysticism and Talmudic Tradition*, New York 1960, pp. 101–17. The title has been given to this text by Scholem, based on a medieval quotation.

22. Edited with an introduction, translation, and extensive commentary by Hugo Odeberg, *Third Enoch or The Hebrew Apocalypse of Enoch*, Cambridge 1928. The original Hebrew title of the work was just *Sefer hekhalot*; the title connecting it with the library of the pseudepigrapha was given by Odeberg. A new translation and commentary by Philip Alexander is included in James H. Charlesworth, *The Old Testament Pseudepigrapha*, vol. I, Garden City, N.Y.: Doubleday 1983, pp. 223–316.

23. The Greek term *pleroma* was used by some Gnostic writers to indicate the unity within the multiplicity of divine powers, and adopted analogically to describe any concept of several divine powers constituting together the divine realm.

24. This subject has been studied in detail by A. Kuyt, *The Descent to the Chariot*, Tübingen: J. C. B. Mohr (Paul Siebeck), 1997. The question of the meaning of the term "descent," which is insistently employed by these mystics when referring to their ascent, has not been satisfactorily resolved.

25. The various texts of this treatise have been published by M. S. Cohen, *The Shiur Qomah: Texts and Recensions*, Tübingen: J. C. B. Mohr (Paul Siebeck) 1985; and see Cohen's monograph on the subject: *The Shiur Qomah: Liturgy and Theurgy in Pre-Kabbalistic Jewish Mysticism*, Latham and New York, 1983. The text is included in Schaefer's *Synopse*, sections 688–704. Concerning its significance see Dan, *Ancient Jewish Mysticism*, pp. 48–58, and *Jewish Mysticism*, vol. I, pp. 205–16.

26. This view is held by R. Elior, who in a series of studies emphasized the priestly element in Hekhalot literature; see: "From Earthly Temple to Heavenly Shrines: Prayer and Sacred Song in the Hekhalot Literature and Its Relation to Temple Traditions," *Jewish Studies Quarterly* 4 (1997), pp. 217–67.

27. This interpretation of the Song of Songs is not connected with the allegorical concept of that work that developed both in Judaism and in Christianity somewhat later in the third century and viewed the biblical treatise as the narrative of the love relationship between God and Israel or God and the church.

28. J. Dan, *Jewish Mysticism* I, pp. 189–204. There is one section in Bavli Berkhot 7a, which describes Rabbi Ishmael as a high priest and refers to God as Akhatriel Yah Adonai Zevaot; it is rather obvious that in this case Hekhalot is the source; see Scholem, *Major Trends*, p. 356 n. 3.

29. See concerning this treatise in detail: J. Dan, *Jewish Mysticism*, vol. I, pp. 109–28.

30. Concerning the role of the Song in early Christian mysticism see McGinn, *Foundations of Mysticism*, pp. 20–22, 121–26 et passim.

31. Concerning the Sefer Yezira see Dan, *Jewish Mysticism*, vol. I, pp. 129–87, and detailed biblography there.

32. Many of these circles and the history of their emergence and their teachings are described in most of the chapters of J. Dan, *Jewish Mysticism*, vol. II. See also: G. Scholem, *Major Trends in Jewish Mysticism*, New York, 1954, pp. 80–118; I. Marcus, *Piety and Society*, Leiden: Brill 1980; J. Dan, *The Unique Cherub Circle*, Tübingen: J. C. B. Mohr (Paul Siebeck), 1999.

33. Abraham Ibn Ezra (c. 1089–1164) was a neo-Platonic philosopher, scientist, and exegete, one of the first Jewish philosophers from Spain to write in Hebrew and to visit many communities, in the East and in the West. Some of his work was done in London. The impact of his work on Jewish esoterics was very meaningful, both in Germany and in Spain and Provence.

34. Published in four volumes by E. E. Urbach, Jerusalem: Mekizei Nirdamim 1939–1964.

35. *Sefer Hasidim*, Wistinetzki-Freiman edition, Frankfurt a/M 1924, sections 1–26.

36. Concerning the emergence of the kabbalah and its early history see the magnificent monograph by Gershom Scholem, *The Origins of the Kabbalah* (first published in Hebrew, Tel Aviv: Schocken 1948, then in an extended form in German, Berlin: De Gruyter 1962, then again in a four-volume Hebrew version based on his university lectures, Jerusalem: Academon 1960–65, and then, after the author's death, in an English translation edited by R. J. Zwi Werblowsky, Princeton 1987). It should be regarded, I believe, as the finest work of historiography produced in Jewish studies in the twentieth century (though a close runner-up is Scholem's Shabbatai Zevi).

37. On the book *Bahir* as an original, medieval myth, see the introduction to vol. II of *Jewish Mysticism*, pp. xiv–ix and 1–16.

38. See Eliot R. Wolfson, "The Doctrine of Sefirot in the Prophetic Kabbalah of Abraham Abulafia," *Jewish Quarterly Review* 2 (1995), pp. 336–71; 3 (1996), pp. 47–84.

39. Y. Liebes suggested that the *Zohar* should be viewed as a colloaborative work of several mystics. See his *Studies in the Zohar*, Albany, N.Y.: SUNY Press, 1994.

40. A summary of this period, and the establishment of the community in Safed and the teachings of Issac Luria, is presented in ch. 7 in Scholem's *Major Trends in Jewish Mysticism*, pp. 244–86. On the mystical atmosphere in Safed in that period see Lawrence Fine, *Safed Spirituality*, New York: Paulist Press 1984.

41. It is debatable whether the teachings of Rabbi Abraham Yehuda ha-Cohen Kook, in the first third of the twentieth century, constitute such an alternative. There is disagreement among scholars concerning the characterisation of this vast body of writings. It can be viewed, however, as a restatement, in modern terms, of the Lurianic worldview.

42. A brief description of this upheaval was presented by Scholem in his famous article, "Redemption Through Sin," first published in Hebrew in 1937, and an English translation is included in his book: *The Messianic Idea in Judaism*, New York: Schocken 1971, pp. 78–141. See also his *Major Trends in Jewish Mysticism*, pp. 287–324. The history and teachings of Shabbatai Zevi and his prophet, Nathan of Gaza, are presented in Scholem's *Shabbatai Zevi: The Mystical Messiah*, published in Hebrew in 1957, and an English translation by R. J. Zwi Werblowsky, Princeton: Princeton University Press 1973.

43. A recent historical study of his life and teaching is presented in: *Abraham Isaak Kook*, by Ben Zion Bokser, New York: Paulist Press 1978; see especially the preface by Rivkah Shatz-Uffenheimer, pp. xvii–xxv.

44. S. Dubnow wrote the only comprehensive history of Hasidism, published in Hebrew, Tel Aviv 1936.

45. Chapter 9, pp. 325–50.

46. See my two articles: "A Bow to Frumkinian Hasidism," Modern Judaism 11 (1991), pp. 175–93; and "The End of Frumkinian Hasidism," *Studies in Hasidism*, ed. David Assaf, E. Etkes, and J. Dan, *Jerusalem Studies in Jewish Thought* 15, 1999, pp. 261–74. "Frumkinian" is a reference to Michael ha-Levi Frumkin, who in 1863 began publishing collections of Hasidic narratives and portrayed the movement in nostalgic, literary terms, which served as a basis to Buber's and others' nostalgic images.

47. This includes even the extensive article "Hasidism: Its teachings

and literature" in the *Hebrew Encyclopedia*, vol. 17 (1969), written by I. Tishby and me.

48. Their teachings have been presented in Rachel Elior's monograph, *The Paradoxical Ascent to God*, Albany, N.Y.: SUNY Press, 1994.

49. *Mishnat ha-Zohar*, Jerusalem: The Bialik Institute; vol. I (1949), vol. II (1961), translated into English as *The Wisdom of the Zohar*, I–III, Oxford: Oxford University Press, 1989.

50. Chaim Wirszubski, *Pico della Mirandola's Encounter with Jewish Mysticism*, Jerusalem: Israel Academy of Sciences and Humanities, 1989.

51. The great scholar who studied this phenomenon, Frances Yates, wrote an article dedicated to understanding what Pico meant by the term *magic* in this formula. Her conclusion was that there is no meaningful difference in Pico's terminology between *magic* and *kabbalah*, and that actually *magic* here is just another reference to the secrets of the kabbalah. See her study: "Giovanni Pico Della Mirandola and Magic" in: *L'opera e il pensiero di Giovanni Pico della Mirandola nella storia dell 'Umanesimo*, Firenze 1965, vol. I, pp. 159–203. This study was included in her well-known work, *Giordano Bruno and the Hermetic Tradition*, London, 1964.

52. The association with Martin Luther does not end here. Reuchlin was denounced by the pope in the same edict that denounced Luther. Some historians described Reuchlin as the father of the Reformation, yet this is very doubtful. Reuchlin did not join the reformation until his death (1526). Concerning *De arte kabbalistica*, see the English translation by Martin and Sarah Goodman, Lincoln (Nebraska) and London: University of Nebraska Press 1993; the best edition, however, is the Italian translation, with notes and introduction, by Giolio Busi and Saverio Campanini, Firenze: Opus Libri 1995.

53. This conflict is described in detail in the classical study of Reuchlin's life: L. Geiger, *Johann Reuchlin, sein Leben und seine Werke, Leipzig*, 1871.

54. See J. Dan (editor), *The Christian Kabbalah: Jewish Mystical Books and Their Christian Interpreters*, Cambridge, Mass.: Harvard University Press, 1997.

55. See his article: "The Assyrian Tree of Life: Tracing the Origins of Jewish Monotheism and Greek Philosophy," *Journal of Near Eastern Studies* 52 (1993), pp. 161–208. This article was followed by several others, in which the Christian character of the concept of the ancient origins of Judaism, kabbalah, the tetragrammaton, and Greek philosophy were connected to the "true" teachings of Christ.

56. A distressing example of this phenomenon is the vast enterprise of "kabbalistic" publications initiated and directed by "kabbalist Rav Berg." Originally he based his teachings on the work of one of the last authentic kabbalists of the twentieth century, Rabbi Ashlag, who wrote a voluminous commentary on the *Zohar*, based on the teachings of Isaac Luria. It was heartbreaking to observe how this authentic enterprise deteriorated into a New Age mishmash of nonsense.

57. Another distressing phenomenon is connected with the numerous books concerning kabbalah, its history, nature, and traditions, as instruction for modern living, published by "Z'Ev ben Shimon Halevi" who is a nice English gentleman from Hampstead who does not know any Hebrew. His books were used as authentic, scholarly sources by many, including Simo Parpola.

Chapter 1

1. Concerning the relationship between these two treatises see J. Dan, *The Ancient Jewish Mysticism*, Tel Aviv: MOD 1991, ch. 10. A scholarly edition of these texts from all available sources is to be found in: Gottfried Reeg, *Die Geschichte von den Zehn Martyrern*, Tübingen: J. C. B. Mohr (Paul Siebeck) 1985, and there also a detailed bibliography.

2. Exod. 21:16.

3. Concerning the history of Samael as an evil figure in the mystical texts, see my studies included in *Jewish Mysticism*, vol. III, pp. 253–82, 367–414.

4. In Hekhalot Rabbati Ch. 6 a story is told of Rabbi Hanina ben Tradyon, who was sentenced to death by the emperor. He used his magical powers and exchanged his features with those of the

emperor, and the Roman was the one who was executed. Rabbi Hanina then ruled Rome and used his powers to destroy it.

5. This is very strange, as both Rabbi Nehunia and Rabbi Ishamel were born after the temple in Jerusalem was destroyed by the Emperor Titus in 70 C.E. On the peculiar, mystical concept of history evident here and in other tests of this literature see J. Dan, *Jewish Mysticism*, vol. I, pp. 189–204.

6. One example from the *Zohar* is translated below, ch. 13.

7. See Mor Altshuler, *Messianism in Hasidism*, Haifa: Haifa University Press (in press).

8. See Ezek. 1:27.

9. The heavenly realm, according to the descriptions in this literature, contains numerous rivers of fire (comp. Dan. 7:10), over which there are many bridges.

10. The name of the seventh heaven, based on the phrase in Ps. 68:5.

11. The title "Prince of the Countenance" is given in talmudic and Hekhalot literature to a prominent angel who stands in front of God (and not to his left or right). In many texts his name is Metatron, but in Hekhalot Rabbati he is called Soria.

12. Totrochiel, or Totrosia, is the highest appellation of the divine power in this part of Hekhalot Rabbati (in the first part of the work it is Zaharriel). The name may have been derived from *tetra*, denoting the tetragrammaton.

13. Rabbi Ishmael is often called in this literature "son of the proud," *ben geim*.

14. Sanhedrin was the name of the highest rabbinic court during the period of the second temple. The full assembly included seventy-one sages and the "small" one, twenty-three.

15. This statement is impossible from a historical point of view, as the temple was destroyed sixty or more years before the narrated events.

16. This is the list of the martyrs who will be executed by the Romans according to this narrative. While the persons on the list are prominent sages, they lived and died in different times, and assembling them together is pure fiction.

17. A list of divine names, most of them seemingly meaningless, follows.

18. This sentence seems to denote that there is a historical-apocalyptic meaning to the mystical practice, if God waits for the people of Israel to perform it, probably connecting it—as indicated in the next paragraph—with the future redemption.

19. "Seals" (*hotam*) is a common term in this literature, probably indicating secret divine names written on some kind of precious material, invoking magically the power inherent in that name.

20. The unruly, arbitrary guardians of the gate of the six palace are described in detail both in Hekhalot Rabbati and in Hekhalot Zutarti, and it is evident that the authors of these works incorporated in them traditions that they themselves did not understand. See an analysis of the available sources in my study on the subject, in *Jewish Mysticism*, vol. I, pp. 261–310.

Chapter 2

1. New York: The Jewish Theological Seminary 1960, pp. 103–117 (using the version found in ms. Oxford, Bodleian Library 1531). The text was included in Schaefer's *Synopse zur Hekhalot-Literatur*, no. 544–96. Two English editions of this text have been published recently: Naomi Janowitz, *The Poetics of Ascent: Theories of Language in a Rabbinic Ascent Text*, Albany, N.Y.: SUNY Press 1989; Michael D. Swartz, *Mystical Prayer in Ancient Judaism: An Analysis of Ma'aseh Merkavah*, Tübingen: J. C. B. Mohr (Paul Siebeck), 1992.

2. The Hebrew language does not have a term for a number greater than ten thousand, which is indicated by the biblical term *revavah*. I have kept the "accurate" number recounted by the text because it seems that the numbers were meaningful for the early mystics. "Thousand of ten thousand," that is, units of ten million, are the standard ones in this literature, often used to describe the magnitude of the limbs of God in the *Shiur Komah*.

3. It is difficult to imagine what the mystic intended by the term *shalhaviot*; obviously, it must be an entity counterpart to a chariot.

4. The Oxford manuscript is incomplete here, presenting five letters that may have been an abbreviation that is incomprehensible

now. It is obvious that all other sources did not have any further information, and tried to reconstruct the missing text or omit it. The text in ms. New York 8128 is just a guess. Only one manuscript probably reached Europe, and ms. Oxford is its closest copy; when it is corrupt, the others have no information.

5. The text of ms. Oxford reads here, in Schaefer's copy, "seventh"; the similarity of the Hebrew letters *vav* and *zayin* explains the mistake.

6. The verse in Ez. 3, which is included in the daily prayer of sanctification in the Jewish ritual.

7. This is the author's interpretation of the difficult phrase in the verse, which reads: "blessed is the glory of God from its place." The writer understands this phrase as a reference to his shekhinah. Scholem pointed out (p. 106, note 11) parallels to this phrase-interpretation in the Midrash and in the Aramaic translation.

8. The American writer Chaim Potok preserved a meaningful item of information concerning Scholem's views on this subject. Potok described in his novel *The Book of Lights* his studies with "Dr. Keter," obviously Gershom Scholem, at the Jewish Theological Seminary, during which they read some of these texts. Potok relates that he asked Scholem whether the writers really meant what they expressed, and Scholem responded that he believed that they meant it literally. I tend to agree with Scholem, provided that we distinguish between "what they meant" and "what they really envisioned."

9. The tradition that Rabbi Akibah acquired this secret is recorded in the beginning of *Hekhalot Zutarti*, a text that belongs to an earlier stratum of Hekhalot literature.

10. The actual word used here is *signs* (*otot*), which may be a mistake instead of *letters* (*otiot*). Scholem read *otiot*. As far as the meaning is concerned, there is no difference.

Chapter 3

1. While this edition deserved praise (it was republished by Ktav Publishing House in New York, 1973, with a new introduction by Jonas Greenfield), the author does not. After writing this work he

became one of the leaders of the Nazi party in Sweden and wrote theological works that displayed deep anti-Semitic prejudice.

2. Attributing to Metatron the name of God is not new. This figure was identified with the angel leading Israel in the desert after the exodus, about whom it is said "for my name is within him." The name Metatron should be understood as "including the tetra," that is the tetragrammaton, YHVH.

3. This episode is told in the Talmud (Bavli Hagiga 15a), and is retold, with some embellishments, in this text.

4. See P. Alexander, "The Historical Setting of the Hebrew Book of Enoch," *Journal of Jewish Studies* 28 (1977), pp. 156–80; J. Dan, *The Ancient Jewish Mysticism*, Tel Aviv: MOD 1991, pp. 101–14.

Chapter 4

1. The few known details have been analyzed by David Kaufman, in his *Mehkarim ba-Sifrut ha-Ivrit shel Yemey ha-Beynayim*, Jerusalem 1962, pp. 11–77.

2. See G. Vajda, *La Theologie ascetique de Bahya ibn Pakuda*, Paris 1947; I. Tishby and J. Dan, *Mivhar Sifrut ha-Musar*, Jerusalem: Newman 1971, pp. 109–204; A. Lazaroff, "Bahya's Asceticism against its Rabbinic and Islamic Background," *JJS* XXI (1970), pp. 11–38; J. Dan, *Sifrut ha-Musar veha-Derush*, Jerusalem: Keter 1975, pp. 47–68.

3. Some of these early expressions have been surveyed by Gershom Scholem, *Kabbalah*, Jerusalem: Keter 1974, pp. 35–37.

4. Bavli Ta'anit 2a.

Chapter 5

1. William R. Inge, *Christian Mysticism*, London: Methuen 1899.

2. See: Colm Luibheid and Paul Rorem, *Pseudo-Dionysius: The Complete Works*, New York: Paulist Press 1987.

3. See: Bernard McGinn, The Growth of Mysticism (vol. II of the series *The Presence of God: A History of Western Christian Mysticism*), London: SCM Press 1995, pp. 80–118.

4. One way to distinguish between the two is the different relation-

ship to linguistic expression. The neo-Platonists were rationalistic philosophers, who held that their statements reflect reality as it really is. The mystics, on the other hand, viewed any semantic statement as an approximation, a feeble, inherently unsuccessful attempt to express the inexpressible. It is not always easy to categorize a given text into the first group or the second.

5. The exact date of his death is uncertain; it is between 1053 and 1058, that is, when he was either thirty-two or thirty-seven.

6. S. Munk, *Melanges de philosophie Juive et Arabe*, Paris 1857–59.

7. The one Jewish source used by Gabirol is a quotation from the *Sefer Yezira*, the ancient Jewish work on cosmogony; the source is not identified in the treatise.

8. Many of Gabirol's contemporaries, Jewish scientists, esoterics, and rationalists of the tenth to the twelfth centuries, used the *Sefer Yezira* in this way, including Saadia Gaon and Rabbi Yehuda ha-Levi.

9. A detailed study of Gabirol's esotericism and mysticism and its sources is found in a monograph by Israel Levin, *Mystical Trends in the Poetry of Solomon Ibn Gabirol*, Lod: Haberman Institute 1986 (in Hebrew).

10. The Hebrew text, including a commentary and the sources used by the author, is found in Hayim Schirman's *Anthology of Hebrew Poetry in Spain and the Provence*, Jerusalem: The Bialik Institute 1955, vol. I, pp. 257–85.

Chapter 6

1. A monograph on this circle, including translations of some of its key texts, is found in my book: *The Unique Cherub Circle*, Tübingen: J. C. B. Mohr (Paul Siebeck) 1998.

2. This is particularly strange because the legend connecting Jeremiah, Ben Sira, and Joseph ben Uzziel is found in a satyrical, heretical collection of narratives known as the *Alphabet of ben Sira*. According to this narrative, Ben Sira was both the son and the grandson of Jeremiah, because his mother was Jeremiah's daughter who was impregnated from the prophet's semen in a bizarre, obscene way. We do not know of any way to explain how

such a narrative became sanctified by the circle of esoterics in Europe. See concerning the whole problem: *The Unique Cherub Circle*, pp. 16–35.

3. The divine figure described in the *Shiur Komah* is identified by these esoterics as the Unique Cherub, whereas in the writings of other esoterics in this period, like the Kalonymus circle in the Rhineland, it is identified with the divine glory.

4. This is a formula quoted from *Sefer Yezira*, 1:9, where the three terms, *voice*, *wind* (meaning the air used for speaking), and *speech* are the three elements of the divine pronouncements that were used to create the world.

5. This is an example of the use of the hermeneutic system of *temurah*, for which *etbash* is the best-known method: writing the last letter of the alphabet instead of the first, the one-before-last instead of the second, etc. The letters of the tetragrammaton thus are replaced by the letters MZPZ.

6. Bavli Kiddushin 49a.

7. This is the rabbinic interpretation of Exod. 33:20.

8. Tanhuma Pequdey 3; see Urbach, *Hazal*, pp. 206–8.

Chapter 7

1. The book *Bahir*, the earliest work of the kabbalah, contains an explicit series of instructions on how to derive this name from the verses, a fact that contributed to the centrality of the name in medieval kabbalah (see *Bahir* sections 107–10). The name was known before the late twelfth century when the *Bahir* was written, and it probably originated in the Gaonic period (seventh or eight century?).

2. Concerning Nachmanides and other kabbalists' concept of the divine name see: G. Scholem, "The Name of God and the Linguistic Theory of the Kabbalah," *Diogenes* 79 (Fall 1972), pp. 59–80; 80 (Winter 1972), pp. 164–94. J. Dan, "The Name of God, the Name of the Rose, and the Concept of Language in Jewish Mysticism," *Medieval Enconters* vol. 2 (Brill, Leiden 1996), pp. 228–48.

3. The Hebrew title includes a reference by *gematria* to Eleazar.

Concerning this work see J. Dan, *Jewish Mysticism*, vol. II, Northvale, N.J.: Aronson 1999, pp. 135–36.

4. Gershom Scholem published this introduction in his study of the rituals of the Jewish mystics, and the following text is based on the English translation of his (originally German) article. See: *On the Kabbalah and Its Symbolism*, New York: Schocken 1964, pp. 136–37. The text of the first portion of *Sefer ha-Shem*, with an English translation and commentary, was published by me in *Jewish Mysticism*, vol. II, pp. 129–78.

5. This text is found in several manuscripts, like British Library Cat. Margulioth 752 (add. 15,299) and Oxford, Bodleian Library, Michaelis 473 (Cat. Neubauer 1960). A detailed study of the text has been prepared by Irina Wandrey in a Ph.D. dissertation at the Institut für Judaistik, Freie Universität Berlin, 1997.

6. A reference to the ritual immersion demanded by Jewish law, which should contain no less water than this measure.

Chapter 8

1. This Eleazar explained in the introduction to the first theological treatise that he wrote in 1217, *Sefer ha-Hokhmah* ("The Book of Wisdom"). I published and analyzed this introduction in a study in Hebrew (*Zion*, vol. 29, 1964, pp. 173–77), and see *Jewish Mysticism*, vol. II, pp. 89–96 et passim.

2. Ivan Marcus was the first to point out the differences between Rabbi Eleazar and Rabbi Judah, especially concerning repentance, a central subject in the writings of both of them. See his *Piety and Society*, Leiden: Brill 1980.

3. This metaphor is derived from the *Sefer Yezira*, ch. 1, par. 7.

4. This introduction was printed in an anthology of esoteric texts called *Raziel ha-Malach* ("The Angel of Secrets"), Amsterdam 1601, p. 7a. See also J. Dan, *Ethical and Homiletical Literature*, Jerusalem: Keter 1975, pp. 135–36.

5. The Hebrew term *rokeach* (= provider of medicine and perfumes) has a numerical value identical to the name Eleazar. The same is true about the title of the esoteric work, *Sodey Razaya*.

6. It is possible that Rabbi Eleazar was following here the norm set

by Maimonides who began his great book of law with chapters dealing with theology and ethics.

7. These most unusual terms combine in their acronym to form the name "Eleazar." Using such highly literate words is characteristic of hymns written in the East in late antiquity, most notably in the poetry of Rabbi Eleazar ha-Kalir (sixth or seventh century).

8. This is the classical interpretation of the tetragrammaton as the combination of the three tenses of the verb "to be"—was, is, will be. In the Hebrew bible the name YHVH is vocalized according to this interpretation. Rabbi Eleazar dedicated his most detailed book, hundreds of pages, to the interpretations of this name and other sacred names of God.

9. The acronym of these last four words is YHVH.

10. This is a paraphrase of the *Sefer Yezira* 1:6.

11. This argument is derived from the "secret of the unity" by Rabbi Judah the Pious, who used the ability of God to hear everything at the same time to demonstrate the difference between creatures and their creator. According to him, God gave people the ability to see everything together to indicate and prove that God can do the same concerning hearing.

12. Paraphrasing Is. 40:18, 25.

13. Praphrasing Ps. 63:7.

14. Paraphrasing Prov. 10:1.

15. There follows a paraphrase of several sections from the *Sefer Yezira*.

16. Ps. 16:8.

17. Job 23:13.

18. The full names of these four letters equal 44, as does the phrase "he is one."

19. ETBS is one of the many systems of transmutation (temurah), in which every letter is exchanged for another letter that has the same place in the alphabet when it is recited from end to beginning, e.g., tav for aleph, shin for beth, etc. In this system the tetragrammaton, YHVH, is comprised of the letters MZPZ, which has the numerical value (*gematria*) of 300. The phrase "the creator, exists in everything" has the same numerical value.

20. The insistent repetition of this phrase throughout this text is

intended to deny the literal meaning of Gen. 1:27, from which one may surmise that God created man in his own form and image.

21. This is a denial that the anthropomorphic descriptions in the Bible are relevant to the creator.

22. Rabbi Eleazar used the Saadian formula concerning the three attributes of God: living, wise, and able.

23. Paraphrasing several verses, like Ps. 145:3, Job 11:7.

24. The acronym of these words is YHVH (indicating a new paragraph).

25. Again, four words the acronym of which is YHVH, here for the purpose of emphasis.

26. Saadia makes the linguistic statement that the biblical term *glory* is identical to the rabbinic *shekhinah*.

27. Like Isa. 6:1.

28. Ps. 147:5.

29. The author, following the *Shiur Komah* tradition, reads the verse as "our master is large" and the next phrase, and powerful, as the measurement of his greatness, [236.] Rabbi Eleazar paraphrases in the continuation of the paragraph several sentences from the *Shiur Komah*.

30. The Kalonymus circle theologians developed and elaborated a midrashic tradition, according to which the vision of God as seen by the prophets expresses the nature of the prophecy: if it is war, the glory looks like a soldier, if it is religious instruction, it looks like an old teacher.

Chapter 9

1. See Evelyn Underhill, *Mysticism*, New York: Meridian 1955, pp. 306–7 et passim (the term used here for this concept is *orison*).

2. See, for instance, *The Cloud of Unknowing*, as described in the introduction to this volume, p. 278, note 5.

3. E.g., the Sufi Abdul Kader al-Jillani, see my discussion in *On Sanctity*, Jerusalem: Magnes 1997 (Hebrew), pp. 395–410.

4. This is similar to some extent to the description of "seeing without eyes, hearing without ears" by Bahya Ibn Paquda's *Duties of the Heart*; see above, ch. 4.

5. The *kedushah* in the Bahir in sections 124–32, and see the analysis presented in my *Jewish Mysticism*, vol. II, pp. 6–14.
6. See Gabrielle Sed-Rajna, *Azriel de Gerona, Commentaire sur la liturgie quotidienne*, Leiden: Brill 1974.
7. See Meir of Narbonne's treatise against kabbalistic prayer, included in G. Scholem, *Origins of the Kabbalah*, pp. 398–400.
8. See I. Tishby's detailed discussion in *Wisdom of the Zohar*, vol. II, Oxford: Oxford University Press, 1989.
9. MGWJ 78 (1934), pp. 511–12, and a translation is included also in his *Origins of the Kabbalah*, pp. 417–19. The English text is taken from that book.
10. *Hasidim ha-Rishonim* are mentioned in Mishnah Berakhot 5:1 and several other ancient sources.
11. Scholem noted the connection between the atmosphere prevailing in this text the writings of the nonkabbalistic Iyyun circle, and indeed, but for a few phrases, this text could be read as emerging from prekabbalistic circles of Jewish mystics in Europe.
12. En Sof, literally: "without end," infinite, is the negative term that kabbalists used to indicate the uppermost realm within the Godhead, the eternal spirit that preceded the processes of emanation and creation.
13. These sentences, indicating the fusion of human will and divine will, are among the most radical expression of union with the divine in early Jewish mystical literature.
14. These three terms are essentially synonyms meaning "wisdom." In kabbalistic terminology they represent the supreme powers in the divine world, following the divine will, which is the highest emanated power.

Chapter 10

1. Gershom Scholem, *Major Trends in Jewish Mysticism*, pp. 119–55; idem, *Kabbalah*, Jerusalem: Keter 1974, pp. 52–56; Moshe Idel, *The Mystical Experience in Abraham Abulafia*, Albany, N.Y.: SUNY Press 1988; idem, *Studies in Ecstatic Kabbalah*, SUNY 1988.
2. Published by A. Jellinek, "Sefer ha-Oth, Apocalypse des Pseudo-

Propheten und Pseudo-Messias Abraham Abulafia," *Jubelschrift zum siebzigsten Geburstage des H. Graetz*, Breslau 1887, pp. 65–88 (Hebrew section).

3. This may be based on the image described in *Sefer Yezira*, 1.

4. An unclear phrase describes the sign. One possible reading would be that "seventy tongues" are emerging from that sign.

Chapter 11

1. Kiryat Sefer 1 (1924/25), pp. 127–39.

2. See the introduction to this volume, pp. 21–22.

Chapter 12

1. It should be noted that one of the names given in the thirteenth century to the kabbalists is *menakdim*, those who deal with the vowel-points, which were conceived as the soul of language: This idea is present also in the text presented here.

2. The author integrates here the verse in Exod. 3:14, in which God answers the question of Moses concerning his name saying *ehyeh asher ehyeh* ("I will ever be what I now am"), using the three words of the phrase as names of God.

3. These are not letters but marks that indicate the way to pronounce them, nekudot, which in Hebrew serve as substitutes to vowels. *Holam* indicates the sound O, *shuruk* indicates U, and *hirik* is EE.

4. In the phrase in Exod. 3:14 that is understood as three words that comprise the secret name of God.

5. The three-part phrase of the name of God in Deut. 6:4, "Hear O Israel," which was adopted as the center of Jewish prayer and the declaration of Jewish faith.

6. The author, following earlier midrashic-esoteric traditions, divides the word *bereshit*, "in the beginning," into two words, *bara shit*—"created six."

7. The term *six extensions* or *ends* and the cosmological picture presented here are derived from the ancient *Sefer Yezira* ("Book of Creation"), chapter 1.

8. This is a reference to an esoteric divine name, comprised of seven groups of six letters each, which do not have any linguistic meaning.
9. *Teamim*, small signs that accompany the words of the scriptures and indicate the melody by which they are sung in the synagogue.
10. The holy name of Yh (Yah, as in hallelujah, "praise Yah"), comprised of two letters that represent the divine father and mother.
11. This is a reference to the primeval light, which is described in Gen. 1:3, long before the sources of light, the sun and moon, were created.
12. The tenth letter of the Hebrew alphabet, *yod*, is written as a small mark that is sometimes described as a dot or point.
13. This picture—the emergence of all from a tiny point that extends into infinite light—has often been compared to the contemporary concept of the Big Bang as the beginning of the universe.
14. El in Hebrew is a general term for the divinity, while Elohim is conceived here as a particular one.
15. The system of the ten divine emanations, the *sefirot*, are often arranged in three columns, left, right, and center; three on each side and four in the middle.
16. The name, often regarded as the most mysterious and elevated name of God, actually consists of 216 letters, 72 groups of three letters each. The name is derived from the three verses in Exod. 14:19–21, each of which, surprisingly, consists of exactly 72 letters. The name is structured by writing the first verse, and below it the second in an inverse manner, that is, the last letter first and the first letter last, and then below them the third verse in the regular manner. Then the columns are read downward, 72 columns of 3 letters. This name is known to us several centuries before the *Zohar*, and it was used by all circles of Jewish esoterics in Europe.

Chapter 13

1. Three centuries later, the early death of Rabbi Isaac Luria Ashkenazi, the great kabbalist in Safed (died 1572 at the age of 38), was attributed to his revealing secrets that he learned in his studies in the celestial academy.

2. *Atik Yomin* (Daniel 7:9) is one of the most exalted terms in the kabbalistic description of the Godhead, and it refers to the highest power in the divine structure, the *sefirah Keter* (Crown).

3. Masach, the curtain that separates the divine world from the regions below it.

4. The word *forever* (*le-olam*) is written in this verse without the vowel vav, and it can thus be read as "to conceal" (*le-alem*), that is: this is my name that has to be secret.

5. A fictional figure that reveals great secrets in the *Zohar* (he is portrayed as the father of the miraculous child, the *yenuka*, who is described in the next chapter in this anthology).

Chapter 14

1. Bavli Hagiga 13a; Ezek. 1:27. The term has been appropriately adopted in modern Hebrew to denote electricity.

2. See A. Z. Aescoly, *Jewish Messianic Movements*, Jerusalem: The Bialik Institute 1987, pp. 305–8 (in Hebrew).

3. Zohar I, 5a–7a.

4. See above, ch. 4.

5. "Hear O Israel" (Deut. 5:4), a main section of the daily prayers.

6. Exod. 17:11, when Moses raised his hands to support Israel's fight against Amalek.

7. This is a reference to a midrashic exegesis in Bereshit Rabba 15:6, according to which the Tree of Life in the Garden of Eden had the size of five hundred years' walk.

8. The right side is the side of holiness; the left—the *sitra ahra*—is the realm of evil.

9. The author uses the two meanings of this Hebrew term: "obligation" and "sin." The halakhah defines these waters as an obligation, but the "child" uses the term to indicate that they belong to the realm of evil.

10. The Jewish custom is to declare the intention to say the blessing on the food before actually doing so; the homily explains why.

11. Berachot 20a.

12. The usual dwelling place of the shekhinah is between the two cherubs on the holy ark in the Temple.

Chapter 15

1. Part of which was published under the title *Maggid Meisharim* ("The Maggid of Righteousness"), see below, p. 224.
2. See below, pp. 118, 214.
3. G. Scholem, "The Maggid of Rabbi Joseph Taitazak," Sefunot 11 (1978), pp. 67–112 (in Hebrew). The text translated here is found in pp. 90–93.
4. See Exod. 31:18.
5. Yad Daniel.
6. That is, the current form of the Hebrew alphabet, and not the ancient Hebrew script that preceded the Babylonian exile.
7. It is not clear who is this "Joseph," who is mentioned several times in the text as a colleague of the writer. Depending on the date in which it was written, it could be Rabbi Joseph Della Reina.
8. This word is probably unnecessary.
9. Here follows a word that Scholem could not decipher.
10. The author uses the phrase in Exod. 32:16, concerning the divine writing.
11. Following Zach. 14:9.
12. "Point" here is the unit of which the vocalization marks are constituted.
13. Halves of a ball.
14. A reference to the supreme sefirah in the kabbalistic system.
15. Their names are listed; they are perfume plants used in Spain, the names are given in Spanish and Arabic (see Scholem, p. 91, note 4).
16. Isa. 59:19.
17. There are several magical practicers of "questions" addressed to heaven, some using the interpretation of biblical verses chosen arbitrarily, or asking a question before going to sleep and interpreting a dream as a response. "Written question" is another variation.
18. This also is a well-known practice, based on the belief that there is a particular secret magical name that enables a person to write automatically, his hand being guided by celestial powers.

Chapter 16

1. See Scholem, "Li-yediat ha-Kabbalah Erev ha-Gerush, *Tarbiz* 24 (1955), pp. 167–206.
2. The text was published by G. Scholem in *Zion* 5 (1933), pp. 124–130; an extended version in: *Studies in Jewish Religious and Intellectual History, Presented to Alexander Altmann,* edited by S. Stein and R. Loewe, University of Alabama: University of Alabama Press, 1979, pp. 101–108 (of the Hebrew section).
3. I analyzed this aspect in the development of the story in my study: Rabbi Joseph Della Reina, *Sefunot,* vol. VI (1962), pp. 313–326; see also *The Hebrew Story in the Middle Ages,* Jerusalem: Keter Publishing Co. 1974, pp. 222–237.
4. Published by Zalman Shazar, the third president of the State of Israel, in: *Eder ha-Yekar, Studies Dedicated to S. A. Horodetzki,* Tel Aviv: Devir 1947, pp. 97–117.

Chapter 17

1. A brief description of his work and ideas can be found in G. Scholem, *Kabbalah,* Jerusalem: Keter 1974, pp. 401–405 (written by Joseph Ben Shlomo).
2. A detailed analysis of this section is found in my *Jewish Mysticism and Jewish Ethics,* 2nd edition, Northvale, NJ: Aronson 1996, pp. 92–100.
3. The term used here is *gerushin,* literally: divorce, but the meaning is to take a journey away from home, going to the empty fields surrounding the town, and thus symbolically identify both with the exiled Shekhinah and the expulsion of Jews who live in exile. Cordovero wrote a treatise entitled *Sefer Gerushin,* in which he recounted his group's experiences during such journeys-expulsions. The term is repeated in the continuation of this paragraph.
4. The phrase is based on Mal. 2:14.
5. The duties of the husband to his wife according to Exod. 21:10.
6. Reflecting the basic Jewish concept that man is not complete unless he is married. A bachelor is often called *plag gufa,* "half a body." In the absence of the wife — if it is a justified absence — the

Shekhinah steps in. Man's obligations toward the Shekhinah are analogous to those of a husband toward his wife.

7. Reference to the kabbalistic work *Tikkuney Zohar*, which was written in the early fourteenth century in language and style of the *Zohar*, and published usually as the fourth volume of that work. Cordovero included it in his *Commentary on the Zohar, Or Yakar*. It is composed of seventy chapters, and the reference here is to *tikkun* 69.

8. Philacteries.

9. Threads of cloth attached to the corners of a garment. When one is wearing this and philacteries he is supposed to be in a state of sanctity.

Chapter 18

1. Within this circle Vital insisted on his leadership role. After Luria's death he compelled the other disciples to sign an agreement not to publish Luria's teachings and not to study them without him being present. See G. Scholem, *Major Trends in Jewish Mysticism*, pp. 254–257.

2. Houses in the East often have niches in the form of windows that are just cavities in the wall, which do not lead outside.

3. The term used here, *sitra ahra*, literally: "the other side," meaning the left side, is the usual Zoharic term for the powers of evil.

4. Metatron is the ancient name of the celestial "prince of the countenance," often regarded, both in Talmudic traditions and in ancient Jewish mysticism, as second to God. See about him the text describing Enoch being transformed to Metatron, above, ch. 3.

5. Killing two snakes, a male and a female, and thus overcoming the powers of evil, is described in the story of the attempt to bring forth the redemption by Rabbi Joseph Della Reina. This version of the story was known in Safed in Vital's time, and he mentions it in another work of his, the ethical treatise *Shaarey Kedushah* ("The Gates of Holiness").

6. This is a reference to the conflict between Jacob and Esau (= Rome, evil), described in Gen. 32.

7. This list in Gen. 36 was regarded in Zoharic kabbalah as the

ancient powers of evil. Esau was associated with Edom = Rome.
8. The prophecy of Ovadia about Edom was regarded as referring to Rome.
9. The Book of Zerubavel is an ancient Hebrew apocalyptic-messianic work, written probably in the sixth century, and was very popular in the Middle Ages as a description of the age of redemption, including the upheavals preceding it. The quotation is not found in the extant versions of this work.
10. Ezek. 1, 14.
11. Gen. 3, 24.
12. Vital uses the phraise *atik yomin*, Dan. 7:9, which in kabbalistic terminology was interpreted as referring to the highest stage within the Godhead.
13. Literally, sons of the tower, those who are elevated.
14. Bavli Berachot 57a.
15. A paragraph is omitted here, in which God explains to Rabbi Hayyim why the masters of the mishnah appear like birds, following verses, talmudic statements, and kabbalistic texts.
16. Rabbi Hayyim uses the term *seor she-ba-issah*, literally: yeast, meaning: the core of goodness in a particular context.

Chapter 19

1. Gershom Scholem analyzed in detail the first meeting and the emergence of the intricate relationship between Shabbatai Zevi and Nathan: *Shabbatai Sevi: The Mystical Messiah*, translated by R. J. Zwi Werblowsky, Princeton: Princeton University Press 1973, pp. 199–327.
2. Mechilta de-Rabbi Ishmael [portion Bo,] ch. 1.
3. Shabbatai Zevi, p. 223.
4. Scholem notes: There follow some untranslatable kabbalistic puns that imply a reference to Moses, the first redeemer.

Chapter 20

1. Scholem's Hebrew studies of the Sabbatian movement were edited and republished by Yehuda Liebes in a large volume,

Mehekerey Shabtaut, Tel Aviv: Am Oved 1992. The studies concerning the Donmeh sect are presented mainly in pp. 289–390.

2. Another section from this manuscript, written probably by the same author, was published in English by Scholem: "The Sprouting of the Horn of David: A New Source from the Beginning of the Doenme Sect in Salonica," in: *The Time of Harvest, Essays in Honor of Abba Hillel Silver*, New York 1963, pp. 368–386.

3. An English translation of this work with commentary and analysis was presented by Martha Himmelfarb, "Sefer Zerubavel," in: D. Stern and M. J. Mirsky (eds.), *Rabbinic Fantasies: Immaginative Narratives from Classical Hebrew Literature*, Philadelphia: The Jewish Publications Society 1990, pp. 67–90.

4. Concerning this figure see: J. Dan, "Armilus: The Jewish Anti-Christ" in: P. Schaefer and Mark R. Cohen (eds.), *Toward the Millenium: Messianic Expectations from the Bible to Waco*, Leiden: Brill 1998, pp. 73–104.

5. "Prince" in this context means the celestial power in charge of that nation or religion.

6. Shabbatai Zevi's wife (see Scholem's note, p. 310 note. 7).

7. As Scholem notes, it is probably the date of the revelation of the Messiah (p. 310, note 10).

8. Scholem explains that this may be a reference to the first group of believers who converted to Islam following Shabbatai Zevi (311, note. 1).

9. Scholem suggests that this may be a reference to the city of Adreanopol.

10. As Scholem points out, this is an apocryphal book attributed to Nathan of Gaza by the Doenmeh author.

11. Scholem notes that the name can be read also as Admeal, indicating that he sought to connect the name with Edom. It is rather clear, however, that the name is derived from the *Sefer Zerubavel* apocalyptic myth, in which the demonic emperor, the son of Beliyal and a statue of a beautiful woman in Rome, is called Armilos. The Greek ending has been replaced by the Hebrew one, -el instead of -los. He is described as the emperor of Rome and the whole world in the ancient apocalypse, destined to be vanquished by the Messiah.

12. This is further proof that the author follows here the apocalypse of *Zerubavel*.

13. Literally, "yihhud" is the declaration of God's unity. The meaning has been extended first to prayers that declare the unity, and then to powerful prayers, accompanied with deep mystical intentions, that have magical qualities.

14. The context is that of the destruction of Edom, which was identified with Rome in Jewish tradition.

Chapter 21

1. This material has been presented in a brief biography by Simon Ginzburg, in his *The Life and Works of Moses Hayyim Luzzatto*, Philadelphia: Dropsie College 1931. A much larger collection of the documents was published by the same author in a two-volume Hebrew work: *Igrot Ramhal u-Vney Doro*, Jerusalem: Mosad Bilaik 1937. Another collection of writings and analysis is that by Meir Benayahu, *Kitvey ha-Kabbala sheleRamhal*, Jerusalem 1979. The most important study and publication of texts is that of Isaiah Tishby, in his *Mehkerey Kabbala u-Shluhoteha*, vol. III, Jerusalem: Magnes Press 1993, which presents the author's nearly forty years of study of Luzzatto, his circle, and his influence.

2. Tishby, op, cit. pp. 809–910.

3. Tishby, op.cit., 756–808.

4. The main accuser of Luzzatto was Rabbi Moses Hagiz, whose anti-Sabbatian crusade, including his conflict with Luzzatto, has been presented in a monograph by Elisheva Caelebach, *Rabbi Moses Hagiz and the Sabbatian Controversies*, New York: Columbia University Press 1990.

5. Published from a manuscript by Tishby, op. cit., pp. 740–744.

6. See Bavli Yoma 39a.

7. The Hebrew term translated here as *messenger* is *mal'ach*, an angel.

8. Again, the Hebrew term is "angels of God."

9. This is a reference to Enoch, who was elevated to the divine world while still alive, as proved by the verse quoted in the following sentence. Concerning Enoch's transformation, compare the text from ancient Jewish mysticism translated above, ch. 6.

10. These are entities that seem to be earthly, but in truth they are sacred and divine.

11. See Bereshit Rabba 82:6 (and compare 47:6, 10). The midrash concludes from the language concerning God's "lifting himself" from Jacob (and a similar statement concerning Abraham) that the patriarchs have a similar status to that of the holy chariot described by Ezekiel.

12. See Ketubot 108b.

13. Gen. 28:14.

14. Bavli Hulin 91b.

15. This is a reference to the last, highest human attribute before holiness.

16. A reference to the verse, Lev. 16:3.

17. This term has several meanings in Hebrew (all different from the one given to it in the Christian Trinity); the most important one, which is its essential meaning here, is the power of prophecy, or the powers of prophets.

18. Bavli Ta'anit 2a. If these powers are not given to messengers, it means that those who can employ them have acquired divine attributes. The second "key" refers to the power to make a woman able to conceive.

19. These three elements are the ones that conclude the barayta of rabbi Pinhas ben Yair, around which the whole book is structured.

Chapter 22

1. This book was the second Hasidic work ever to be published. The first was the same author's *Toledot Ya'akov Yosef*, published in Koretz, 1780. The Besht's epistle was the subject of intensive scholarly study. See most recently: Mor Altshuler, "Messianic Strains in Rabbi Israel Ba'al Shem Tov's Holy Epistle," *Jewish Studies Quartely* 6 (1999), pp. 55–70, and detailed bibliography there.

2. To the Besht's question: "When will you come? The Messiah responded: When your teachings will engulf the whole earth." Scholars are divided in the interpretation of this answer, whether

it indicated an imminent redemption in which the Besht, or at least his teachings, are involved, or whether it means an indefinite delay. See Altshuler's analysis in her study (note 1).

3. An English edition of this work, *In Praise of the Besht*, was published by Dan Ben Amos and Jerry Mintz, Bloomington: Indiana University Press 1970.

4. While there is very little doubt that the first narrative is a historically reliable document, the second one may be a jocular tale, trying to belittle Rabbi Gershon, whose relationship with the Besht was not always amicable.

5. It is very difficult to understand to what exactly the Besht was referring. The terms used here are unusual ones.

6. This seems to be the meaning of the sentence, but, with some difficulty, it could also be read as "the rabbis will be put to trial before all the sages of the Talmud."

7. A day, including a holiday, in Judaism is counted from sundown to sundown. A holiday begins in the evening, and is "out" the next evening.

8. The process of ascension is described here in terms derived from the ancient Hekhalot mysticism. For an example of such a mystical journey, see above, ch. 1, *The Secret of the World*.

9. This is the narrator's note, refering the reader to a section in the first published book of Hasidism, *Toledot Ya'akov Yosef*, written by the Besht's disciple, Rabbi Jacob Joseph of Polonoi, printed in Koretz, 1780. According to that book, the Besht's teacher was the prophet Ahia ha-Shiloni, who was also the teacher of the prophet Elijah according to rabbinic tradition.

10. A holy name composed of two letters of the alphabet.

11. The term used here, *reshimah*, is better known in the history of Jewish mysticism in the Aramaic form, *reshimu*; it can be translated also as residue, what remains after something has been discarded in spiritual terms. See Scholem, *Major Trends*, pp. 264, 267.

12. Kan Zippor, see Deut. 22:6, the commandment to extend mercy on a bird's nest. The *Zohar* (vol. 2, page 8a, and compare *Tikkuney Zohar tikkun* 6) says that in the bird's nest, the place of divine mercy, God has hidden the Messiah.

13. The narrator emphasized that both of them used the same prayer

book, so that the difference in the time cannot be explained by
different versions. Luria's prayer book, which included many kabbalistic additions and instructions for intentions, was used in the
eighteenth century by kabbalists and "intellectual aristocracy"; the
Hasidic movement later adopted it for all its adherents.

14. After the last words of this prayer a person has to step three little
    paces backward.
15. The conversation is recorded in the third person.
16. Housing wheat, a barn.
17. It is tempting to find an analogy between the Besht's shaking dur-
    ing prayer (which is attested in several other narratives as well)
    and the Protestant mystical movement of the Shakers. Yet the
    analogy is incomplete: The Shakers express their devotion to God
    by shaking, instead of praying, while the Besht's shaking accom-
    panies formal, traditional prayer.

Chapter 23

1. A detailed analysis of these two stories and the messianic meaning
   of the missing conclusions is included in my monograph *The
   Hasidic Story* (Jerusalem: Keter 1975, in Hebrew), pp. 132–172.
   A. Band was kind to include my suggestions in his presentation of
   these stories.
2. It is remarkable that Rabbi Nahman began to tell these stories in
   1806, after his only son died, an event that intensified his messianic pretensions (as pointed out by M. Piekarz, "Ha-mifneh be-
   Derech Haba'to shel Rabbi Nahman of Brtslav in 1806," Tarbiz
   40 (1971), pp. 226–54; and see his monograph, *Hasidut Bratslav:
   Perakim be-Hayey Mehollelah ibi-Ketaveh*, Jerusalem: The Bialik
   Institute 1972). It should be noted that this tragedy represented
   the end of the line of the founder of Hasidism and Rabbi
   Nahman's grandfather, Rabbi Israel ba'al Shem Tov. The messianic meaning of childlessness has been demonstrated very
   clearly in the contemporary messianism of the Habad Hasidism,
   which was led in ther last generation by a childless Zaddik, and is
   now leaderless. See J. Dan, *Modern Jewish Messianism*, Tel Aviv:
   MOD 1999, pp. 189–203 (in Hebrew).

3. See G. Scholem, *Major Trends in Jewish Mysticism*, New York: Schocken 1954, pp. 260–268; idem, "Kabbalah and Myth," in his: *On the Kabbalah and Its Symbolism*, New York: Schocken 1965, pp. 110–117; I. Tishby, *Torah ha-Ra veha-Kelipah be-Kabbalat ha-Ari*, Jerusalem: Schocken 1942.

4. It is thus incorrect to present the present expectation of many Habad Hasidim that Rabbi Menahem Mendel Shneersohn will return and redeem the world as a "first" in Jewish messianic thought. These Lubavitch believers are now joining the Btaslav Hasidim, who adopted this belief 190 years ago. The Bratslav Hasidim were called by other groups "dead Hasidim," because of their faithfulness to a dead leader; there are now tens of thousands of new "dead Hasidim" of the Lubavitch kind. Early Bratslav believers were encouraged by computations concerning the date of Rabbi Nahman's return—in twelve years, then forty years, etc.

5. The name of this person can be understood also as "the Man of Truth and Kindness." The terms are part of the usual kabbalistic list of divine powers.

6. *Komah shelemah*, a reference to the concept of the divine world in anthropomorphic terms as a complete human stature, when every aspect and power is represented as a limb. It is derived from the ancient (prekabbalistic) text known as *Shiur Komah*, the measurement of the height. See G. *Scholem, On the Mystical Shape of the Godhead, New York: Schocken 1991, pp. 1–45;* J. Dan, *Jewish Mysticism*, vol. I, Northvale, N.J.: Aronson 1998, pp. 205–216.

7. The term *riddles* (*hidot*) should not be understood in a narrow sense. This Hebrew term was used by the Tibbonite translators of Jewish philosophical texts from the Arabic to Hebrew in the late twelfth and the early thirteenth centuries also to represent narratives in general, tales that often carry ethical or ideological messages.

8. See in detail: I. Tishby, *The Wisdom of the Zohar*, Oxford: Oxford University Press 1989, vol. I, especially pages 423–430.

9. See G. Scholem, *Major Trends in Jewish Mysticism*, New York: Schocken 1954, pp. 232–234 et passim.

10. Among the main studies of the doctrine of the Zaddik in Hasidism see: G. Scholem, "The Zaddik," in his *On the Mystical Shape of the Godhead* (above, note 6); Arthur Green, "The Zaddik as Axis Mundi in Later Judaism," PAAJR vol. XLV (1977), pp. 327–47; idem, "Typologies of Leadership and the Hasidic Zaddik," in: Arthur Green (editor), *Jewish Spirituality*, vol. II, New York 1987, pp. 127–56; Rivkah Shatz-Uffenheimer, "Le-Mahuto shel ha-Zaddik ba-Hasidut," in: *Molad* 18 (1960), pp. 365–78; Samuel H. Dresner, *The Zaddik: The Doctrine of the Zaddik According to the Writings of Rabbi Yaakov Yosef of Polnoy*, London: Abelard-Schiman 1960; Rachel Elior, "Between Yesh and Ayin: The Doctrine of the Zaddik in the Works of Rabbi Jacob Isaac, the Seer of Lublin," in: A. Rapport-Albert and S. J. Zipperstein (editors), *Jewish History: Essays in Honor of Chimen Abramsky*, London 1988, pp. 391–456; David Assaf, *Derekh ha-Malkhut: The Life of Rabbi Israel of Rizhin*, Jerusalem: Magness Press 1996; Ada Rapoport-Albert, "God and the Zaddik as the Two Focal Points of Hasidic Worship," *History and Religion*, vol. XVIII (1979), pp. 296–325; I. Tishby and J. Dan, "Hasidic Doctrine and Literature," *The Hebrew Encyclopaedia*, vol. 17 (1969), pp. 769–821; J. Dan, *Jewish Mysticism* (above, note 6), vol. IV, pp. 67–86, 111–30.
11. This is an addition by the narrator, Rabbi Nathan of Nemirov.
12. Rabbi Nahman of Horodenka, who immigrated to Eretz Yisrael in 1764.
13. Meaning: infirm, unhealthy.
14. Suffering in this world sometimes is interpreted as assuring that one will be admitted to the reward in the next world.
15. This may be a reference to the story in *Shivhey ha-Besht*.
16. Isa. 4:2: "In that day shall the plant of the Lord be beautiful and glorious and the fruit of the land shall be excellent and comely for them that are escaped of Yisrael."

Chapter 24

1. It seems that it is just an accident that the title is also the title of the greatest work of Jewish mysticism. There is no inherent con-

nection between the two; Bialik's poem is dedicated to expressing his emotions when touched by many kinds of light that a boy meets in his daily life.

2. "The Four Sages Who Entered the Pardes," see above, p. 63.
3. This poem has been studied and interpreted in various ways. See an analysis and bibliography in my article on the subject in my book *The Outsider and the Mandarin*, Ramat-Gan: Massada 1975 (in Hebrew), pp. 160–166.
4. This poem, like many others, has been translated into English in an elegant, moving way by Ruth Nevo (*Cahim Nachman Bialik: Selected Poems*, Bilingual Edition, 1981). For the purpose of this anthology I translated it in a more literal manner, emphasizing the use of traditional Jewish esoteric and mystical terms. Thus, for instance, Nevo translated the title as "Gazed and Died"; I preferred the traditional translation of *heziz*, "peeked," which is derived from the phrase used in the parable of the Four Sages.
5. A supreme class of angels.
6. See: J. Dan, "The Gate to the Sixth Palace," *Jewish Mysticism*, vol. I, pp. 261–310.
7. First published in *Ariel* 50, 1979, pp. 108–114.

Chapter 25

1. This poem follows the scheme of the emergence of the elements of which the universe was created in the *Sefer Yezira*, ch. 1.
2. Throughout the history of Jewish mystical expression the homonyms indicating the tetragrammaton and the verb "to be" has been used. The poet does it again here, but instead of using YHVH, the traditional supreme apellation of God, she uses an original form indicating that YHVH "is mine" and is a feminine entity.

PERMISSIONS

Band, Arnold. Excerpt from *Rabbi Nahman of Bratslav: The Tales.* Reprinted by permission of Paulist Press.

Bialik, H. N. "Language Closing and Disclosing." Translated by Yael Lotan. Published in *Ariel: A Quarterly of Arts and Letters in Israel,* No. 50, 1979. Reprinted by permission of the translator and *Ariel.*

Bejerano, Maya. "Suddenly I was stabbed from behind," "My garment is empty of body bereft of life," and "Job: I was cast onto a new life cycle" from *The Hymns of Job.* Reprinted by permission of the Association of Composers, Authors, and Publishers of Music in Israel (ACUM).

Charlesworth, James H. "The Hebrew Apocalypse of Enoch" from *The Old Testament Pseudepigrapha.* Copyright © 1983, 1985 by James H. Charlesworth. Reprinted by permission of Doubleday, a division of Random House, Inc.

Cordovero, Moses. Excerpt from *The Psalm Tree of Deborah by Moses Cordovero.* Translated by Louis Jacobs. Reprinted by permission of Sepher-Hermon Press.

Gabirol, Solomon Ibn. Excerpt from *The Kingly Crown.* Translated by Bernard Lewis Reprinted by permission of Frank Cass Publishers.

Gorion, E. Bin, and D. Ben Amos. Excerpt from *Mimekor Yisrael: Classical Jewish Folktales.* Collected by M. J. Bin Gorion. Translated by I. M. Lask. Reprinted by permission of Indiana University Press.

Mishol, Agi. "Meditation" and "A Love Song." Reprinted by permission of the author.

Scholem, Gershom. Excerpt from *Major Trends in Jewish Mysticism.* Copyright © 1946, 1954 by Schocken Books. Copyright renewed 1974 by Schocken Books. Reprinted by permission of Schocken Books, a division of Random House. Excerpt from *Origins of the Kabbalah.* Translated by Allan Arkush. Edited by R. J. Zwi Werblowsky. Reprinted by permission of The Jewish Publication Society. Exerpt from *Shabbatai Sevi: The Mystical Messiah.* Translated by R. J. Zwi Werblowsky. Reprinted by permission of Pora Fanieth Sholem.

Schvili, Benyamin. "Creation," and "With the Lines of Ibn El Arabi." Reprinted by permission of Schocken Publishing House, Ltd. "A Song of Desire for Krishna" and "God Has Touched Me" published by permission of the author.

Tishby, I. Excerpt from *The Wisdom of Zohar.* Reprinted by permission of The Littman Library of Jewish Civilization.

Wollach, Yona. "When You Will Come to Sleep with Me Like God," "I Shall Never Hear the Sweet Voice of the Lord," "Tefilin," and "When You Will Come to Sleep with Me Come Like My Father" from *Yona Wallach: Selected Poems 1963–1985.* Reprinted by permission of Hakibbutz Hameuchad Publishing House, Ltd.

INDEX

Donmeh/Doenmeh sect, 303(n1)
    myth of, 217–222
Dubnow, S., 39
Dumah, 158
The Duties of the Heart (Ibn Paquda),
    75–80, 294(n4)
"duties of the limbs," 76

Ecclesiasticus, 96
Edom, 221, 301(n7;n8), 303(n11),
    304(n14)
Effacement, 130
Egypt, Jewish settlement in, 31
Ehyeh, 143, 186, 296(n2)
El, 297(n14)
Eleazar ben Judah of Worms, Rabbi,
    24, 25, 26, 27, 102–103, 107,
    121, 150, 151, 155, 156, 157,
    158, 159, 170, 171, 172, 173,
    185, 291(n2), 292(n1;n2),
    293(n7;n8), 294(n22)
Eleazar ha-Kalir, Rabbi, 293(n7)
Eleazer the Great, Rabbi, 52
"elevation of the soul," as mystical
    experience, 232–233
El gadol, 145
"Eli eli lama shavaktami," as Jesus's
    words, 10
Elijah the Prophet, 185, 186, 209,
    210, 230, 306(n9)
Elior, R., 284(n48)
Elisha, 230
Elohim, 99, 143, 144, 145, 146,
    297(n14)
emanation, 142–143
Emancipation, 39
emet, 247
Emunot ve-Deot (Gaon), 110
end of prophecy, 12–13, 15
Enlightenment, 39, 42
Enoch, 18, 280(n22)
    deification of, 61–73, 301(n4),
    304(n9)

Enosh, 68
En-sof, 118, 119, 142, 143, 295(n12)
ephod, 261
eroticism
    in modern Israeli poetry, 264–269,
        270, 271–273
    Shekhinah and, 197, 200, 201,
        225–226
    in Sodey Razaya, 108–109
    in Wollach poetry, 264–269
Esau, 301(n6;n7)
Eshkoly, A. Z., 203–204
esotericism
    Greek, 45
    Jewish, 24, 27, 46, 101, 107, 121
etbash, 99, 112, 291(n5), 293(n19)
Etz Hayyim (Vital), 203
exegesis
    in Christianity, 14
    in Judaism, 13, 14
Exodus, 25
expulsion, of Spanish Jews, 31–36,
    176, 182, 195, 213
extensions/ends, 296(n7)
Ezekiel, 17, 57, 161, 305(n11)

Falaqueira, Shem-Tov, 82
Falk, Rabbi, 236
Farber-Ginat, Asi, 263
Ficino, Marcilio, 44–45
fire
    bridges of, 286(n9)
    chariots of, 55–56
The Flood, 66
Florence, humanism in, 44
Fons Vitae (Avicebron), 82
"Four Sages who Entered the Pardes,"
    20, 150, 255, 310(n2)
Frank, Jacob, 37
Frumkin, Michael ha-Levi, 283(n46)

Gabirol, 81–94, 290(n7;n8;n9)
Gabriel [angel], 177, 179

Hasidism
emergence of, 33, 38, 51, 231
history of, 283(n44)
literature of, 195, 232, 305(n1),
306(n9)
Lubavitch, 41
modern, 38–41
prayer ritual in, 117, 120
Rabbi Nahman as leader of,
239–249
Zaddik doctrine in, 309(n10)
Havvayah, 185
Ha-Zarfati, Rabbi Avigdor, 99
Hebrew
language, 43, 299(n6)
midrashic methodologies in, 14
numbers in, 57, 287(n2)
postmodern poetry in, 264–275
Hebrew Book of Enoch, 18
hekhal, 18, 19
Hekhalot, 16, 17, 18, 22, 28, 29, 58,
82, 255, 280(n14), 281(n26)
mysticism in, 20, 21, 110
Hekhalot Rabbati, 17–18, 20, 49–54,
62, 150, 285(n4), 287(n20)
Hekhalot Zutarti, 20, 287(n20),
288(n9)
Hermetic treatises, 44–45
hesed, 196, 246
Hesed le-Abraham, 177
Heziz va-Met, 43
hieroglyphics, 47
High Middle Ages
Jewish mysticism in, 23, 29
kabbalah in, 9
Hinduism, 44, 48, 269
Hiyya, Rabbi, 151, 154, 157, 170
hokhmah, 119, 196, 245
The Holocaust, 39–40, 231
Holy Land, Jewish settlement in, 31
Holy Name, worship of, 101–105,
132, 227
holy names, 22

hovah, 164
humanism, 44, 45
Hungary, Hasidism in, 39
HVH, 110
HVYH, 190
HYH, 110

Ibn Ezra, Rabbi Abraham, 25, 99,
282(n33)
Ibn Gabirol, Solomon. See Gabirol
Ibn Paquda, Rabbi Bahya, 23, 75–80,
294(n4)
Ibn Tabul, Rabbi Joseph, 34
Ibn Tibbon, Judah, 75
Iddo the Prophet, 158
imitatio dei, 195
immersion ritual, 104–105, 292(n6)
Inge, William, 81
"In Praise of Rabbi Hayyim Vital,"
203
"In Praise of Rabbi Isaak Luria,"
203
"In Praise of the Besht," 232
In Praise of the Besht (Ben Amos &
Mintz), 306(n3)
Internet, as kabbalah source, 48
Isaac, 167, 248
Isaac ben Abraham "the blind," 29
Isaac, Rabbi, 30, 151, 157, 162, 164,
228
Isaiah, 2, 12
"I Shall Never Hear the Sweet Voice
of the Lord" (Wollach), 266
Ishmael, Prince of, 221
Ishmael, Rabbi, 18, 19, 20, 25, 49, 50,
51, 52, 53, 60, 62, 64, 65–66, 69,
70, 71, 97, 98, 150, 281(n28),
286(n13)
visions of, 55–60
Islam, 22, 81, 178
Jewish conversion to, 217, 303(n8)
mysticism of, 7, 23, 75, 121, 130,
269

Name of Forty-two Letters, 185, 186
Name of Power, 188
names, mystical significance of, 129,
   179–180
Naphtali, tribe of, 221
Nathan of Gaza, 37, 181, 283(n42),
   302(n1), 303(n10)
   prophetic vision of, 213–215,
   217–222
Nathan of Nemirov, Rabbi, 247,
   309(n11)
Navarro, Shlomo, 183, 184
Near East
   Jewish settlement in, 31
   kabbalism in, 31
Nearness of the Messiah, 220
nefesh, 98
Nehunia. See Ben ha-Kanah, Rabbi
   Nehunia
ne'ilah [prayer], 233, 234
nekudot, 11, 140, 296(n3)
neo-Platonism, 27, 81, 282(n33),
   289(n4)
Nero, 15
Netivot, kabbalism in, 42
Nevo, Ruth, 310(n4)
New Age sects, kabbalah in, 44, 48,
   285(n56)
New Testament, 15
   language of, 10
Newton, Isaac, 48
New York, Hasidism in, 39
Nicholas III, Pope, 122
Nine Hundred Theses (Pico), 45
Ninevah, 207
Noah, 112
North Africa
   Jewish settlement in, 31
   kabbalism in, 31
notaricon, 47

Odeberg, Hugo, 62, 280(n22),
   288(n1)

ophanim, 68, 69
oral tradition, role in mythology,
   29
"An Orchard of Pomegranites"
   (Cordovero), 32, 196
The Origins of the Kabbalah
   (Scholem), 282(n36)
Or Yakar (Cordovero), 32, 196
Oslo agreements, 39
Ottoman Empire, Jewish settlement
   in, 31
The Outsider and the Mandarin
   (Dan), 310(n3)
Ovadia, 207, 302(n8)

Padaya, Haviva, 263
"The Palm Tree of Devorah"
   (Cordovero), 195–201
Paradise, 254
pardes, 253, 255
Pardes Rimonim (Cordovero), 32
pargod, 98
Parpola, Simo, 48, 285(n7)
"Path of the Names," 132
"The Path of the Righteous"
   (Luzzatto), 226
"Paths of the book Yetsirah," 132
Patros [Salonica], Nathan of Gaza in,
   220
"Peeked and Died" (Bialik), 252–254,
   310(n4)
Pentateuch, 30
Pesaq ha-Yira'ah veha-Emunah, 93
pessimism, mysticism and, 3
philacteries, 201, 301(n8;n9)
Pico della Mirandola, Giovanni, 45,
   46, 284(n50;n51)
Pico della Mirandola's Encounter
   with Jewish Mysticism
   (Wirszubski), 284(n50)
Piekarz, Mendel, 240
pietism, in Jewish mysticism, 27
Pietists, Jewish, 23, 107, 108

tikkun, 34, 35, 37, 200–201, 242, 246m301(n7)

Tishby, Isaiah, 43, 139, 141, 149, 263

Toledot Ya'akov Yosef, 234

Tomer Devorah (Cordovero), 193–201

Topiel, Prince, 54

Torah, 13, 58, 69, 70, 78, 102, 120, 125, 131, 132, 136, 137, 138, 140, 149, 151, 164, 172, 199, 233

Toriel, 127

Totrochiel, 51, 52, 286(n12)

Totrosia, 53, 54, 286(n12)

Totrosiai Zortak, 53

traklin, 255

tree, as image of divine world, 28

Tree of Life, 163, 170, 203, 298(n7)

trisaggion, 116

Trismegistus, Hermes, 44–45

"The True Man of Kindness" (Nahman), 242–244, 246

Tummim, 138

Turkey
    Jewish settlement in, 31, 176
    Sabbatian movement in, 217–218

tzimtzum, 242

Ukraine, Hasidism in, 39

Unique Cherub, 96, 97, 98, 99

unique cherub circle, 24, 25, 96, 290(n1), 291(n3)

The Unique Cherub Circle (Dan), 96, 290(n1)

Urim, 138

Uzzah, 66, 68

Valle, Rabbi Moshe David, 223, 224

Va-yomer, 145

virginity, Christian concept of, 20

"The Visions of Ezekiel," 17

Vital, Rabbi Hayyim, 33, 34, 35, 301(n1), 302(n12;n15;n16)
    messianic dreams of, 203–212

The Voice of God Over the Water," 101–105

vowels, signifiers for, 140

"wave-offering," 173

"The Way of God" (Luzzatto), 226

Weiss, Joseph, 240

"When You Will Come to Sleep with Me Come like My Father" (Wollach), 268–269

"When You Will Come to Sleep With Me Like God" (Wollach), 264–265

The Wisdom of the Zohar (Tishby), 149

"With the Lines of Ibn El Arabi" (Shvili), 270–271

Wollach, Yona, poetry of, 264–269

women
    depiction as evil, 221, 222
    kabbalistic poetry by, 264–269, 271–274

"The Wonders of Creation" (Gabirol), 87–94

"The Work of the Chariot," 18, 55

World War I, 39

writing, "automatic," 176, 177–180, 299(n18)

Yah Akhatriel, 97

Yahoel, 127

YAVH, 123

Yefehfia, 58

"Yehi or," as word of God, 10–11

yenuka, 161, 298(n5)

Yesa, Rabbi, 151, 152

yesod, 40, 147

Yetsirah, 135

YHVA, 123

YHVH, 59, 61, 63, 73, 99, 104, 110, 111, 123, 144, 146, 289(n2), 293(n8;n9;n19), 294(n24;n25), 310(n2)